COMHAIRLE CHONTAE ROSCOMÁIN
LEABHARLANNA CHONTAE ROSCOMÁIN

1. This book may be retained for three weeks.
2. This book may be renewed if not requested
   by another borrower.
3. Fines on overdue books will be charged by
   overdue notices.

Yesterday's Country Village

Memories of Village Life from 1900-1960

STOURTON CAUNDLE, CHOIR, BELL RINGERS, &
CHURCH WORKERS' OUTING TO WEYMOUTH, AUG 15TH 1922.

YESTERDAY'S COUNTRY VILLAGE

HENRY BUCKTON

David and Charles

Frontispiece, previous page: Three young girls with bunches of wildflowers outside a house in Winster village near Windermere in the Lake District. It's June 1947, two years after the end of the war.

A DAVID & CHARLES BOOK

Copyright © David & Charles Limited 2005, 2008

David & Charles is an F+W Publications Inc. company
4700 East Galbraith Road
Cincinnati, OH 45236

First published in 2005
This UK paperback edition published in 2008

Text copyright © Henry Buckton 2005, 2008

A catalogue record for this book is available from the British Library.

ISBN-13: 978-0-7153-2095-2 hardback
ISBN-10: 0-7153-2095-5 hardback

ISBN-13: 978-0-7153-2881-1 paperback
ISBN-10: 0-7153-2881-6 paperback

Printed in Singapore by KHL
for David & Charles
Brunel House, Newton Abbot, Devon

Commissioning Editor: Jane Trollope
Editor: Jennifer Proverbs
Art Editor: Lisa Wyman
Production Controller: Beverley Richardson
Project Editor: Joan Gubbin

Visit our website at www.davidandcharles.co.uk

David & Charles books are available from all good bookshops; alternatively you can contact our Orderline on 0870 9908222 or write to us at FREEPOST EX2 110, D&C Direct, Newton Abbot, TQ12 4ZZ (no stamp required UK only); US customers call 800-289-0963 and Canadian customers call 800-840-5220.

CONTENTS

INTRODUCTION

British rural life between 1900 and 1960, a time which nestles between periods of huge social and industrial change, is a time still fondly remembered by much of the population, instilling a strong sense of nostalgia for a gentler segment of our nation's recent domestic history, now sadly gone forever. But this period was full of changes in the way that village people lived and worked, while at the same time maintaining a strong sense of community and tradition.

At the turn of the 20th century, many villages were centered on a large country estate that provided work and sometimes accommodation for local men and women. Villages thrived, as most people were able to secure employment in the vicinity. It was a time when grand houses still employed legions of staff, and in tiny village communities the benevolence of the local gentry might affect a large proportion of its inhabitants.

Then there were the large farms, many of which belonged to the same land-owning gentry, or smaller farms that cultivated most of the country's productive land. Farming was still largely unmechanized, and a vast workforce was required for tasks that within a few short years would be done by machines alone. Perhaps, contrary to the popular perception of country life, there were also local industries other than farming which sustained the workforce of small communities. These varied around Britain, from coal mining in the Welsh valleys, to peat cutting on the Somerset Levels. Many villages also had a mill, bakery, slaughterhouse, or smithy, all of which provided work.

World War I brought unimaginable changes to village life. A look at the memorials in rural settlements to observe the numbers that perished makes one begin to appreciate how the adult

Left: Widdecombe in the Moor in Devon is often thought to be one of England's most delightful villages. The magnificent perpendicular church dominates and unifies the little community set in the middle of Dartmoor.

Below: Maypole dancers dancing around a maypole during the May Day celebrations in the village of Elstow, Bedfordshire in 1952.

British troops march down a village street in May 1944. A woman farm worker pauses to watch them pass.

male population in some villages was decimated. Following the war, during the 1920s and 1930s, young men barely out of school had, therefore, to replenish the workforce that had been cruelly taken away.

In the 1920s, changes began to occur that would have a profound effect on village life. The land-owning gentry had themselves been affected by the war; many of their brightest sons had been sacrificed, and stately homes and country houses went into steady decline. Before long a proportion of rural villages were starved of their benefaction, as there were fewer jobs to go around. This was accompanied by rapidly improving farm technology, which meant that fewer jobs were available on the land as well. However, the decline of jobs within the village itself, coincided with transport improvements, enabling villagers to make train journeys or bus rides into local towns for work. Transport helped to maintain communities, as people could still live in their ancestral village homes, but travel to work in the town.

And later, motorcycles and cars further aided the independence of villagers. Having said that, there is no doubt that at this point there was already a shift in the population from the country to the towns as people moved to find, not only work, but also a better quality of life.

In 1929, the world entered the Great Depression. Britain's export markets almost totally dried up and by 1931 there were three million unemployed. It was a terrible time for everyone, but particularly for those in villages. By the mid-1930s things had slowly recovered, but

Three trainee land girls take a ride on a carthorse's back while others carry on working on the hay stack during harvest time in west Suffolk during World War II.

Welcome home! Sergeant F Tucker with his wife and young son is given a heart warming welcome by flag waving villagers in Oreston, south Devon, after his return home from a POW camp in May 1945.

only in time for the next major event of the 20th century: World War II.

Once again, most adult males from rural villages, between the ages of 20 and 40, found themselves employed by the Crown. In the countryside, farming became intensive, and

tranquil villages were transformed into bustling communities. Hordes of land army girls worked the fields. Then there was the evacuation scheme, when children from towns and cities were relocated to the countryside. These children resided with local families and went to

The main street of Wykeham, North Yorkshire, in the early 20th century. Mrs Peacock, who grew up in the nearby village of Cayton, said that her husband was born in the house on the left, where the people are standing. He could remember tanks rolling through the village during the war and his mother frantically trying to stop everything falling off the shelves. The house has since been demolished to make the road wider.

the village schools. After 1942, some parts of
rural Britain, notably East Anglia and the West
Country hosted tens of thousands of American
servicemen, during the build up to D-Day. The
war years were an interesting and exciting time
for many rural communities, but of course, in the
remotest parts of the UK, the war passed by
relatively unnoticed.

The final period in this village story, from the
euphoria of VE Day and the less celebrated VJ
Day, to the 1960s, started with a period of relative
prosperity, but burdened by the financial
consequences of the war, British industry slowly
went into decline. Mining, steel, fishing,
shipbuilding, and other mainstay industries
began to disappear. Villagers were more than
ever forced away from their homes to find work.

By the mid-1970s, the future course of village
life was set. As young people moved away and
the older generations began to disappear, village
properties were increasingly bought by people
from outside the community, often commuters
from towns and cities who sought a more
pleasant life in the countryside, pushing up
prices. Then came the housing boom, with every
available village plot used to build new houses,
which were often unaffordable for local people.
At the same time towns and cities expanded

relentlessly, and many villages on their outskirts
were swallowed up by the urban sprawl.

In numerous villages today, few of the old
families remain, while in others they cling on in
small pockets. However, village life is constantly
evolving and the new residents often bring their
own sense of community, refilling the church
pews and starting new activities in the village
hall as well as reviving old traditions.

Told through the memories of those who lived
in rural communities, *Yesterday's Country Village*
studies the time before traditional village life
altered forever, and attempts to recapture a very
special and much-loved period in Britain's
history. All aspects of village life are examined
through these memories, photographs and
period postcards. It details the daily lives of
village people and looks at the rural industries
that provided work for village folk, as well as
other occupations that made each settlement
self-sufficient. It also looks at the public services
that villages enjoyed, the type of transport that
people used for work and pleasure, and the
institutions such as the school, church and public
house with the many clubs and organizations
enjoyed by children and adults. But ultimately, it
examines the wonderful community spirit that
existed in Britain's rural villages in bygone days.

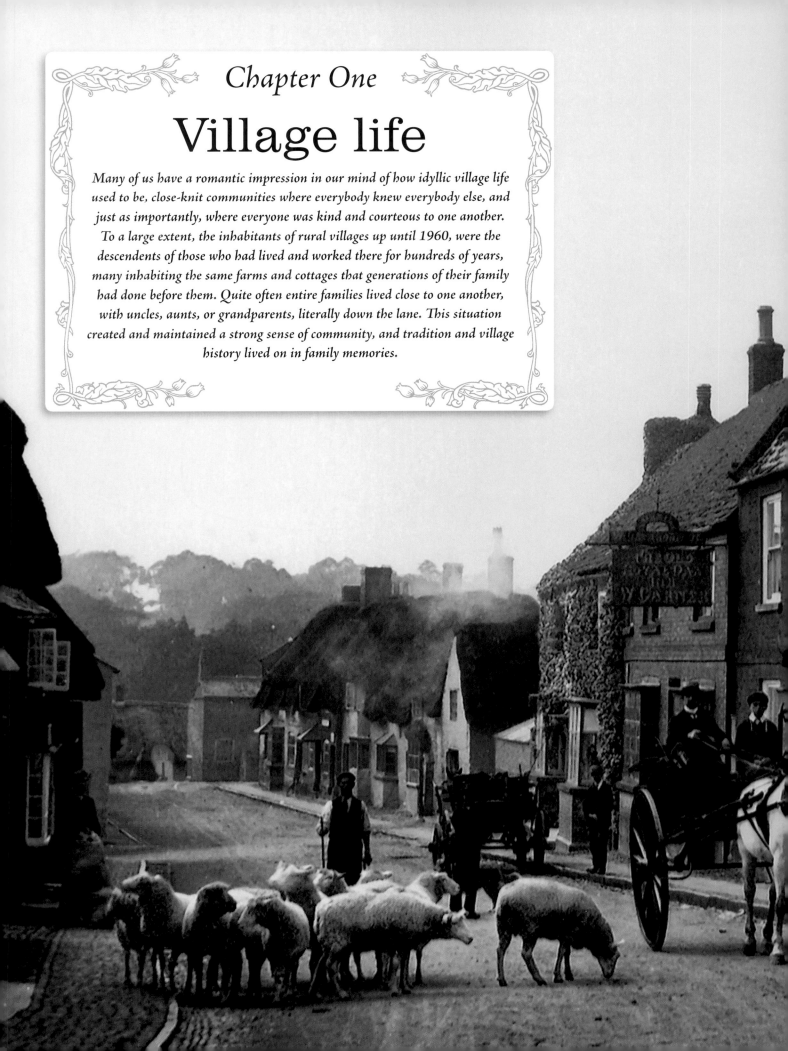

Chapter One

Village life

Many of us have a romantic impression in our mind of how idyllic village life used to be, close-knit communities where everybody knew everybody else, and just as importantly, where everyone was kind and courteous to one another. To a large extent, the inhabitants of rural villages up until 1960, were the descendents of those who had lived and worked there for hundreds of years, many inhabiting the same farms and cottages that generations of their family had done before them. Quite often entire families lived close to one another, with uncles, aunts, or grandparents, literally down the lane. This situation created and maintained a strong sense of community, and tradition and village history lived on in family memories.

Life in the average home

A look back at the home life of people living in rural communities in many parts of the United Kingdom, to see what it was really like. People remember their houses, how they organized their weekly routine, how they carried out day-to-day tasks like cooking and washing, and how they were far more self-sufficient than we are today.

A typical village house at Oving in Buckinghamshire, around 1923, with farmer's wife Mrs Watts, her son Jim, and two village lads, Harold Cheshire and Ernie Clarke outside the front porch.

Margaret Wilce was born at Forest Green in the village of Walford near Ross-on-Wye in Herefordshire in 1933. Both sets of grandparents, the Morgans and the Symonds, came from the village and she lived with her parents in a small cottage that comprised of two rooms downstairs, with a lean-to kitchen, and two bedrooms upstairs. It was situated at the top of a hill, and they had no electricity or mains water. Her mother would frequently go down into the woods to collect sticks to light the fire and she would drag larger pieces home to keep the fire going, or to cook their food. 'She was an expert with an axe,' recalls Margaret, 'and could swing it above her head and bring it down with such force it split the wood in two.'

Coal was also used for heating and cooking, but it was a luxury that the family could only afford from time to time. Later they purchased a Primus stove, which was started with methylated spirit, but it could only accommodate one item at a time,

This old photograph shows the High Street of the Dorset village of Winfrith, reproduced from a postcard, which was posted in 1936, publisher unknown. At the time when this photograph was taken, most of these cottages would still have been heated by an open fire and lit by candles.

so it was a choice of the kettle or the flat iron.

'We used oil lamps or candles to light the house,' Margaret explains. 'The lamp had to be filled with paraffin, the wicks trimmed and the lamp glasses washed.'

For entertainment they had a wireless, powered with a glass accumulator and a dry exide battery. However, its use was very restricted and it was only ever switched on to hear the news. This was because the accumulator wouldn't last for a whole week. 'We needed two accumulators, one in use and the other being charged in a shop in town.'

Most people in the village faced similar problems with their accumulators. The floor covering at the front of the local bus was completely rotted away by the acid that had spilt out of the many accumulators that passengers ferried to and from the town.

David Andrews recollects that his parents had one of the first wireless sets in the village. On Derby Day his mother would put the speaker on the windowsill and open the window. 'Quite a crowd gathered,' he notes, 'some indoors and some outside. They were able to hear the race live without having to wait for the next day's newspapers, to know the result. The aerial wire was mounted on a pole at the end of the garden; the height and distance were important for good reception. There was also a copper rod installed into the ground outside the window to act as an earth wire.'

Above left: Harry Foster and his brother-in-law, Albert Crawley, two country gentlemen from a village in Buckinghamshire pictured in 1930.

Below right: Home entertainment in the 1930s at Edithmead in Somerset. The wireless was listened to through headphones, and the reception was best outside with an aerial attached to the branch of a tree.

As well as radios, people were beginning to buy gramophones to entertain themselves at home. Molly Kinghorn's father is enjoying some music of the day at Throstle Nest Farm, Beckwithshaw near Harrogate.

Water – the essence of life

But what about water, an essential commodity we all need to survive? Very few houses in rural communities anywhere in the country were connected to the mains at that time. Most villages had a pump and many homes had their own well, or shared one with neighbours, but most water used in the home had to be carried inside in pails.

Margaret Wilce recalls, 'My father, who was in the building trade, sunk a well in our garden with the help of a water diviner who came with a hazel twig and located the spring. Father dug down, stoning the sides all the way until he found the spring water. He built low walls on the top, then he put a wooden roller resting on the walls with a rope chain attached to it and a bucket attached to the other end. The bucket was lowered empty and brought up full.'

Rainwater was also collected from the roof of the cottage and Margaret's father built an underground tank for it to be stored in. He included a pump, with a pipe leading down into the tank. The water was then pumped into an

Postcard showing the village pump at Falmer in East Sussex.

earthenware sink. But not many people had access to such tanks, and most had to carry all the water they required for drinking, washing, and cooking, either from a communal tap, or a well, somewhere in the village.

Mr E Fairweather who lived in Acton, a hamlet near Newcastle-under-Lyme in Staffordshire recalls, 'I was born in 1928. My father was a gamekeeper to the Mainwaring family at Whitmore Hall. There was no electricity or water in the hamlet. All drinking water had to be fetched from an open well, which was easily one mile from the house.' His mother had to carry their water by using a yoke on her shoulders, with two buckets hanging underneath.

Diana Phillips lived in a farm worker's cottage at Winterbourne Abbas in Dorset, where water came from a pump by the back door, which froze in the winter. 'Mother took the Primus stove out,' she says, 'and lit it beside the pump to thaw it out before we could have water to heat for breakfast. The heat from the Primus sometimes melted the

Above left: With no mains water supply connected to village houses, rainwater was collected straight off the roof in as many makeshift tanks, tin baths and barrels as possible.

Below left: Tom Knott drawing water from the River Stour to fill the barrel mounted on a horse-drawn cart in Dorset, circa 1930.

Left: Ron Foster collects water from the village pump in the early 1920s, at Oving in Buckinghamshire.

Right: Rosa Hibbert at the entrance to the family cottage in East Ilsley, Berkshire in 1940. A light-hearted scene, but it shows the yoke that was used to carry water buckets filled up from the well in the yard, or from the well by the pond. It was also used to carry the milk pails from the local farm.

lead pipes, then we had to wait for an estate worker to come to repair it.'

Living on the outskirts of the village of Buttercrambe in North Yorkshire, Ken Rennison remembers having to carry drinking water from a well, about 200 yards down the road. When that well dried up in the summer, he had to walk to the village, where there was another well. When that also dried, he would have to cross three fields to a spring coming straight out of the hillside.

The variety of water sources inevitably contributed to the fact that diseases of different kinds often raised their head. 'There were occasional scares when a contagious illness struck – such as scarlet fever or diphtheria,' notes Ernest Hawkins, who grew up in Barlaston in Staffordshire. 'We were warned to keep away from the home of those affected. Seeing the conditions we lived in, although clean, were most unhygienic, it was remarkable what a strong and healthy lot we were. Most of the small cottages in the village were full of happy children and all the illnesses passed over without much fuss. It was just a fact of life that we accepted.'

Mr Hawkins goes on to explain, 'There was also no plumbed water to our cottages – only one outside tap at the rear to serve five of the Queen's Row Cottages. Before we went to school on Mondays, we had to carry the water in buckets for washing day.'

Pussy's in the well

Imagine if your one source of drinking water had been contaminated by something dead and decaying. Beryl Haywood lived in a group of labourers' cottages, known as The Castle, in Essington, Staffordshire. One of her earliest recollections, around 1925, centres on the well from which they drew their water. 'With a crowd of other children, I was watching the men from The Castle who were trying to empty the well. No easy task when it had five or six springs in the bottom. The men were working like beavers, sweating in the hot sun. They emptied the big iron bucket over and over again, all the time swearing and cursing the lad who had caused all the trouble. The lad, Norman Hinks, was nowhere to be found, and no wonder, as it was he who had thrown the cat into the well and drowned it.' Let's hope the water was thoroughly boiled thereafter!

This photograph was taken outside the village shop at Huggate in the Yorkshire Wolds when piped water was brought to the village for the first time, circa 1936.

Being self-sufficient

Many people kept their own poultry and livestock to help supplement their diets, and quite often the gardens of village houses resembled mini farmyards. The poultry were fed on household scraps and it should be remembered that often the vegetable plots were tended after a hard day's work.

Margaret Wilce's parents kept fowls, geese, and ducks at Walford. 'I remember my mother putting eggs under the broody hens,' says Margaret, 'and hatching lovely baby chickens, ducklings and goslings. We were heart-broken when the fox broke into the hen house and killed many fowls. The eggs were sold and mother killed and dressed the fowls and ducks for the wealthy landowners, or gentry. We only ever had poultry at Christmas, what a treat that was.'

They also kept a pig, which was killed by a local man. It was tied to a bench and had its throat cut, and the poor creature's shrieks could be heard throughout the village. Later, humane killing was made compulsory, which meant that the pig was first shot, and then had its throat cut. Margaret recalls 'I was given the job of catching the blood for black puddings. Every part of the pig was used! The intestines were cleaned and put into salt water; they were eventually plaited and were fried in the frying pan – a great delicacy. Even the bladder was used as a football.'

Right: The majority of rural households had either a productive vegetable garden at their home, or an allotment somewhere else in the village. Margaret Wilce's grandfather Andrew Symonds, and his son Leslie are hard at work gardening in theirs.

The pig could only be killed when there was an R in the month because it was too hot during the summer months of the year, and in those days there were no fridges or freezers. The sides of bacon were salted and saltpeter was put round the ham bone to stop flies laying their eggs. The sides were then hung on the walls of the kitchen to cure, but the salt and fat marks came through the wallpaper forever after.

From the village of Cattistock in Dorset, Marie Langford also has childhood memories of pig-killing day, when the squeals of the pigs would be silenced by the pig-killer's knife. 'After scalding and scraping to remove their hair, the carcasses were hung from a beam in the cart shed, waiting to be dressed. They were carried there on a pig jib, which was a long wooden slatted bier-like object with wooden handles at each end. We still have it, but not in use.'

Hunting and fishing were popular methods of contributing to the family diet and many fathers owned a shotgun. Rosa Bowler grew up in the

Above: Avarina Jane Evans feeding the chickens with grain in the field opposite the shop her husband James Pearce Evans had built in the village of Bontgoch in north Ceredigion, Wales.

Rabbits for the pot

In the 1950s, when Frank Hind was growing up at Chipstable in the Brendon Hills of Somerset, he was able to wander where he liked, either on horseback or on foot, 'as long as you shut gates and respected stock,' he points out. As a boy he loved to get up early on a summer's morning and go shooting rabbits with his .22 air rifle. Later he would cycle down to the butcher in Wiveliscombe who gave him half-a-crown for each animal.

village of East Ilsley in Berkshire and her father was allowed to go shooting in the surrounding fields or nearby woods. Rabbit, hare and pigeon were frequently on the menu. He also kept ferrets, which he would take out into the fields with him to catch rabbits by chasing them straight from their burrows.

For those who lived in a coastal village, the sea itself could provide extra food supplies. Richard Shimmin, who lived in Dalby on the Isle of Man notes that, 'some of the villagers would tie baited lobster pots to the rocks at low tide to catch crab and lobster, and go line fishing at full tide off the coast in small boats. They also hunted rabbits and hares in the hills and collected mushrooms and berries in season, all to supplement the diet, living off the land and sea.'

Most villagers throughout the country also had a productive vegetable garden or allotment and fruit and vegetables were grown all the year round for family use; what was available depended on what was in season.

Martin Skin, who lived in the small hamlet of Doddycross near Menheniot in Cornwall, remembers how villagers tried to keep the worst of the pests under control. 'There were no pest control sprays in those days, most people used to have jam jars half filled with water and a little sugar.' The jars would have a hole in the lid, through which wasps would crawl to obtain the sweet nectar. However, once in the jar they would be unable to get out again, and would always meet their demise.

'To keep birds off newly planted seeds and

shoots,' says Martin, 'gardeners would have strings with silver and gold milk bottle tops on them. When these blew in the wind they did a reasonably good job of scaring the birds away. Scarecrows were also a common sight in fields and gardens, and farmers would hang up shot pigeons, crows and rabbits, to keep pests off the crops. I have no idea if it worked!'

This postcard of an old cottage at West Horsley in Surrey, shows how important gardening was to ordinary village people. This gentleman's modestly sized garden is full of flower borders and elaborate hedges.

The weekly routine

Before modern life was made easy, with hot and cold running water, dishwashers, washing machines, and all the other household items that have revolutionized the way in which we live, people often dedicated a whole day to particular tasks. The domestic week followed a common pattern and Margaret Wilce describes the week of her own family.

We don't care if it snows.

'Monday was washday. Mother filled the copper with water, which she had either got from the well or pumped up into the kitchen from the underground tank. She got sticks and lit the fire, and then stood nearly all day rubbing the clothes, starting with the whites. Then, putting them into the copper to boil, she went on rubbing the coloured items, finishing with the socks. When the white clothes were removed from the boiler, towels and tablecloths were put in their place. All of these had to be swilled and the white clothes put through water which had been turned blue with the aid of a cube of Blue, which had been put into a piece of cloth and immersed in the clean water.'

Having finished the washing, the water that had been so painstakingly collected and heated, would be used for other tasks before being thrown away. First the kitchen floor would be washed, then the seat and floor of the outside lavatory, which was situated in the garden underneath a yew tree.

Monday's dinner, in most village households around the country, would have been bubble and squeak. This was made from the leftover vegetables from Sunday lunch, fried up and served with cold meat and pickles. Tarts would also be made from whatever fruits were in season and easily obtainable from the woods or hedgerows, or grown in the garden.

On Tuesday the ironing would be done, assuming that the clothes had dried from the previous day. The flat iron was heated on the fire, until the Primus stove made life a little easier. 'Despite mother cleaning the iron thoroughly,' says Margaret, 'there was always an inevitable black streak on the clothes, which upset her terribly.'

Also on Tuesday, the pigsty, fowl and duck houses had to be cleaned out. And for Tuesday dinner, the remainder of the meat from Sunday lunch would be minced, and cooked with onions, carrots, swede, and parsnip, and eaten with dry bread. Most of the vegetables came from their own garden, with the exception of the swede. Margaret's mother obtained this by crawling through a hole in the farmer's hedge. Apparently all the mums did this, and although the farmer was probably aware of the practice, he didn't seem to mind.

On Wednesday a few special cleaning jobs were done. Margaret was made to dust the iron base and ornate ironwork of the treadle sewing machine, which she did with hen feathers, tied in a bundle. Her father would shoot a rabbit for

Left: Before people had baths in their homes, a big tub in the yard would do the trick, or inside in front of the fire on colder days. A postcard, postmarked 1927, published by Misch & Co Ltd.

Below: A mother and daughter prepare a simple supper in a village house in Wales in 1944, towards the end of the war.

Wednesday dinner and her mother had various methods of cooking and presenting it, so that it was slightly different each week.

Thursday was usually shopping day and the village wives went to town. The Co-op was the place for discerning housewives in those days, because of the dividend they offered. They also provided a next day delivery service. Before she was of school age Margaret would always accompany her mother when she went to town on the bus. They would meet up with her grandmother who would treat them to a lunch of faggots and peas. They would also collect her waste food, which was later boiled, mixed with mash, and fed to the animals. Thursday's dinner was usually fish, bought in town earlier that day.

Friday was an important cleaning day in the house, with the bedrooms, stairs and front room being taken care of. For dinner there would be liver, stuffed hearts, or stew, the main ingredients having been bought the previous day. The groceries would be delivered from town and Margaret's mother maintained that saving up the Co-op dividend helped her to pay the rates or tithes.

On Saturday the fire was made up in the range, so the oven was ready for when the butcher delivered the joint of meat, which was nearly always a rib of beef. While the joint was cooking, Mrs Morgan baked cakes, tarts, and a large pie made from corned beef mixed with potato, carrot, and onions, baked in pastry. 'I used to love bread dipped in the meat juice (dripping) in the meat baking-tin,' admits Margaret. 'If there was a football match played locally my father used to go to watch it. On Saturday nights he met up with all his friends in the local pub. Water was heated in the copper and put in a tin bath in front of the fire where I was given a bath.'

Finally on Sunday, after all the animals were fed and the vegetables prepared for lunch, Margaret would go to Sunday-school at the local chapel. Later in the day the whole family went to church, where they met her grandparents. Everybody had their regular seats and her grandmother would always pass peppermints back to her discreetly. Her father and grandfather were sidesmen and did the collection together, in fact her great grandfather had helped in the building of the church, which was completed in 1875 – today like so many others in rural villages, it is closed and being considered for conversion into a private house.

So that's very much how the week was organized in Walford, and from discussions with many other people, a similar pattern was followed all around Britain. Of course things were made more difficult for housewives during the war years, as their partners were frequently away. As

Below: A group of village men pictured tree felling at Deep Dean in Herefordshire. Wood was an important aid to both cooking and heating and men and women would spend a great deal of their spare time gathering kindling and splitting logs.

Margaret's father was in the building trade, he was sent to Coventry to repair bomb-damaged buildings, which left her mother at home with all the animals to look after. As well as their own daughter, who was eight or nine at the time, she took in two evacuees.

When time allowed in their busy routine, enjoying a walk in the country was always a favourite pastime with rural people. This picture, taken during World War II, shows Phyllis Wyatt, standing here on the right, enjoying a Christmas stroll to the top of Brent Knoll in Somerset, accompanied by her mother, sisters and brother-in-law.

Cleaning and cooking

Looking at this weekly routine in detail, it's evident that cleaning and cooking were the two most important and time-consuming activities of the week. A varied range of implements were used to try and keep the family's clothes clean, ranging from washboards and mangles to possers and flat irons.

Many houses had a scullery, where most of the cleaning chores were carried out. Water had to be heated in the copper over a fire before use. Then there were things such as the washing dolly and the posser, which were used to agitate the clothes to remove dirt and stains. The clothes would be dried outside, weather permitting, or in front of the fire. Afterwards they were pressed with a variety of flat irons, which took an incredible amount of time and effort.

Geoffrey Charge, who lived in the village of Eight Ash Green in Essex, said that his father had built a shed at the bottom of the garden to house the copper boiler that his mother did their washing in. 'I helped him to measure and cut the pieces of wood for the main framework,' he recalls. 'All went well until I marked out one piece too short. Dad cut it with his saw, and when he went to fit it in place it was two inches too short. He called me a "cuckoo" and had to cut a separate two-inch piece, and somehow join the pieces together. The old boiler was a cast-iron casing on legs with a grate for wood or coal, and a door to keep the fire in. The heat went all round an inner galvanized drum, in which all the clothes were put when the water in the drum was hot enough. Then soap flakes were added, and it was all left to cook for an hour or so, with an occasional stir with a wooden stick. Then the clothes were placed in a galvanized bathtub and

rinsed with loads of clean water. Next they were put through a mangle, to squeeze out all the water before hanging them out to dry on a line stretched between two posts in the garden. The whole affair took all day on a Monday, always Monday, never any other day of the week. When the clothes were dry, a large solid metal iron was heated up on the coal fire trivet, and everything was ironed. On one occasion I was helping Mum feed wet clothes into the mangle when my finger

Above: The contents of a typical rural scullery between 1920 and 1940.

Below: This Raphael Tuck & Sons postcard gives an idea of the many barrels, buckets and tubs that rural people used in their weekly washday routine.

Spring-cleaning

As well as the weekly clean, once a year there was spring-cleaning, when the entire house was freshened from top to bottom. 'The curtains came down for washing,' writes Rosa Bowler from East Ilsley, 'the rugs went out on the washing line, and were beaten to get the dust out. The blankets were washed, walls washed – sometimes distempered. Everything was cleaned, one room at a time, it took weeks. The village chimney sweep Mr Welch came to sweep all the chimneys. My father hated the disruption of spring-cleaning and disappeared to the garden or fields.'

Above: The isolated
village of Oving was
completely snowbound
between 21st and 25th
December, 1938 when this
picture was taken. With
little transport available,
village houses had to be
well stocked with essential
supplies.

Below: With her husband
a pilot fighting in World
War II this woman, like so
many others in Britain, was
left alone to care for the
children and probably also
went out to work.

went into the rollers as well. To this day that
finger will not bend at the first joint.'

Mrs J Peacock, who grew up in Cayton, in
North Yorkshire, recalls the famous posser, an
invaluable cleaning aid. 'In those days,' she
explains, 'the poshy tub was used instead of a
washing machine, along with a long-handled
posser. This had a large metal cone shape on the
end, and was used to agitate all the washing in
the tub. After this the washing went through a
huge mangle, which was so large it almost took
up the whole kitchen. We also had a huge black
range that had an open fire with an oven at the
side to do all the cooking. You didn't need to go
and keep fit in those days – hard housework took
care of that.'

If there was no shop, and with few people
owning transport, isolated village houses would
normally have been well stocked with essential
items. William Moore, who grew up in the village
of Tasburgh in Norfolk says, 'A considerable

amount of households kept a reserve stock of
flour, as many housewives made their own bread.'
During the war, as with most other commodities,
flour was rationed. This meant that personal
stocks began to dwindle, and if you had no flour,
you had no bread. 'We were actually cut off
completely by snow for three weeks,' recalls Mr
Moore. 'During this time the local council
arranged for prisoners of war (Italians from Long
Stratton) and all other able-bodied men, to go out
daily with a pick and shovel just to cut pathways.
Our household must have been almost out of
food. We had eaten our chickens, except two,
which were to provide eggs. In the mornings we
enticed birds by feeding them scraps, then set
mousetraps in the late afternoon to catch them.
Yes, we lived on blackbird and sparrow pie.
Sometimes a robin was caught. It was sad, we just
buried it with a prayer for our sin.'

During the war years, with the added burden of
rationing, the ability to make ends meet was even
more essential. Mrs M Williams, who lived in the
tiny mining village of Betws near Ammanford in
Carmarthenshire, explains that all the local
housewives had to create meals from anything
they had to hand and hearty vegetable soups
were a staple dish in most people's diet. 'Cawl
soup, made in a huge saucepan would be dinner
for two to three days.' The humble potato proved
its versatility beyond doubt. 'Potatoes that were
scrubbed in the morning and put in the oven
were ready for supper. You could have them with
a little butter if you were lucky. Potatoes made
lots of meals! There were chips, if you had
dripping, or they could be boiled, mashed, fried
or made into rissoles.'

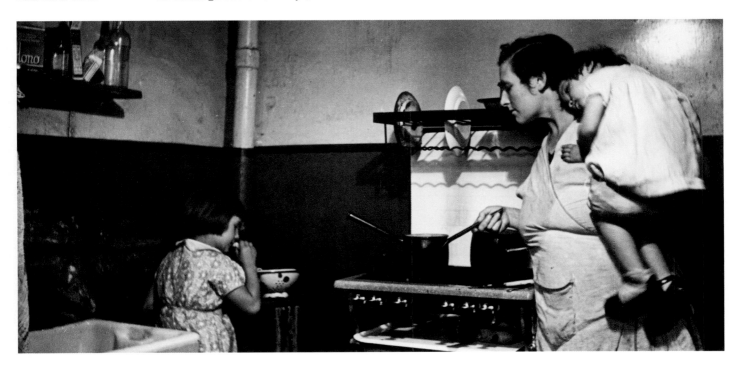

Domestic skills

Another important aspect of home life, were the many domestic skills that had been handed down through generations. As well as cooking, women were expected to be able to knit, sew and crochet and use these skills to make clothes and household items. Men picked up practical skills such as carpentry from their fathers.

Margaret Wilce's mother would knit, sew, or crochet, in the winter evenings. Her mother made all Margaret's clothes and she remembers her unstitching a navy coat that had belonged to her grandmother, turning the material inside out and making a new school coat from it. She was also good at re-upholstering furniture and they had a mat in front of the fire, which her mother had made out of rags. To make these mats, which were known as peg or rag mats, women would save all the old clothes that were too far gone to repair again. These would be cut into strips and pushed through hessian sacking with a thing known as a peg. The finished mat would then be backed with sacking.

Peter Waite, who grew up in the village of Little Addington in Northamptonshire, remembers his grandmother, Sarah Jane Flawn, who lived to be 100 years and six months old. She was still living alone in her cottage and making pillowcases on her 97th birthday. Her first husband Thomas Waite died in a typhoid epidemic leaving her to bring up seven children. Another victim of the same epidemic was the wife of William Flawn, who was left with five children to raise. Sarah and William married in January 1900 and together successfully raised their 12 children as one family. Peter Waite says, 'She was known as Grandma to all in Little Addington until the time of her death in April 1959.'

While the wives made cakes and tarts, the men often provided the household with beer or cider. Margaret Wilce's grandfather made cider with his friend the village policeman. They had a hand-

Sarah Jane Flawn making lace pillowcases on her 97th birthday. She was still living alone in her cottage in Little Addington in Northamptonshire when she died aged 100 years and six months. Almost everyone in the village called her Grandma.

Baskets were used for storage and in agriculture and basket making was another skill handed down through the generations. This picture, taken around 1950, shows Francis Joseph Ashton, who lived in the village of Gowdall near Snaith, and worked as a master basket maker. He picked up the skill from his own father, also a basket maker. Notice the missing fingers on his right hand; he lost these while working in the Clog Mill in Snaith.

operated press in a disused cottage, and the juice was collected in a stone
trough in the floor, and then stored in large wooden barrels. During the
war her grandmother saved their sugar ration to help her husband's cider
production. He was known for sharing his cider with the village menfolk
and often, as they returned home from work, he invited them into the small
disused cottage where they all sat around and enjoyed stories. The same
cottage is now a very desirable residence called The Old Cider House.

A traditional craft

*Mrs McInnes at her spinning wheel near the
hamlet of Portnalong on the Isle of Skye, in 1952.
She came from South Uist in the Shetlands and
married a man from Skye, and worked at the
spinning wheel at every opportunity. Gaelic was
the first language of the entire family and she
possessed an endless repertoire of sad-sounding
Gaelic songs. The spun wool would have been
knitted into traditional jerseys through the long
winter evenings.*

Farmhouse and cottage cider was brewed in many parts of rural Britain, although traditionally the West Country had become most associated with its manufacture. Many villagers had their own apple trees, and if they didn't wish to make their own cider, they could take their apples along to a local farmer who operated a press, who would make it for them for a small charge. There were also men who travelled around the villages collecting apples, offering a similar service. Cider apples were of a particular type, and had names like Dabinetts, Somerset Redsteak, Tremletts Bitter, Yarlington Mill and Kingston Black. Traditionally, the apples were ground into pulp, which was then laid between cider cloths in a rack, and squeezed in a press. The juice was left to ferment and mature in wooden barrels, and was considered ready when the farmer or cottager might consider it so.

Andrew Symonds, seen here on the left holding a jug, would make cider in a disused cottage with his friend the village policeman. The village men folk would gather there to drink and tell stories.

Cider was drunk at local festivals, family occasions, or any other social gatherings when the conversation would flow. It was also used to quench the thirst of the harvesters during the hot dry days of summer. It was quite a weak brew and often safer than drinking the water.

Best Somerset cider

Cider houses were common in many parts of the countryside. If a village didn't have a pub, quite often a farmhouse would provide its own facility, so that members of the community, especially the farm labourers, could congregate and relax after a hard day's work in the fields. At Edithmead in Somerset, Phyllis Wyatt, recalls, 'Most farms boasted a cider house and our house was no exception. Built as a lean-to against the main dwelling it was just an outhouse with an earth floor and one small window. Below the pantiles of the sloping roof, its timbers were clad in a shroud of thick, black cobwebs. Quite a considerable amount of floor space was taken up by two 70-gallon barrels. These contained my father's best brew of Somerset cider and stood on a platform made of old railway sleepers.' Sacks of barley meal served as seats for the visitors, as the old cider mug was passed around. 'I don't believe it was ever washed,' she admits, 'from one drinking session to another.'

The outside loo

When people talk about the old days, and how things have improved, the one memory that invariably enters the conversation, is the outside toilet.

Margaret Wilce recalls that the lavatory for their cottage in Walford had a wooden seat and a door at the front from which a large bucket, purchased from the ironmongers especially for this purpose, could be removed. The bucket was emptied into a large hole dug in the garden. Margaret herself, as did most other village children, had her own smaller version of the lavatory, as the grown-up one was two high for them to sit on. The children's version had a potty under it, instead of a bucket. Margaret's parents would cut old newspapers into squares, and thread them on to string that hung from a nail on the wall. 'It was a real luxury,' she states, 'when some soft tissue paper was obtained from an old dress pattern, or the wrapping from the occasional orange.'

At Eight Ash Green in Essex, Geoffrey Charge remembers the tiny building at the bottom of the garden with a large metal bucket under a wooden seat. Geoffrey lived in a row of cottages, so the privy wasn't that private. 'Of course you could hear the person next door when they came to use the toilet,' he admits. 'Sometimes two of the girls next door would come down together if it was dark, and I heard some odd conversations at times. There was often a large harvest spider lurking in the corner. I was quite frightened of them and on one occasion a spider dropped on to my face and ran round my shoulder. The contents of the bucket had to be buried in the garden when it became full up. This gave rise to some superb fruit and vegetables for the village annual show.'

On a lighter note, Mrs Peacock from Cayton says, 'I remember the earth toilets which were in the yard at the front of the house, and how you dreaded having to go there when it was cold and wet. I remember as a child being told to take Moss, our Old English sheepdog puppy, to pay a call, so I thought it used our facilities and promptly popped it in the earth closet. I can still hear my mother's cries of anguish, but we had the cleanest dog in Cayton when she set to with the carbolic soap in the poshy tub.'

And for those who couldn't face going into the garden at night to relieve themselves, there was always the chamber pot under the bed. Poor Marie Litchfield, at Ashcott in Somerset, had a nasty experience with one of these, explaining that like many of their household posessions, it was old and badly cracked. Consequently, when she sat on it one night, it broke. 'The contents,' she writes, 'ran down the sloping bedroom floor, through the cracks and into the hall below.'

Marie and her sister hurried downstairs and went into the front room to tell their parents what had happened. 'You must have been playing about!' scolded her mother accusingly, until she noticed that her daughter was standing barefoot in a pool of blood.

'I must have been cut by the broken pot,' she explains, 'but by such a sharp edge that I hadn't felt it. Mother fled into the kitchen – she couldn't bear the sight of blood, especially on her own children. Father had seen such a lot of it during his lifetime, so he always took command on such occasions. He gently helped me to lie down, and kneeling beside me, wiped the blood away with a piece of rag.' Marie's father had lost the use of his right arm, smashed by a shell in October 1917, while serving in the trenches.

Following Marie's accident, the girls were given an old paint can to use until such time as her father could afford to buy another chamber pot to replace the broken one!

Muck spreading

Where did all the human waste go? Stanley Church, from Yardley Gobion in Northamptonshire recalls that on Saturday nights, at around midnight, a couple of volunteer farm labourers would visit the outside lavatories with a sludge tank pulled by a horse. Each lavatory had its own galvanized bucket and these would be emptied by hand into the sludge tank. The contents of the tank would then be disposed of by opening the valves and driving the horse across the farmer's field, thankfully a mile away from the cottages. This would be ploughed in as soon as possible. 'Surprisingly,' he recalls, 'after a few days, the smell had almost disappeared.'

The outside lavatory might have been situated in a shed at the bottom of the garden, or in a small lean-to attached to the side of the house like this one at Willow Cottage at Oving in Buckinghamshire.

A time of large families

Another surprising aspect about rural life between 1900 and 1960 was the number of large families that existed. Considering there was very little assistance in the form of child support, it seems almost a miracle that relatively poor people could successfully raise a large family of happy and well cared for children. Yet they did!

Christine Harber was one of a family of 12 children who grew up in Little Missenden, in Buckinghamshire. There were seven girls and five boys and they lived in a three-bedroom house, with the boys in one bedroom and all the girls in another. 'We had two sittings for meals because our living room wasn't that big.' Having said that, she admits that they were always well fed, with lots of mashed potato and stews, and the occasional pig's trotter. 'Also bread and jam,' she notes, 'we used to have a lot of that.'

At Christmas, her father made wooden dolls for all the girls, which her mother would knit clothes for, and other things for the boys, working out in his shed. 'If we were really lucky we would have an apple or orange.' Her father died from a heart attack when he was only 57 and two and a half years later her mother died of cancer – she was only 52. 'Sadly Mum and Dad didn't live to see all the children growing up,' says Christine.

Jessie Lockhart was born in 1929 on the Isle of Lewis in the Outer Hebrides, and was one of five children who lived with their parents in the village of Lower Coll. Her mother died when she was only three years old, leaving her father to raise the children by himself. 'No easy job in those days,' she explains, 'before child benefit.' She was sent to live with her aunt in Glasgow, leaving her father with the other two boys and two girls. He was a shoemaker and repairer, and worked in a small shop in Stornoway, having to cycle 15 miles there, and 15 miles back each day. While he was at work, aunts, uncles, and neighbours looked after the children.

Every year for the long school holidays, Jessie would return to Lewis, where she stayed with another aunt who lived in a croft house. 'Those were wonderful times,' she recalls. She had been born in a traditional 'black house', a strong dwelling built with large stones, with a thatched roof. Even in those days, black houses were going out of fashion, and there are now very few left. Those that remain are mostly museums, helping to preserve the island's heritage, and recapture the spirit of a bygone age.

Village people: Joseph Morgan and his wife and family in 1914. They lived at Howle Green in the village of Walford, near Ross-on-Wye. His son Fred is in uniform and Charlie stands behind his mother. Charlie married the daughter of another villager, Andrew Symonds, and remained in the village; their daughter Margaret still lives nearby today.

Keith Watkins, who grew up in the Welsh village of Varteg in Gwent, came from a large extended family, and explains, 'We were a large family, nine children and at this time in the 1930's there were many of my father's family living at Varteg.'

His grandmother, Mary Ann, who had formerly lived at number 17 Salisbury Terrace in the village, had been married to his grandfather James Watkins, who died in 1901. A few years later, she married again to Charles Thomas. Mary already had eight children by James, and Charles had another four from his first marriage. The couple went on to have a further three children, so that between them, they had a total of fifteen children.

Just down the road, at number 11 Salisbury Terrace lived his grandmother's sister, Martha, who was married to George Malsom, and they also had a large family.

He seemed to have relatives everywhere in the village. For instance, his eldest sister lived in Post Office Row; his dad's sister, who was married to Irvine Malsom, lived in Incline Row; Will Thomas his father's stepbrother also lived in Incline Row; at Ten Houses, sometimes called Chapel Row, lived his father's brother Charles and his wife Florence, with their children, Gethin and Ida, his cousins; at Spring Gardens lived his father's cousin, Roy Malsom, with Mary, his wife and children; and at Summerhill North, lived his father's half-sister, Ethel, who was always called Nin, and was married to Harold Malsom.

'The family connections with Varteg go back until 1850 at least,' he explains. 'Grandmother was born in Cross Row (Mary Ann Morgan); James Watkins married Mary Ann in 1885 at Trevethin. He came from just over the border in Herefordshire. My mother's father and mother also both came from Herefordshire, but the north of the county. He was Robert Davies, and I was named after both my grandfathers, so I became Robert James Keith Watkins.'

A bridal couple on the Isle of Lewis, which shows the type of house that island people built after the era of the 'black houses'. The story of this particular couple was very sad, as the bride died in childbirth, with their first child, a daughter. The groom was heartbroken and refused to return to the house. The contents were left undisturbed, until sometime later when he sold the house. He went back to live with his family with the little girl, where his sisters helped to raise her. Sadly they are all gone now.

Making ends meet

Without the state benefits, pensions and income support available today it was important that members of a village community cared for each other as much as possible. Times were often hard and while people trusted each other more, leaving their doors unlocked, this may also have indicated that they didn't have anything worth stealing.

In the main, rural jobs were very poorly paid, and it was a time when the man of the house was still the main breadwinner. Ernest Hawkins reveals that, 'most survived on a pittance of a wage, which you would hardly think possible. There was no financial help such as income support or other benefits that we know today. I remember the excitement when the first old age pension of ten shillings a week came into force (in the early 1920s I believe). The Lloyd George they called it after its instigator – people had never been so rich! However, if a family did fall on very hard times and were not able to carry on, it was the workhouse for them, but I never remember any family from Barlaston having to go in. Everyone seemed to look after one another in those days with very little fuss.'

Geoffrey Charge recalls that the rent on their cottage at Eight Ash Green was seven shillings and sixpence per week. 'The landlady's son used to call every month to collect the money,' he explains. 'Dad used to get paid every Friday, and after tea he would set out all his wages on the table and write on the back of the wage packet the amounts of all the bills that needed paying. I don't ever remember seeing any money left over.'

Even though times were difficult, it is already becoming evident, that in rural Britain between 1900-1960, there was a caring society. Ruth Bennett, who lived in the hamlet of Stowe near Bucknell in Shropshire, was born in 1926 in one of four almshouses and remembers an elderly neighbour called Miss Hyde. 'She was bedridden and in my mind's eye I can see her in bed, wearing a little flat hat. At one stage my mother cared for Miss Hyde and I remember her toasting slices of fat bacon in front of the open fire for her midday meal.' When the old lady passed away in January 1935 at the ripe old age of 88, Ruth and her mother continued to put fresh flowers on her grave every Saturday.

During the war, this tendency to help each other became even more apparent. Mary Cave lived with her husband Stan and four children in the Somerset village of Ashcott. When Stan was called up for military service, life became very hard. 'I had registered for my rations with Mr Willcox,' she writes, 'who had a mobile delivery van. I would get all my shopping for the week for ten shillings but I

A beautiful Dorset village of thatched cottages, photographed in the early part of the 20th century. For many people life wasn't always as idyllic as it might have seemed.

Trust and mistrust

Jean Pearse recalls two elderly ladies who lived together in the village, and who died within a short time of one another. 'Their house was cleared out and £4,000 in £1 notes were found all over the house. Some notes were found stuffed in drawers, some under mattresses and in cupboards. That was an awful lot of money in those days.' Not that this was a case of the old ladies trusting the community, more an example of their distrust of banks and the encroaching modern world.

A small boy shows off his new scooter in 1916. Children had very few toys at that time and most of them were home-made.

usually found that by about Tuesday, I would be running out. So I would send my son Jim on the bus to ask Mr Willcox for some more. Mr Willcox was very kind to me and would often say, "I don't know which week's rations these are, Mrs Cave. Next week's I think!" He never minded and was always very good to me. He would save the end of the ham bone for me. It had quite a bit of meat left on it and he would give me a big tin of fruit sometimes.'

Mary reflects on how her neighbours were kind, even willing to share their rations, especially with those who had young children. 'People were always very kind and helpful when I was alone with all the children.' When the war ended and she heard that her husband was coming home, her son Jim went out to try and snare a rabbit for her to cook. He was unsuccessful, but on the way home he met a man from the village, and when he told him of his

disappointment, the man went out and got a rabbit for them. 'Times were very hard,' she admits, 'but everyone was kind and helped each other. We had to stick together, to get through it.'

People also trusted one other, much more than they do today. Jean Pearse, who grew up at Holbeton in Devon says, 'If the people of the village went to Plymouth for the day they would leave their doors open. My mother used to leave her key in a hole in the wall beside the front door where everyone could see it.'

Coming of the modern age

Two faces of the future – Lynda Dear and her sister Maureen have their picture taken in 1959. In the fullness of time, advances in technology began to improve village life for everyone. Margaret Wilce remembers how electricity was put into their cottage in 1952. 'It altered our way of life completely,' she reflects. 'There was no more fetching wood, or attending to the lamps for light. Mother was so relieved that she put all the lamps out for the dustman, a service that had started the year before.' Previous to that little was thrown away, unlike in our modern society, recycling within the household was standard practice. Prior to the arrival of the first dustmen in the village in 1951, rubbish was thrown on to a tip in the woods. Then, a year later, her father bought their first television set, which was like a large piece of furniture and had a small screen in the middle about ten inches across. They had it in time to watch the Coronation of Her Majesty Queen Elizabeth II in 1953, and invited family, friends and neighbours around to their cottage to watch it in comfort. And the last major improvement to their lifestyle took place in the early 1960s, when mains water was eventually connected to all the cottages in the village. Luxury at last!

Chapter Two

Working the land

At one time agriculture provided the main source of employment for village people throughout Britain. Many owned or leased their own small farms, some of which were located within the village boundary itself. Others ran smallholdings, but the majority of farm labourers sought employment on the larger farms that dominated the countryside around them.

There were many different jobs to be done and some were more specialized than others. Agriculture was both arable, and livestock based. Arable farming was concerned with the growing of crops such as cereals, root vegetables and peas, and livestock would mainly be cattle, sheep and pigs. Some work was seasonal, which meant a farm worker might have to adapt himself to other types of work, at different times of the year.

Harvesting and haymaking

While researching this book, what comes across time and time again is the community spirit that village people had in earlier times, and their willingness to help one another. Perhaps the best illustration of this came during harvesting and haymaking on local farms, when people pulled together in a way that would be unimaginable today.

People from all around the village would come to lend a hand, whether they worked on the farm or not. They might have been the village schoolteacher, or blacksmith, and their ages ranged from children to grandparents. It was almost as though rural people had an inherent instinct, handed down through the generations, to help the farmer make hay or harvest his corn before the winter weather began to set in.

At Walford in Herefordshire Margaret Wilce recalls, 'In the summer all the men used to help the local farmers get the hay and corn in. The grass was cut by hand with a scythe, or a horse-drawn grass-cutting machine. When the grass had dried the horse and cart was brought into the field and we, yes I helped in my own small way, had to throw the hay up on to the cart where one of the men flattened it. It was eventually put into a rick and a man known as the thatcher came and thatched it to keep the wet out.'

At harvest time after the men, and often the women as well, had cut the corn with their scythes it was collected into sheaves. The sheaves were stacked in bundles of about five or six ready for a cart to come and take them to the farm where the threshing machine would separate the

corn from the straw. In those days the straw was not baled, but left loose, and would be used for winter bedding for the animals.

Farming was very labour intensive, particularly so during the summer months when the haymaking and harvesting took place. Luckily for the farmers these activities coincided with the long school holidays, and the older boys couldn't wait to get to work to earn some money. Jack Gee who lived on a farm at Thorney in the Isle of Ely says, 'At harvest time we had six weeks holiday from school and any boys over 12 were allowed to work on the farms. They did such jobs as leading the horse and wagon from the fields loaded with wheat sheaves to the stackyard, where a gang of men would build them into sugar-loaf stacks, so named because of their shape. They received about 12 shillings for a 70-hour week. If it rained there was no pay, unless there were jobs vacant in the barn or stables.'

For the menfolk of the village who came to lend a hand, it was almost as though corn harvesting and haymaking were celebrations in the rural calendar, which they enjoyed as social occasions helped along with draughts of cider. 'In between loads,' says Margaret Wilce, 'the men drank

Previous page: Harvesting at Hoggard's Farm near the village of Huggate in the Yorkshire Wolds.

Below: 'Harvest Time' from a postcard, postmarked 1930.

The harvest at Brunsell Farm, Stourton Caundle in Dorset, in the 1920s.

home-made cider from a stone jar, drunk out of a cow's horn which was passed from man to man.'

Richard Shimmin, who lived at Dalby on the Isle of Man recalls that on the day the threshing machine visited the farm, some of the farmers' wives would help each other to cook a big midday meal for all the men who had assisted. Afterwards the men would gather outside to smoke a pipe of strong Battleaxe tobacco. For obvious reasons

Meal breaks

Matt Hatham (left) and Edward Peacock on the traction engine at Middle Deepdale Farm in about 1930. The girl in the front is Monica Mosley, who would bring the workers their mid-morning lunch (pronounced lauenchen in broad Yorkshire). This would consist of pork pies, apple pies, bread and so on, all home-baked. There was also a billycan or a bucket of tea with tin mugs. Many a mouth was burnt on the tin mugs. Lunch was taken at the farm, and then another lauenchen was taken mid-afternoon. Plenty of tea was needed as it was a very dusty job.

Hay Time, Brounsell Farm, Stourton Gaundle.

they couldn't smoke while near the straw itself.

Other than a sense of community obligation and the satisfaction of helping the farmer, what else did the village people get from their efforts during haymaking and harvesting? One thing was a rabbit for the pot. Margaret Wilce recalls that the first tractor she ever saw was used during the corn harvest and as the tractor got nearer to the middle of the field the rabbits had to make a run for it. 'The men were waiting with their guns,' she recalls, 'and very few got away. We were all assured of rabbit dinner for the next few days.'

At Murthly in Perthshire, Bill Wilson recalls using catapults as a means of killing rabbits, but during corn harvesting sticks were enough. 'When the corn was being cut,' he says, 'long before the days of combine harvesters, we used to follow the binder, with a stout stick. When the field got to the last little bit it was crawling with rabbits. I once came home with 22 and gave most of them away to old age pensioners.'

At the farm where Jack Gee worked in Thorney, they employed binders to put the cut corn into sheaves, and he too remembers the rabbits. 'When the binders had only a small section left in the field everyone encircled the

area in anticipation, armed with sticks and dogs. The rabbits and hares that had been hiding in the corn would break out and run in all directions as the noise of the binder came near. Some would be lucky and escape the ring of dogs and humans, hiding in the nearest standing corn, only to run the gauntlet of death at a later date.'

Jean Pearse from Holbeton in Devon remembers harvest time as being a very happy time for the village children, as they went into the fields to help stand the sheaves of corn. 'Threshing time was a big day,' she notes. 'Each day the thresher used to call at different farms and all the farm workers from the surrounding

Haymaking at Brunsell Farm, Stourton Caundle in Dorset. Mr Albin Harris, the sitting tenant, purchased Brunsell Farm at the 1911 Stourton Estate sale. It is currently being farmed by the sixth generation of the Harris family.

After the harvest

Jack Gee of Thorney remembers another benefit to the villagers from the corn harvest. It was called gleaning and was another way that children could make a little money. 'After a field had been cleared of sheaves quite a lot of corn ears were left on the ground. Mothers would organize the children into gangs, each wearing an apron with a large deep pocket in the front. We would work across the field in a line with our backs bent double picking up the corn. This was known as gleaning and was appreciated by all the families because the corn they gleaned was later fed to their pigs. Our cash for this task depended on our parents, some could not afford to give any.'

Matt Hatham's steam engine would work the threshing machines, and would be hired out to all the outlying farms on threshing days. The man working the engine would have to get up two hours earlier than everyone else, to get the steam up, at the same time being careful not to set the stacks alight.

Harry Coultas and Edward Peacock threshing grain at Octon Lodge near Driffield in Yorkshire, in about 1938. Barley would be carried into the granary in 16 stone sacks, and wheat, in 18 stone bags. This would involve a walk of about 40 yards across the farmyard, and up 14 steps with the sacks. On threshing days they would have to carry between 60 and 100 sacks. So they needed to be fit and strong.

farms would help and then go into the farmhouse for a midday roast meal. I remember the meals that Mrs Annie Sherrell and Mrs Elma Sherrell, my father's cousins, used to put on the table. There were great platefuls of home-grown vegetables.'

But farming was often hard, unforgiving work, for horses and men alike and accidents while working were not uncommon, and this is perhaps best explained by Mrs Peacock from Cayton in North Yorkshire. 'My dad used to go threshing on the farms. Us children used to rush from school down to the farm just to see him, because by this time my parents had separated. Dad moved out, lack of money being the main fault. He worked hard and carried the corn in huge sacks from the back of the huge threshing machine, which had pulleys run from a tractor to work it, up a flight of steps into the granary, back and forward all day. He had been a ploughman, left home at 13 and went on a farm. He looked after a team of six Shire horses and used to take them to Burniston Show in all the brasses and plumes. He had an accident though when one bolted and trod on his head, bursting his eardrum and fracturing his scull. So after that he just became a farm labourer.'

There is no doubt that the summer months of harvesting and haymaking, were a special time for village folk, and another chance for people to bond together and rededicate their commitment to each other and their community.

A busy scene on a farm near Cobham in Surrey around 1934. The farm was one of several owned by the Combe family of the Cobham Park Estate.

Horses and machines

During the early part of the 20th century, although tractors were becoming increasingly available in British agriculture, on smaller farms that could not afford to buy expensive machinery, horsepower was still the main way of getting things done. Man still relied heavily on the horse, as he had done for centuries.

Machines were constantly being invented to make different farming jobs more efficient, but the horse remained an integral feature of most designs. Haymaking and harvesting involved horses in several ways, but in the agricultural scheme of things, ploughing was another task primarily undertaken by horses.

David Andrews grew up in the rural village of Woodlands St Mary near Newbury in Berkshire and he recalls, 'Ploughing with horses was a slow process. It was thought that a good ploughman could plough an acre a day, and that would mean he walked about ten miles as well as the horses. They had hollow shoulders as they adapted to the shape of the horse collar, as all their lives they pushed into it, to pull ploughs, carts and wagons. It took three horses to pull a two-furrow plough.'

For many of these farm horses, each day was a long and gruelling challenge. 'The horses were very tired by the end of the day,' notes David Andrews, 'but somehow seemed to sense when it was getting near to knocking off time. On one occasion I remember Fred "Timmy" Timms was cutting the corn in the field opposite Fieldridge Cottages at approximately 7pm. The farm manager went to see how much he had done, and said, "I thought you would be nearer the middle." Timmy replied, "These horses are tired boss." The manager answered with, "Once more round the field won't hurt them." It was a hard life for working horses.'

During the year the same horses might be used for several different jobs, so their handlers had to form a special relationship with them, in order to get the best out of them.

'The man driving the horse-drawn binder had to be alert at all times,' Mr Andrews points out. 'He had to control the horses and also adjust the binder controls as necessary, and keep an eye open for any loose or untied sheaves. Sometimes the binder twine would break, or there would be problems with the knotter, which was a clever device which tied the knot of the bind around the sheaf.'

During haymaking, horses would pull the wagons that were laden down with hay, to take

White House Farm near Bradfield in South Yorkshire, 1930. Tom Sanderson raking hay with one of his beloved horses. He never married and left some money in his will to a charity that cared for old farm horses.

them across the fields to the stackyards. They would also pull hay sweeps and rakes, and some farmers had hay loaders, which had an elevator towed behind the wagon. A revolving drum of tines raked the hay from the ground to the base of the machine, where a series of prongs lifted it on to the elevator, which carried it up to the top of the wagon.

For the men who worked with, and looked after both horses and machines, there were often hours of non-productive work, as David Andrews goes on to explain. 'Farm workers put in hours of non-productive work, as each time the haymaking equipment was moved to another field, the hay sweeps and elevators had to be packed up and then unpacked. They usually left off work on the fields at about 4.15pm, then went back to the stables to feed and clean the horses, check and clean their hooves, to finish at five o'clock. The carters made a last check on their horses at around 9.30pm.'

David Andrews pinpoints 1937 as the year that tractors began to arrive on the farms around Woodlands St Mary. 'This made some horses redundant,' he notes, 'but not all farmers could afford the tractors. Mr Hussey at Burgess Farm had a Massey Harris; Mr J Manchester at East End Farm, and Mr Siddy Manchester at Battens

Daddy and Me.

Potato harvesting

Horses worked in all aspects of farming, and Jack Gee recalls how they would haul trucks of potatoes through the muddy fields. This kind of operation shows how important horsepower remained to farming, and the backbreaking work expected of these sturdy animals. Jack Gee describes how one horse could pull three flat trucks, each weighed down with a ton of potatoes. They hauled these across the fields to the road, and on towards the loading platform of a light railway that had been specially built by the farmer. Just before reaching the platform there was a slope, and here the trucks were hauled individually using two horses for safety reasons. The potatoes were then drawn along the little railway track to Thorney station, from where they would be sent to the London markets at Covent Garden. Of course, within a few years of this tractors took over from horses and then road transport took the place of the railways, and haulage lorries would carry the potatoes along with other crops direct from the farm to the markets.

Duncan Lucas with his horse Betsy in 1952. Mr Lucas ran his own farm at Wigston Magna in Leicestershire, and he remembers that Betsy was the last but one working horse in the village.

Left: A small boy takes a ride home with his father after a day's work on the farm. This postcard entitled 'Daddy and Me' was published by Valentine's and posted in 1909.

Ron Foster with a boy from the village photographed in 1950. Ron lived in Oving in Buckinghamshire and worked at Crossroads Farm and even though by this time there was a tractor on the farm, this horse called Captain, was still used. 'Captain was worth his weight in gold,' says Ron's son Bernard, 'he certainly earned his keep, and died of old age in 1959.'

Farm both had Standard Fordsons. The Hussey brothers at Hilldrop Farm also had a Fordson and this was the first tractor I saw which was fitted with rubber tyres. They all had TVO paraffin engines, and with their open exhaust pipe could be heard working over half a mile away. Mr Butler at Poughley Farm had the first power-driven binder I saw and in 1944 he had the first combine harvester and pick-up baler.'

Today these machines are doing the work that many farm workers and their horses would have done in bygone times. There is no doubt that village life and culture has changed dramatically with the advent of agricultural machinery. At one time, farms were important features in the working and social make-up of the village, but now they are completely separate and the two rarely combine, as village people seldom become involved with what goes on in them.

Lending a helping hoof

Frank Hind lived at Chipstable in Somerset's Brendon Hills. His mother was a farmer's daughter, and was a skilled horsewoman and shepherdess. She ran a small riding school and did a bit of horse dealing. 'My mother never did learn to drive a car,' says Frank, 'she always used the pony and trap, but then in those days few country folk had a car.' This photograph shows her in 1952, riding her horse Bracken up and down the silage rick to flatten it down.

Above: Farmer Tom Sanderson (left) at Stores Grange Farm, Stannington, South Yorkshire, in the 1960s, with a Ferguson 35 tractor.

Changes in farming

Just as horses were being replaced by tractors and other machines, so were the tools and equipment they pulled. Farming machinery, both hand-operated and horse-driven, were changing just as drastically as any other aspect of rural life, revolutionizing the way in which farms were managed and reducing the number of people working on them.

The farm machinery used in particular parts of Britain, would of course reflect the type of agriculture that was prevalent in the area. It must also be realized that rural Britain had undergone a technical revolution, over many hundreds of years. This effectively meant that, whereas today, the older generations look back with nostalgic affection for the machinery that was used before the advent of tractors, elder citizens during the early part of the 20th century would have remembered the equipment and processes that were employed during their youth. For instance, just as tractors replaced the work of the threshing machine in harvesting, these had themselves replaced earlier methods of removing the husks from grain.

Although threshing machines had been around for some time, they really began to take off in the middle of the 19th century, after which, this process and equipment remained standard for the next hundred years. Before that time, the cutting of crops was done by hand, with reaping hooks and scythes. This made each process even slower and more costly in terms of manpower. The scythe was the universal tool, used in many agricultural processes for generations.

When mowing machines arrived, communal mowing was already becoming a thing of the past. So therefore, the life of farm workers during the period we cover, although very different from those of today, was equally different from decades before.

Horses now did the bulk of heavy farm work, but there were many processes that involved smaller equipment that would previously have been done by hand, and again these would revolutionize the way that country people would work. By far the biggest effect to many of these jobs, was caused by electricity, and by 1959, the majority of British farms would have been connected to the grid.

Two particular examples of this would have been milking and sheep-shearing. With milking, the advantages were obvious. In many large dairy farms, legions of young local girls would have been employed as dairymaids. Now, thanks to electricity, milk could be collected and processed, both more quickly and more hygienically, and being a dairymaid became an occupation of the past.

Sheep-shearing was itself another communal activity, and on one day a year, or sometimes two, if the flock was large enough, neighbours and villagers would help gather the farmer's flock together in readiness for shearing. From experience gained over the years, numerous farmers, shepherds, and villagers would set about the shearing and the hope would be that by the end of the day the job was done, and the next day or so, everyone would help the next farmer to gather and shear his sheep. With the coming of electricity, fewer and fewer people were required, and often an outside professional would come to the farm with his new tools, and do the job that dozens might have done before.

These are just a few examples of the way in which farming techniques and tools changed from 1900-1960, and the way this affected both the farming community, and the local villages.

It's now the 1960s, and in Wiltshire, beneath the famous White Horse, the tractor has long since replaced real horses working in the fields. From a postcard published by Salmon.

Working in the fields

As well as the cereals, oats, wheat and barley, there were many other crops in British agriculture that demanded a large workforce, and kept many of the villagers employed. One such was potatoes and the flat open fens around Thorney were ideal for their production, as Jack Gee recalls.

'The most distant field on the farm was the 50 acre in Fish Fen and it was also the largest field on the farm. Potatoes were stored in earth clamps and opened in winter to select the seed potatoes from the larger ones for consumption. This job was done regardless of weather and I remember the men shaking the riddle and picking the potatoes with fingers half-frozen and coat collars raised against a blistering east wind. Tarpaulin sheets were rigged on poles as shelter but that didn't stop all the freezing gusts. The bags were sown up with string and loaded on wagons, then hauled by three horses over the deep rutted mud drove to the farm. This transport problem eventually forced the farmer to lay a light railway line from a raised loading platform.'

As with the corn harvest, farmers would often enlist the help of villagers on a casual basis, to work on whichever crop was grown. At Eight Ash Green in Essex, for instance, Geoffrey Charge recalls, 'When the local farmer wanted his crops harvested he would put word round the village, and Mum and several other mums would go and pick peas or potatoes, and after school I would go and help as well. The best crop was the strawberries for I could eat more than I picked, but it was easy to earn a lot of money if you could spend long enough in the fields. The baskets we filled were tipped into big wooden crates and when they were weighed we got paid in cash for each one. Peas paid about one shilling and sixpence for a 28lb sack.'

In Dorset, Ken Knott who worked on a farm near Sturminster Newton, recalls the backbreaking work of harvesting mangolds, another popular crop that was grown to provide fodder for the cattle.

'The mangold harvest was another autumn task starting around mid October, with my brother and myself assisting my father, and my mother joining in between the household chores. We would take three lines apiece, pulling the mangolds up by the leaves from the soil, then twisting the leaves from the top, and throwing them into heaps at mid distance between us. By keeping the heaps in straight lines, and at the right distance apart, hauling would be made a lot

A busy scene in the fields, for all except the man dressed in black sitting in the back of the upturned cart. From a postcard, publisher unknown.

easier. A horse and putt was used to haul the mangolds, and handling them on a cold frosty morning was a very unpleasant job indeed, my hands would become numb, and I can remember a lot of arm swinging and rubbing of hands on mornings such as this.'

Another problem associated with harvesting crops such as mangolds in the autumn, was the effect of the weather. By this time the rain had begun to set in, especially in the more exposed areas, and with the constant movement of men, horses and machines, if farms had them, the whole area became a quagmire and a very unpleasant environment in which to work. Being a farm worker was, therefore, often a messy, cold and dirty job.

Soon after these crops had been gathered in, the winter began in earnest, bringing another problem – frost. 'In cold weather,' writes Ken Knott, 'the mangold heaps left out in the field were protected from the frost by covering them with the leaves removed from their tops. The mangolds were stored in a clamp, located in a suitable place near the cow stall. On arrival of the horse-drawn putt at the site identified for the clamp they were tipped on to the ground. They were then thrown back by hand into the clamp,

Carting the mangolds. Reproduced from a postcard published by Raphael Tuck & Sons.

Tom Sanderson, with a load of swedes for animal feed at White House Farm, near Bradfield, South Yorkshire, in the 1920s. The swedes would be put through a turnip cutter before feeding them to the sheep, cows and calves. Horses would eat them whole.

Taking a lunch break during harvesting on Hoggard's Farm, near the village of Huggate in the Yorkshire Wolds.

which was constructed in the form of a gable roof. The completed clamp was then thatched in the same way as a haystack. This ensured that the mangolds remained in good condition throughout the hardest winter weather.'

For the cows, all this effort was well worth the trouble, as they apparently loved the flavour of the mangolds. Some farmers took the mangolds out to the fields, and simply tossed them whole on to the ground for the cows to eat. Others, such as Mr Knott's father would pulp them in a hand-operated machine. This mangold pulp was then carried in buckets to the cow stall, and tipped into the cribs. 'In fact he was so particular,' says Ken Knott of his father, 'that when the mangolds were taken from the clamp, all the soil was removed before they were placed in the pulping machine. This was a time absorbing exercise especially at the weekends when a double lot was prepared on a Saturday, to run over the Sunday. This meant that on Sunday afternoons before milking, I would only have to pulp the mangolds, and then carry them across the farmyard to the cow stalls, using two four-gallon buckets.'

Perthshire and Angus in Scotland were two of the most concentrated areas for soft fruit production in the UK, which seasonally provided

employment opportunities for village residents, both young and old. Bill Wilson from Murthly recalls that there were two particular classics in Scottish village culture in those parts, one was picking berries, known as 'rasps', and the other was the 'tattie holidays', introduced during the war to help the farmers get the crops lifted.

'You went to the berries and worked your butt off for a penny-halfpenny old money per pound, when the crop was heavy at the start of the season. The object was to earn one pound per day. This was so that you could go back to school with a new pair of trousers and blazer. The object of the exercise was to weigh in at mid morning for five bob, and hopefully repeat that for the rest of the day. Now it is all pick your own and there is no supervision. In my young days the gaffer would stride up the dreel and send you back to pick your bottom berries.'

Richard Shimmin explains that on the Isle of Man the fields were cultivated on a five-year rotation system, where everything was done by hand and horse.

'The first year,' he says, 'the field would be ploughed, harrowed (raked) and rolled, prior to seed, oats, wheat or barley being sown on it. Some four months later it would be cut with a binder, pulled by two horses, which cut the crops and tied it into sheaves, which were stood on end in stooks of eight and left to dry. They would be carried in and stacked in the hacket (stackyard) on a cut gorse base, about nine yards by three yards, and covered with thatch cut from the mountain tops. They were then left until the winter, when the threshing machine and baler, pulled by a steam engine belonging to a contractor, would come round from farm to farm. About 14 men from neighbouring farms would help each other to feed sheaves into the top of the machine, which separated the grain from the straw.'

The grain itself would be stored in sacks, and put in a warm place that was used as a granary, such as above the cow-house or the stables. The straw would be tied into bundles, or if a farmer had a baler, it would be made into bales and stacked for winter use, normally as fresh bedding for farm animals.

During the second year of this rotation process, in the winter, the field would be ploughed, cross-ploughed and harrowed into ridges, which would all be done by horses. In the spring, the manure that had piled up during the winter while the animals were in the sheds would be put into these ridges, ready for the crops. Potatoes were the main crop on the Isle of Man, and would be planted ten inches apart and then covered with the ridging plough. But other ridges would be reserved for growing turnips, carrots, cabbages and cauliflowers, all of which would be later dug by hand, and presented for sale.

'For the third year,' continues Richard

Shimmin, 'the field would be ploughed, harrowed and rolled again, and grain sown on to it, and a week or two later grass seed would be scattered on top with a fiddle.'

In harvest time during the summer of the third year, the grain would be cut and handled as in the first year, and then the grass would be left to grow. In the fourth year the grass would be cut with a reaping machine and stacked in heaps to dry, then brought into the hacket and stacked for winter feed. The field would then be left unplanted and simply used for grazing stock during the fifth year and then the sequence would start again. To operate this system the farmer would obviously need more than one field, in order to alternate the process.

This old postcard of a hand-painted photograph, published by *Weekly Tale-Teller*, is titled 'Threshing.'

Crofting in Skye

The family of Ewen Gillies lived on a croft in the small village of Edinbane on the Isle of Skye, which must have been one of the most inhospitable places to try and eke out an existence from the land, but even here the land and, of course, the surrounding sea, provided for most of their needs.

'On the croft we grew vegetables, kept a few cattle and some hens, which along with the occasional wild rabbit and fish from the sea or river, met most of our dietary needs. There were berries and fruits growing on the crofts and by the roadside that could be harvested for jam making. Most crofts grew a variety of crops that were shared or bartered, which meant that few people went without and the need for crop rotation was reduced to a minimum. We also had access to a steady and bountiful supply of fish that could be stored in salt, smoked or dried.'

Crofters houses on the Isle of Skye, from a postcard published by Valentine's. The family of Ewen Gillies lived in a similar croft at the small village of Edinbane on Skye. These sturdy stone houses with their thatched roofs had few, small windows to keep out the winter storms.

Livestock farming

In terms of livestock, different parts of Britain were always known for their varied and particular breeds of cattle. Hereford, Aberdeen Angus and Jersey cows were all named after their area of origin but today the breeds are scattered throughout Britain and can also be found worldwide.

Prize winning heifers with the presentation cup at Taunton market in 1961.

Billy Morris, a bachelor shepherd of the 1920s from the Hackleton area of Northamptonshire.

On his farm at Thorney in the Isle of Ely, Jack Gee's father often ran 100 or more beef cattle, which at that time were Herefords. It was a popular breed on which his father was quite an authority and Jack remembers how he would regularly check his stock.

'My dog Pip and I would accompany him to inspect the stock and gently drive them past him while he ran his expert eyes over each animal. This task was usually done when they were almost ready for market, but when October came around, a more intensive inspection was carried out. The chosen animal was tied to the manger and allowed to eat while my father ran his hand over the animal. Horns, hooves, eyes, nostrils, teeth and tail had to be perfect to secure his approval for entry into the Peterborough Fat Stock Show at Christmas.'

As the show approached, Mr Gee would normally select six animals, and from then onwards they would receive special attention. First of all, if they were going to be led around a show ring, they would have to become used to being handled. In order to achieve this the first week after selection would be devoted to handling these nervous animals, which until then had only known the freedom of the herd.

'Once they became happy to wear a halter,' he continues, 'they were led around the yard with the handler quietly talking to them, or humming a tune. While the beast was feeding the handler lifted a foreleg for the first time and then lowered it gently. Within a week it would be completely docile and accept handling as being normal. Any beast that proved difficult at first would require two men to train it to be led, with one man each

Molly Kinghorn's Uncle Jack with Auntie Jessie leading a bull. Jack was the manager of a farm that ran a herd of Shorthorn dairy cattle in Yorkshire, which won many prizes at shows in the area around Harrogate.

side holding a rope tied to the leather halter. Sometimes a pole would be clipped to the nose ring if it proved to be difficult and he usually gave up the fight and the pole was discarded. Every day until the show, those magnificent animals were walked around the farmyard twice a day with my father casting an expert eye over each one.'

As well as teaching these animals to become docile, in order to take part in the show, a great deal of attention had to be given to their appearance. There would be intensive grooming of their coats, hooves and horns. By the time they were ready for Peterborough, they were a picture of perfection and their handlers had good reason to be proud of their charges. 'Sadly,' admits Jack, 'the aim was to produce the best beef bullock to grace the Christmas dinner plates.'

The show was always held on Wednesday, a week before Christmas and the farm staff all had the day off, and so did their children. Quite a procession would make its way towards Thorney station; show beasts, farm workers and their families dressed in their best, boarded the train for Peterborough. It was a great day, and a great occasion in the lives of rural people living in a relatively remote area of the Fens.

Back at the farm itself, for the rest of the herd it was a different routine. Sometimes they would need to be treated for different things, such as warble fly. To do this the bullocks were driven into the stable yard, which was an enclosed area with a gate in just one wall. Around the walls of this enclosure were stable boxes, each of which contained a fodder manger with an iron ring set into it. A stockman would then separate a bullock

from the herd by dropping the looped end of a rope attached to a long ash stick over its horns. The other end of the rope was passed through the iron ring on the manger, and once this was done, the men in the yard would pull on the rope, thus drawing the bullock tightly against the manger, and the treatment was administered.

As well as farming beef cattle, there were of course dairy farms, which supplied milk to the community. In the winter the cows and calves would often be taken in at night, which resulted in a lot of work, cleaning out each morning, carrying hay for consumption, and fresh straw for bedding. Another job that Ken Knott remembered doing was loading a wheelbarrow with the dung and straw from the cow stalls and pushing each load to the dunghill, or midden as it was known.

Cows on the shore of Lake Windermere near Bowness. From a postcard published by G D & D, London.

BOWNESS FROM NEAR THE FERRY HOTEL.

John Watts farmed at Crossroads Farm, Oving in Buckinghamshire, in the 1930s. According to Bernard Foster, whose father worked on the farm, they did the milking by hand until 1957, when they went over to machine milking. The milk was put into churns that were left on a stand in the lane for collection. The lorry arrived at the farm at about 8am, seven days a week, to take the churns to the Nestles milk factory in Aylesbury, where it was bottled.

The tiled single-storey building without windows was the village pound at Stourton Caundle in Dorset. It was used for penning up any stray cattle or sheep.

'After cleaning out the stalls,' writes Mr Knott, 'I would carry in straw to provide fresh bedding for the cows. On fine and dry winter days the cattle could be let outside into the yard for some exercise. However, on cold and wet days they were kept inside the cow stalls, only going outside for a drink of water, and then straight back in to be tied up and have a feed of hay. On days such as this, the stalls would be cleaned out a second time in the afternoon prior to milking.'

Richard Shimmin recalls that on the Isle of Man milking was the first job in the morning all year round, and was done before breakfast. Some of the milk was sold locally and some was collected by a dairy company for town delivery. 'The rest,' he explains, 'would be kept in earthenware dishes for a couple of days on stone shelves in a dairy, as good as any fridge, then put into a churn.'

One of Richard's evening jobs was to deliver half a pint of milk to two sisters who lived in a little cottage under the Foxdale railway bridge. He recalls that the sisters were always dressed in long black clothes, with shawls and bonnets, and they would always like a chat. He doesn't ever remember being paid for the milk but points out, 'such was life in the country in those days.'

After cattle, sheep were very common on British farms, and in many parts were, and still are, the main type of livestock. Frank Hind's mother was a farmer's daughter and a skilled horsewoman and shepherdess. She ran a small riding school at Chipstable in Somerset's Brendon Hills and did a bit of horse dealing, as well as buying in around 50 acres of grass keep each year, on which to run a flock of 50 breeding ewes. 'Many's the time,' says Frank, 'I've been out in the cold early hours with a lantern in the lambing shed. We used to walk the sheep to be sold to the sheep fair at Raleigh's Cross, some eight miles across country. We used a pony and collie dog to round up the sheep for foot rotting and dagging. My mother never did learn to drive a car; she always used the pony and trap, but then in those days few country folk had a car.'

In order for people to take their sheep to market, the West Country in particular was criss-crossed by droves or green lanes. It was a common sight, reminiscent of a scene from a Thomas Hardy novel, to see a flock of sheep being shepherded along these grassy lanes, right up until World War II, and in some places even beyond that.

Joanne Cousins lived at Salmonby in Lincolnshire, where her father was a sheep dealer; an occupation that she says has completely gone due to changing farming practices. He bought and sold sheep and sometimes cattle, both for himself and other farmers. He travelled up and down the country to attend the markets at places like Banbury, Carlisle, and Northampton, which at the time in question were great distances to cover. He also used the more local markets, at the likes of Alford, Horncastle, and Sleaford, all of which have since disappeared.

'Living on a sheep farm meant hard work,' says Joanne. 'I had to walk sheep, with my friends, up and down the villages to different pastures. I would have pet lambs

Frank Hind's mother with horse and foal at Newhouse Farm on the Brendons in 1958. Mrs Hind was a skilled horsewoman, who among other things, ran a small riding school and also did a bit of horse dealing.

Edward Lewis and his wife Louisa Hardisty were the tenant farmers of Throstle Nest Farm, on the Haverah Park Estate at Beckwithshaw near Harrogate. Mr Lewis is seen working in the backyard of the farm where they kept pigs, hens and a few other animals.

to look after and feed. In the lambing season we would have old drawers and boxes with lambs in around the fire in the kitchen. There would always be ducks, geese, chickens and so on, around the back door.'

David Andrews says that in the farms around Woodlands St Mary, in Devon, sheep were pitched in pens formed by hurdles that were made of hazel sticks. 'To watch a hurdle-maker or a thatcher effortlessly split a hazel stick in half from end to end, required a knack which was handed down from father to son. The shepherd made a hole in the ground with a pointed iron bar, and then drove a post into it with a beetle, which was a long-handled mallet. The hurdles were fixed to the posts with a loop of hazel stick. While the sheep were grazing in that pen, the shepherd pitched out more hurdles for a pen adjoining the first one, so that when the first pen was cropped, he was able to open a hurdle to move them into the second one. He then dismantled the first pen and carried the hurdles to make a third one, and so on, until the whole field was cropped. To move the hurdles he laid one on top of another, wriggled the iron bar through the middle of them and then carried them on his shoulder, sometimes over a hundred yards. I often wonder how many tons of hurdles

Far right: Mrs Aitchison's father worked as a shepherd for 60 years, on a farm at Ancroft in Northumberland.

he carried during his working lifetime.'

The huge pig breeding companies of today really began to develop in the 1950s. Before then, pigs and poultry were just as likely to be kept by the villagers themselves, in village gardens or on small-holdings, as they were by the farmers. Duncan Lucas, who was born in Wigston Magna in Leicestershire in 1929, was still a teenager when he bought his first animals.

'I kept my first pigs on the allotments on Horsewell Lane. My allotment was just outside the Council field at the side of the old stream, fed from the horse wells from which the name of the lane was derived. I built two sties. I was 16 or 17 at the time and Frankie Woodward lent me some money to buy this allotment. In my spare time, which was mainly at night, I used to fetch the bricks, sand and cement from Albert Lowe's yard in Bull Head Street, load them on my barrow and push it to where I was building my sties. The brickwork was uneven, but it did its job and I was so proud when eventually I took my own pig up to Freck's to be killed. I was taught how to take the leaf (fat) out and to render it down. I also learnt the art of curing bacon and ham – and I still do it.'

When Duncan Lucas kept pigs he discovered that when the older animals were off colour, or were bored and biting each other, if he threw them coal, they would chew it and push it around with their noses. Once, a pig was kept in the cellar, where it thrived, 'until mother asked for some coal to be brought up and they found that the pig had eaten the coal!'

The farming life

In the main, agriculture was thriving in Britain, but the constant invention of better machinery reduced the number of staff required to a bare minimum. Today most farms offer little opportunity for the regular employment of villagers, but in earlier times they had a special place at the heart of the community.

Richard Shimmin says that on the Isle of Man, 'the farmer's wife was known as the lady of the house. She had her own very important role to play in the life of the farm. As well as running the house and family she would keep a large flock of hens to provide fresh eggs every day for the kitchen, and to sell to neighbours. She would also breed geese and turkeys for the Christmas market. There would be a large fruit orchard full of apple, pear, plum and cherry trees and in the spring and summer, the farm garden would grow lettuce, onions, leeks and mint.'

The farmer's wife was a very busy person, but Richard admits that she would always have plenty of willing help from the local children in return for gifts of fruit and flowers to take home. Most of the fruit would be used in jam and pudding making. 'She also liked a bit of skeet (gossip),' he says, 'at the local tea fights and social evenings.'

'A popular dinner in the winter,' he explains, 'was vegetable soup followed by boiled salt herring and spuds. Flour was bought in 56lb bags and used in cooking almost every day with fresh milk and home-grown fruit to make large cakes and Manx bonnagh.' Other Manx meals included broth and dumplings followed with bread and butter pudding; or soda and potato cakes that were cooked on a flat iron plate, known as a griddle plate, which was laid on top of the fire.

In the winter evenings the family would sit around the fireplace, with dad, mum and grandparents in rocking chairs, while the children sat on thick rugs listening to stories from the past. 'There was no TV or radio in those days,' Richard

points out, 'but there were always big jugs of tea, coffee and cocoa sitting on the hearth for family and friends with a slice of bonnagh.'

Born on the Isle of Lewis, Jessie Lockhart recalls that every croft had its own patch of peat lane, which had to be cut and dried. Every spring the peat would be brought back to the croft and made into a peat stack ready to be used in the winter. These stacks were built in a special way so that the rain did not soak through and make the peat too wet to burn.

Above: Church Farm, Ashcott, in the 1930s. From the left: Stanley Cave, his father William, brother Frederick and Tom Durden.

Below: Southlands Farm, in Buckinghamshire from a postcard, published by Lucy & Birch of Uxbridge.

Manx farmhouse fare

Farmhouse food was basic but wholesome and varied around the country. Of the diet on the Isle of Man Richard Shimmin recalls pinjane, an old-fashioned yoghurt; and Manx bonnagh, a fruitcake fresh out of the oven, which would be spread with butter and covered in cheese. This was popular in the spring when everyone was busy working in the fields, and needed a quick nourishing snack.

SOUTHLANDS FARM, DENHAM

Mr G Thacker as a child, sitting on the traction engine, while his father stands by a Model T Ford, at Downside Farm in Surrey in 1934. The farm was owned by the Combe family, who lived at Cobham Park, and the Thackers lived in a tied house on the estate.

'After that,' she says, 'the crops had to be harvested. There would be barley, corn, potatoes, cabbage, carrots, turnips, and so on. All the families helped each other in these tasks. When it was your turn everybody had to be fed and this was done with a lot of talk and laughter. Most people had at least two cows, and some sheep. The cows, of course, had to be taken out to the meadow each morning and collected every evening, a task that I loved. The sheep also had to be brought home and sheared. Then there was

weaving, which most of the ladies on crofts and small farms undertook. I remember a lot of gossip and laughter in the loom sheds. The wool came from the warehouse in Stornoway, and was usually left at the end of the road of each village.'

Farmers and crofters were to a large extent in charge of their own destiny, but what was it really like for people living in villages who merely worked on farms. From the southern end of Britain, Marie Litchfield who lived in the village of Ashcott in Somerset gives a good

Sheep-dipping was an annual event at which farmers protected and cleansed their stock of parasites and diseases. This photo was taken in about 1910.

Left: Men threshing wheat in the 1930s at a farm near Henley-on-Thames, Oxfordshire, England, using a Surrell's patent compound steam traction engine (mounted on springs).

Below: Men and women packing asparagus near Evesham, Worcestershire in the 1930s. This was seasonal work as the harvesting period is so short.

Below left: Men weigh and sack potatoes at Rhossili, in the Gower Penninsula in the 1950s. Owing to the mild, wet winters, this part of Wales is noted for its early new potatoes.

indication of their lives as she writes:

'Farm labourers worked from morning until night every day, even part of Sunday, because the milking and feeding of the animals had to go on, yet their wages were only ten shillings and sixpence a week in 1936. This had to pay the rent of their cottages and keep themselves, their wives and their children. If they were ill or off work for some reason, then there was no pay for that day. Even if they were not able to work because of bad weather conditions, it was still "no work – no pay". There was no question of a holiday or even going anywhere. Many of the children were often ragged and dirty and had lice in their hair; they must have been cold in the winter. Even tiny tots played on the roads, and every year impetigo and all the other contagious diseases swept through the village. There were

Children sorting the hops during hop-picking in Kent in 1928.

This Raphael Tuck & Sons postcard is titled 'The Children's Playground' and gives an idea of how pleasant an environment, both farming and the rural life of yesteryear in general, were for kids to grow up in.

no antibiotics; I remember a little boy of six dying of measles. The mothers had a tough time; there were none of the labour-saving gadgets that we are so accustomed to today. Many had no mains water; none of us had hot water on tap. One got hot water by boiling it in a kettle. Washing-up liquids and detergents were unheard of. However, what we now think of as deprivation was by no means seen as such at the time - no doubt future generations will think of these present days as deprived. There were lots of

pleasures, many of which are gone now, to be replaced by television and holidays abroad. Everyone was in the same boat, so to speak, and it was a good boat to be in, and a steady one.'

Although Marie feels that when she was a girl living in Ashcott, times were hard, but good, she concludes by contrasting what the village was like then, and now, admitting that not everything had changed for the worst.

'When I visited the village 50 years later and saw the young mothers popping the toddlers into their car-seats and driving off to town to do the shopping, I realised what a vast change had taken place. The little ones looked so healthy and warmly dressed. I could see that, in some ways at least, it was a change for the better.'

The life of a farm labourer and his family up until 1960 was relatively simple. It was often a harsh, unforgiving life, very far removed from the picture postcard image we have today. However, with the advances in technology that offered things like personal motor transport, television, and better kitchens, people were quite rightly starting to become dissatisfied with their lot, and felt they could improve their standard of living by travelling to the nearest town to find better paid work. This enabled the home life of ordinary village people to improve beyond recognition in just a few short years.

Chapter Three

Up at the Big House

Most village communities were affected in some way by the benevolence of the local gentry, whose wealth often derived from the type of farming or industries prevalent in the area. Quite often large houses or country estates, situated close to a village would provide numerous opportunities for employment. The local gentry were also regarded as an eminent part of the community, giving support and funds to local events and projects. They quite often paid for a village hall to be built, or provided almshouses for the poor. The village fete or fair might have been held in their gardens, and they were always available to officiate at community ceremonies.

Self-contained villages

There were grand country houses throughout Britain, many of which were maintained by their supporting estates. Large country estates, such as the Berwick Estate in Shropshire, employed so many people doing various jobs that they built their own self-contained villages, where accommodation was provided for the people who worked on the estate.

Berwick House was bought from Lord Denbigh in 1878 by James Watson, who was twice MP for Shrewsbury, and the house thereafter remained in his family. The estate, situated three miles west of Shrewsbury covered a picturesque area of 5,000 acres, including a seven-mile section of the river Severn. There was also a 50-acre lake, complete with boathouse and water pumping station. John Stanley Woodcock was born and worked on the estate. His father Jack Woodcock had served with the Army Service Corps during World War I, before he was given the job of running a new pump and accumulator, which provided Berwick House with gas. All the cottages on the estate were still lit by candles. Jack also did odd jobs on the estate, and carried water up to the house.

John Stanley Woodcock's mother, Rose Edwards, also lived on the estate, her brother Bob was the gamekeeper, and she had worked as a helper at Berwick vicarage. Rose and Jack were married in 1921, and when Jack was given his new duties in 1922 his wife was expected to clean the church, and attend at the bothy, for a remuneration of £20 a year. Jack and Rose had three sons, all of whom would work on the estate at some point in their lives. Not only were most people in the village employed by the estate, many were related to one another, through

Above: Front view of Berwick House in Shropshire, photographed across the Hardy Garden. The house was bought from Lord Denbigh by Mr James Watson in 1878 and was thereafter lived in by his descendants. The estate covered an area of 5,000 acres to the west of Shrewsbury, including a seven mile section of the river Severn.

Rose Edwards aged 19 standing at the back of this photograph, on the right, The occasion was a vicarage tea party for the old ladies and gentlemen of the Berwick almshouses, in 1917. Rose would later marry Jack Woodcock, who became the very last resident of the same almshouses.

marriage, like Rose and Jack, and this kept the community close and confined to the estate boundaries. Jack was the last person to live in the estate almshouses, which had originally been provided for in the will of Sir Samual Jones in 1672. Today they have been converted into flats.

To give some idea of the size of the estate, and the employment opportunities it offered, John Stanley Woodcock's brother Fred, who had been a gardener on the estate, compiled the following list. There was Home Farm, which as the name suggests provided the family at the big house and their staff with most of the food and services they required. There was the church, almshouses, sheepcote, brickworks, gravel pit, dower house, tollhouse, tar pit, and limekiln. There was also an ordinance room with balcony and sprung wooden dance floor. There was a game larder, laundry, and a brew house where beer was brewed in large copper vats. There was even an area for drying the salmon nets that were used across the river Severn, and housing for the coracle boats that were used to put the nets in place. There was a boot cleaning room, two large coal and fuel stores, and a dairy with slate slabs and dozens of cream vats, adjoined by a churning room.

The coach house and stables, with an open

The wedding of Jack Woodcock aged 28, and Rose Edwards aged 23, at St Mary's Church, Shrewsbury in 1921. They were provided with accommodation on the Berwick Estate, which was Jack's employer.

fronted hitching area, had housing above it for the stable and coaching staff. There were also several harness and tack rooms, and a dog kennel set in the shape of a U. There was a water tower, on which was a clock, always kept three minutes fast to ensure that the carriage arrived at the front door on time. Near the coaching stables were a blacksmith's shop, a granary, further stables for the Shire workhorses, 15 pigsties, a two-storey mill house, cow house with hayloft over, and houses for the bailiff, wagoner, and gas man. This last was Jack Woodcock's house, of course, where his sons were born. The gas works where Jack worked were part of another group of buildings which included bull pens, loose boxes, and the estate saw shed, where at the time there was a steam-driven circular saw. At the rear was a large stackyard with three rows of Dutch barns, and a steam engine shed.

This list describes half of the buildings, both domestic and working, which constituted the village on the Berwick Estate. One can visualize how busy a place it must have been in its heyday. Some cottages were tied to the job their occupier did but not all the accomodation was provided free to the workers of the estate; some could be rented for an affordable sum.

Above: Jack Woodcock (right) with the footman and head butler from Berwick House, wearing aprons for cleaning the silver.

Below: Fred Woodcock in 1951, aged 18, while serving in the Grenadier Guards. He had previously worked in the gardens of Berwick.

Memories of Berwick

For a young child who spent most of his life in a city, spending the school holidays with relatives who were part of the staff of a large country estate promised that an exciting time would be had. Helping the various estate workers in their daily tasks meant that there was never a dull moment throughout the summer.

Fred Shore lived in Manchester, but spent every holiday with his large family at Berwick. He remembers his Uncle Jack and the unusual work he did, not only producing gas for Berwick House, but other things as well. 'Uncle Jack Woodcock was a mine of information. I watched him remove the coke from the gas retorts – two working and one in reserve. Then refilling with gas coal, burning the coke, scattered with tar underneath. I suppose a kind of baking process. Gas flowed through a series of pipes to the lime purifying beds. Then the tar was extracted and stored. The gasometer indicated, as it floated on water, the quantity of gas produced. It was fascinating to go with him into the woods, to pump water from the river Severn, for washing purposes at the house. I was allowed to try my hand at carrying two enamelled buckets of drinking water from the pump, with the aid of a yoke.'

There was a block of three houses at Home Farm; Jack and Rose lived in one, with Mr Escomb the farm bailiff in another. He had a reputation as a strict disciplinarian. In the third house lived Uncle Art (Arthur Edwards) with his wife Gladys. Arthur was the estate wagoner, and looked after two Shire horses, both strawberry roans, named Dragon and Bowler. Gladys used to help Mr Leek the cowman, with hand milking the herd. Although the Shires worked in the fields, they might have done other jobs as well. One day for instance, Uncle Art asked Fred if he would help him load gas coal from the railway sidings in town. 'With one horse in the shafts, and the other trailing we arrived at the sidings,' he explains, 'where I did my bit, transferring coal to cart.' On the way back to the estate at the top of a hill, Uncle Art got down from the cart and put on the brakes. On his return he didn't climb aboard immediately, but fell about with laughter at the sight of little Fred, covered from head to foot in coal dust, as though he had just climbed down a sooty chimney.

Bob Edwards, the gamekeeper, was uncle to both the Woodcock children and Fred Shore. He resided in the gamekeeper's house with his wife Mary. He also had a hut that overlooked a field full of chicken coops, which was the pheasant-

Jack Woodcock fetching water from the pump on the Berwick Estate in 1931. The water would be carried in the two buckets hung from a yoke up to Berwick House.

rearing field. Each coop contained a broody hen and up to 20 chicks.

Fred Shore remembers the first day Uncle Bob took him hunting on the estate. 'The thought of big game hunting came to mind as Uncle Bob Edwards asked if I would like to go with him one morning. We walked passed Leighton Knowles to a field he called Hell Hole. "Keep behind the gun." I was instructed. Well I thought, it's all right for him in protective leggings – the thistles and

The estate wagoner, Uncle Art (Arthur Edwards), with his two strawberry roan Shire horses, Dragon and Bowler. His own father had been the estate wagoner before him.

nettles were unkind to me in my long stockings and short trousers. Soon the two cartridges were fired from the double-barrelled gun, and the cook at Berwick House was given whatever she requested for the pot.'

Another of Uncles Bob's responsibilities on the estate was to oversee the beaters when the folk from the big house fancied some sport. This was a moment that the young Fred had eagerly awaited, but later remembered for its unpleasant consequences. 'Eventually my turn came to be invited as a beater at the shoot. It was a great day out. My reward was to share a chunk of cheese and crusty bread with a glass of super draft cider.' Satisfied with his lot, he made his way to the stackyard to sleep it off on top of the hay, before eventually making his way home. 'The next day,' he continues, 'I had a bad dose of diarrhoea – it must have been due to the hot hay – only then did I realize the distance from the house to the toilet near the drinking water pump. A dose of brandy soon put me right.'

Everybody knew everybody on the estate, so it must have been a wonderful life. As each holiday came to a close, Fred was left with very special memories. Such as the time the steam tractor in the stackyard was going to have its boiler fired, so that it would be able to drive the circular saw.

Watching for poachers

Gamekeeper Bob Edwards, shown above with his nephew Fred Shore on his left. On one occasion he took Fred out at 11pm on a hot summer's night. They walked to a field at the side of the railway line that ran nearby, where hens were nesting in coops, on pheasant and partridge eggs. They were to guard these from foxes and poachers. In the dark the difficult part of the job was avoiding the trip wires that Bob had placed around the field, attached to detonators. Should an unwelcome visitor stumble into one of these, the bang would alert them. 'The thought of that night still makes sweat run down my back,' says Fred Shore. 'I was too scared to move!'

Charlie Rendall recalls that the country estate where he lived, employed its own outside staff to look after estate worker's cottages. In this old Raphael Tuck & Sons postcard, I don't know if the carpenter is coming or going, but the woman doesn't look particularly happy.

'It was interesting seeing logs, poles and other timber cut to size.' Fred was given a prize for stoking the engine. It was a plank of wood that was six feet long, showing a beautiful grain. All the estate men must surely have thought the plank would never leave Berwick, and for the next few days his treasure was kept well hidden. Then it was time to go home and the usual taxi driver was Alf Baker. 'Yes,' notes Fred, 'my plank fitted in the taxi and at the railway station my parents kept a safe distance from the kid with a plank. I was not challenged at the turnstile and it fitted on the railway carriage rack. At Crewe station the Great Western engine was replaced by LMS (London, Midland and Scottish) for Manchester. The plank has given good service and is still in my shed.'

Shooting parties were all the rage on country estates. The caption to this Raphael Tuck & Sons postcard in their Jokes from 'Punch' series, is as follows: Young Lady (to Fiance, who has rashly promised to teach her to shoot): 'Tell me, George, when you want to take out the little red things, you pull this thing below, don't you?'

Many different jobs

A big house and its estate created many different opportunities for employment for people living in the nearby villages. Skilled workers such as stone masons, carpenters and gardeners were employed full time throughout the year, often living in tied cottages on the estate.

At Rainthorpe Hall at Tasburgh in Norfolk, William Moore remembers there being a butler, valet, housekeeper, cook, two gardeners and a woodman but his own grandfather was more unusually employed.

'At Rainthorpe Hall, my late grandfather was employed as estate bricklayer and chimney sweep to Sir Charles Harvey. My grandfather, who had eight sons and two daughters, would take one of his sons with him, when sweeping the large chimney.'

Sir Charles also employed his grandfather, along with his son Albert, to work on the village church, emphasizing the unity that existed between the gentry and the community. In 1911 they built a new vestry at his instruction. 'After the passing of Sir Charles Harvey,' writes William Moore, 'new owners moved in. My grandfather was retained but not full time however. Grandfather whose reputation had grown enormous, used a two-wheel handcart walking miles from Tasburgh to Poringland sweeping chimneys, repairing brick ovens, and installing cast iron coppers.'

No doubt similar to many other young men from Barlaston, Ernest Hawkins first found employment courtesy of the Wedgwood family, but in his case, not at their factory. 'The recession in 1930,' he points out, 'following the 1926 General Strike wasn't the best of times to leave school and look for a job. I eventually found employment as a garden boy at the home of Mr and Mrs Frank Wedgwood at The Lea. My wages were eight shillings a week, which included daily duties like stoking the boilers, cleaning boots and shoes, gardening, watering the greenhouses and washing cars.'

The father of Mr G Thacker, worked for the Combe family, important brewers living at Cobham Park, a big house in Surrey. The family owned several farms in the area, including Downside Farm, where Mr Thacker grew up. 'We lived in a tied house on the estate,' he recollects, 'father drove the lorry, and also looked after the lock gates on the river Mole.'

When Squire Combe died about 1937, a new man took over the estate, and he brought in his own workers. At this point the Thackers had to leave their farm. 'We were given a cottage on the estate, and dad had to get a job and pay rent.

Charlie Rendall left school at 14 and began work on the Butleigh Wootton Estate in Somerset as an apprentice stone mason, working on the general maintenance of all estate properties. Here he can be seen working on the roof of a farmhouse in about 1955.

Brick ovens

'Ovens were like a tin box about 15 inches across, and 24 inches high,' according to William Moore whose grandfather used to replair them. 'Above the door were two brass handles to operate a draught system.' The heat was regulated by pulling or pushing a metal panel at the back. These ovens were at eye level, encased in brickwork. Beneath the oven, which was next to the kitchen fire, was a firebox that had a grate at the bottom and an opening to the kitchen chimney. It had a small cast iron door, through which the fuel – coal and wood – was placed. 'One would think this primitive today,' he reflects, 'but if you tasted the bread made in one of these ovens, what is produced now bears no comparison!'

A lorry with a trailer of tree trunks pictured outside the big house, Cobham Park, in the 1930s. The Combe family, who were important brewers, owned the house. Mr G Thacker's father worked on the estate and his duties included driving the lorry.

When Elizabeth Crowe left school at 14, she went to work at Crake House in Greenodd, Cumbria, the big house in the village where she lived. She was paid seven shillings and sixpence a week, which rose to seventeen shillings and sixpence at the time she left, four years later. 'Many people went into service in the big houses,' she states. 'The Machels for instance, owned a lot of land including the farm where I was born. They employed maids, cooks, and gardeners. They used to hold a garden party every summer, so that was part of village life too.'

Audrey Blake lived in Bramdean, Hampshire and also left school at 14 and became a nursery housemaid in nearby West Meon. 'I lived in,' she explains, 'and was paid six shillings and eight pence a week.' She had to buy her own uniform, and had one half day a week off, and every other Sunday. 'I was up at seven,' she recalls, 'and

Rose Edwards aged 19 and seen here in the typical clothes of a young girl working in service in 1917. Before she married Jack Woodcock, she had worked as a helper at the vicarage in the village.

didn't finish before ten. It made us grow up fast.'

Stanley Church from Yardley Gobion in Northamptonshire remembers the jobs of his sisters. He states, 'Jobs were scarce. If you were a girl, you had even fewer options. You could go into service employed by the lord of the manor, as a housemaid. Your duties would include cleaning, bed-making, polishing shoes, and so on, for all the inhabitants. You would have to live in, of course, and could be working from 5.30am to maybe 10pm with a few tea breaks in between. Two of my sisters worked in one big mansion and they had a half day off each week. Even that was farcical as they had to cycle several miles home and back again, to return in time to help with dinner for the toffs at 6pm.'

Laundry service

At Fivehead near Taunton in Somerset, Dot Hunt recalls a basket of laundry that was delivered by chauffeur every Monday morning to the cottage opposite their farmhouse where two spinster ladies lived. These two ladies did all the laundry for the big house and their copper was lit early each morning, so that by lunch time, there were snowy-white billowing sheets, tablecloths and shirts, hanging from long lines in the orchard. Reckitts Blue and Robin Starch had seen to that. 'As a child,' she points out, 'it never occurred to me to wonder what on earth happened to the wet clothes if it was rainy or foggy. But come what may, it seemed the basket was ready for collection on the following Saturday. Inside were the results of the most exquisite workmanship.' In the evenings, Dot sometimes watched the ironing in progress. 'The table was very large,' she says, 'and I remember the big damask tablecloths spread over it and polished until they shone. Then the two ladies would fold them with such care and place them, almost reverently, certainly with pride, into the basket. The irons were heated on a square iron box with racks at the sides and filled with glowing coals, which made the box almost red-hot. The two ladies' faces glowed, too, with the almost excessive heat. Stiff collars and shirtfronts were turned and pressed and curved all to perfection and would grace the throats of those who ate their meals from a table laid with the lovely damask tablecloths and napkins. These ladies exuded friendliness and contentment. I wonder how little or how much money they earned?'

The model village at Selworthy in Somerset was built by Sir Thomas Acland of Killerton to provide housing for the aged and infirm of the Holnicote Estate. From a postcard dated 1913.

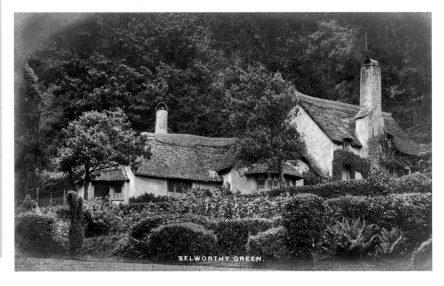

SELWORTHY GREEN.

Part of the community

Rural people who lived near or worked for the gentry were affected by their presence, not merely as their employees, but because they were integral to the community, as much a part of the village, as the vicar or the blacksmith. Many of these large houses are now open to the public, giving visitors an opportunity to see how life was lived in the past.

Flete Castle near Holbeton in Devon was the home of Lord Mildmay. Jean Pearse who lived in Holbeton remembers the family well, and their association with the village.

'Lord Mildmay junior,' she says, 'lived at Mothecombe House. He used to love riding horses and even rode in the Grand National. The Royal Family used to come for short visits to Mothecombe and the children of the village had a chance to see them. We saw the Queen when she was Princess Elizabeth, and Princess Margaret who was on the private beach at Mothecombe. The Queen Mother also stayed and used to go to Newton Abbot races with Lord Mildmay.'

With amusement, Jean remembers one particular occasion, when Lord Mildmay senior came to the village to meet a bus from Plymouth,

having ridden his horse from Flete Castle. He shouted at the conductress, asking if there was a Mrs Jones on board? The conductress told him to 'ask himself'. Lord Mildmay dismounted and boarded the bus, while Jean Pearse and a friend, kindly held his horse. When he told the conductress it was Lord Mildmay she had been rude too, the woman felt quite ill. 'We never saw her on the bus again,' says Jean.

Lynne Oakes grew up in the village of Eaton in Cheshire. Her father had worked on the Eaton Hall Estate, the home of Colonel and Mrs Antrobus. The Hall, now sadly demolished like so many other big houses, had come into the possession of the Antrobus family in the 18th century and several members of the family were appointed High Sheriff of Cheshire.

'Many older members of the village remember

Eaton Hall in Cheshire, home of Colonel and Mrs Antrobus, was a popular venue for hunts and hunt balls. The house was demolished in the 1970s, and the site is now a sand quarry.

Lanhydrock from East

This old postcard published by Valentine's, shows Lanhydrock House in Cornwall, during the early part of the 20th century. The house was presented to the National Trust in the 1950s, and today affords visitors with a glimpse of the many different jobs carried out below stairs, through a warren of kitchens, larders, and sculleries.

happy days spent in the grounds of Eaton Hall,' reflects Lynne. 'Sports and games were held on the spacious lawns, and tea was laid on in the large coach house, specially prepared for the occasion. They were allowed to wander through the lovely gardens and shrubberies and receive gifts of flowers and fruit.'

Not only the children enjoyed these privileges as the Colonel also entertained tenants and villagers at the estate on occasions such as royal weddings, coronations, anniversaries and Empire Days. Hunts and hunt balls took place at the hall right up till its closure. There was even an annual fair for the villagers held in the grounds,

Miss Leah Greatorex, headmistress of Barlaston School, was sister to Bill Greatorex, the village blacksmith. She is seen here with some of her pupils taking part in a school play in the garden of the Wedgwood family home at The Lea, Barlaston.

featuring old-fashioned rides like the Cakewalk.

Following the deaths of both Colonel and Mrs Antrobus, the hall was demolished and a quarry for extracting sand was established on the site. The countryside and the village, not only lost a friend and benefactor, but an important part of its identity. 'Until approximately 1949,' says Lynne, 'most of the village belonged to the estate, and was maintained by it.'

Audrey Blake from Bramdean remembers Lady Gapper, who resided at Bramdean House. 'She was a wonderful lady,' Audrey fondly recalls. 'She took Sunday-school, and gave us all an Easter egg.' On Mother's Day, she would invite the children into her garden, where she would give them two daffodils each for their mums. As Audrey was one of three, they went home with a decent bunch. 'Lady Gapper,' she continues, 'would go round the village, and if anyone was ill, she would take them soup and coal. At Christmas she would give all the children a party. We would go into her billiard room, where there was a gigantic tree and every child in the village had a present.'

Bill Wilson grew up in the tiny village of Murthly in Perthshire, where, as in much of the countryside at that time, there was an unwritten code of respect awarded to the local gentry, this has left him with a slightly different attitude to some of the previous contributors. 'Our local laird,' he recalls, 'had a dreadful stutter but he was always taken by his chauffeur to the village hall to open whist drives. We were always warned not to giggle during his speech on the pain of a good thrashing. There was still a bit of deference shown to so-called toffs in my young days. At school you were, if a boy, expected to salute when accepting a prize from our patron, Lady Lyle (of Tate and Lyle fame). Another estate in Murthly was owned by two spinster twins. They were as mad as hatters but on a Sunday when they passed in their Bentley we were expected to touch our forelock. What rubbish!'

As already mentioned by Fred Shore, shooting parties were another feature of estate life, where the rich and often famous members of society would be invited by the lord of the manor for a weekend of sport, bringing them into full view of the villagers.

Bill McKay, who lived in the village of Migvie in Aberdeenshire, has memories of the shooting seasons at Tornasheen Estate. Prior to the arrival of the shooting parties, his grandfather was approached to be a loader for several of the visiting gentry who occupied a butt on the hill. The butts are the covers dotted in a uniform line throughout the hills which the shooters shelter in while the beaters drive the birds towards them to

Gamekeeper, Joe Morgan, who lived in the village of Walford near Ross-on-Wye. This picture was taken in 1914 when he was the gamekeeper on the Bishopswood Estate.

become sport. At the same time, Bill remembers, he gleaned all sorts of information, useless or otherwise from the toffs. While his grandfather loaded sporting guns the Honourable Mrs Thesinger, owner of the estate, would visit his grandmother, accompanied by her lady-in-waiting, chauffeur and brother-in-law.

His grandmother would make absolutely certain that her appearance, and that of the children was impeccable before her ladyship arrived. She had an array of pinafores, aprons and other suitable overalls, from which one would eventually be decided upon. 'The Rolls

Stallions from Arabia

The local gentry might also provide an element of prestige for a village community, instilling a sense of local pride, especially for those who worked for the estate. For instance, Ken Rennison from Buttercrambe in North Yorkshire notes of the Darley Estate, which owned most of the houses in the village and many farms in the area, 'Buttercrambe has been revered by sporting gentlemen and ladies for bringing one of the first three Arabian stallions to Britain and so helping to sire the line of English thoroughbreds racing today. Aldby Park in Buttercrambe became the home of the Darley Arabian, the most successful sire of the trio. In the Aldby paddocks near the house, the Muniqi Arab that Thomas Darley shipped from Aleppo in 1703–4, may well have had his first taste of English grass and sired his first generation of winners.' Aldby Park remains in the Darley family today, and unlike many other big houses which have since been demolished, has been cherished and restored.

nosed into the close at Ballahullich,' he writes. 'The party of guests had arrived; Grandma offered tea. The visitors thanked her for the offer but declined. Her ladyship had sent her butler earlier in the day to the luncheon hut on the moor with tea provisions. They would be joined by the shooting party around three o'clock.'

That night, his grandfather would return home cold and hungry, and would supper on Brochain, which was a gruel, often taken to ward off a cold. 'The gruel,' explains Bill McKay, 'would prevent him from catching a cold and he would be fit for tomorrow's shoot. The gruel was made up of onions, oatmeal, hot milk sometimes, seasoning and melted cheese, not a regular meal but believed to have medicinal qualities.'

Mr Edwards the gamekeeper with the beaters prior to a shoot around 1934. The bottles contain cold tea. The farm was one of several owned by the Combe family of Cobham Park.

Many country houses, such as Eaton Hall in Cheshire, the home of Colonel and Mrs Antrobus, were popular venues for hunts and hunt balls. Several estates even ran their own pack of hounds. In this photograph, a pack of hounds waits for the chase to begin. From a postcard, published by Raphael Tuck & Sons.

Farming the Estate

Many country estates managed their own Home Farm, which provided for the needs of the big house and its army of staff. The estate might also rent farms to local people. All of these, whether run by the estate itself, or leased to individual farmers, were a rich source of employment for the villagers.

One such estate was Butleigh Wootton in Somerset, where Charlie Rendall lived in a tied cottage. His father worked on a farm belonging to the estate. 'The estate employed its own staff of outside workers,' he recalls. 'There was a foreman carpenter, a mason, and a woodman cum "help out anywhere". They all occupied cottages held by the estate, up until the mid 1950s. The big house itself employed gardeners, chauffeurs and various household staff, who on retirement were allowed to continue living in their cottage.'

'Each cottage had a pigsty and hen house, with toilet facilities at the top of the gardens provided by earth closets. Most grew their own vegetables, and farm workers were usually allowed a line of potatoes in the farmer's field and perhaps swede. Milk came as part of your wages, and sometimes cider, which was made on the farm. And most cottages also had a fruit tree, usually apple and sometimes plum or pear.'

Mr Rendall's father did absolutely everything on the farm: milking, hedging, ditching, hoeing mangolds, harvesting, haymaking and ploughing. His rent was around two to three shillings a week.

'I left school at 14,' he continues, 'and started work on the Butleigh Wootton Estate as an apprentice to the stone mason, starting work at 7am and finishing at 6pm – and 1 o'clock in the afternoon on Saturdays. I worked on the rebuilding of a cottage in the village, and on the general maintenance of all estate properties. The foreman, Mr Norris was a very superior being and kept a tight rein on everything, wasting nothing, even to the point of straightening out bent nails. Eventually I acquired a bicycle, and with estate pay being so poor, after about two years I sought another job.'

Molly Kinghorn's grandparents were tenant farmers on an estate called Haverah Park at Beckwithshaw near Harrogate, at that time owned by Ripley Castle. As well as running his own farm, her grandfather was a woodman on the estate, and she remembers the names of some of the woods in his care: 'Maple Plane, Larch Planting and Bore Holes.' This latter may not be spelt correctly, she admits, due to the fact that she only ever heard it spoken, so it might have been Boar Holes. The fields also had names: Little Meadow, Long Meadow, and Fourteen Acres. The field in front of their farm was called The Garth.

Molly spent a great deal of her childhood on the estate, and gives a colourful and atmospheric description of what it must have been like. Her grandparent's farm was in a valley, with a beck running behind it. 'Not much of a farm,' she states, 'a few cows, pigs, hens and geese, and a horse for pulling the cart.'

There was great excitement when a new horse appeared in August. 'We thought it was an addition to the farmyard,' says Molly, 'but it was the stallion doing his round of duty with hope of a foal the following April.'

The farmhouse had four bedrooms, three at the front and one at the rear with separate stairs.

Pitchforking sheaves on to a farm cart pulled by a team of four horses. From a postcard published by Hildesheimer & Co Ltd.

Firewood

Martin Skin grew up at Doddycross in Cornwall, and recalls that his father was very industrious. He would often go to the Coldrenick Estate, where his mother had once worked, to cut firewood. As a lad he sometimes accompanied his father and says that at first he had a crosscut handsaw, but later bought a chainsaw. 'The smell of the pinewood was magnificent,' he explains. 'I used to collect the pinecones to make Christmas decorations, or to burn.' Martin spent many happy Saturdays with his father cutting wood on the Coldrenick Estate, or working in their garden.

Clearing up after re-thatching, at the Butleigh Wootton Estate near Glastonbury in Somerset. This house was divided into three separate homes.

Downstairs there were two rooms and a large kitchen and half cellar. The fire was kept burning both winter and summer, and all the cooking was done either on the fire itself, or in the oven attached to it. 'Granny made lovely rice pudding in a big enamel bowl with nutmeg topping. Bread was baked when yeast was available but as the nearest shop was some miles away, it couldn't be made each day. I think my very favourite food were the mushrooms we had just gathered and then fried in a big frying pan over the fire. My least favourite was rabbit, especially seeing them skinned and stewed. Occasionally you'd find a pellet in your mouth. To this day I can't eat rabbit, even the smell turns my stomach.'

Her grandfather ran a pipe from the kitchen to the fireplace where the water was heated, so hot water was usually on tap, and the children – and no doubt adults as well – would bathe in an old tin bath in front of the fire. To keep the fire going, sticks would be gathered every day, sometimes twice! Coal was also available, but was only

In the summer, 1945, Molly Kinghorn's father and her Uncle George gather pea sticks on the Haverah Park Estate in Yorkshire.

Right: Grandad Lewis feeding the sheep and lambs on his tenant farm on the Havarah Park Estate at Beckwithshaw.

Far right: Estate worker, Charlie Rendall, up a ladder attempting to evict a swarm of bees from the chimney of the servants' quarters of Wootton House. The picture was taken around 1957.

delivered part of the way to the farm, so they would have to go and fetch it. The only means of lighting at the farmhouse were candles and one paraffin lamp. The wireless was only turned on to hear the news, as the battery had to be taken to the village for recharging.

'Grandad must have been quite clever,' she says with pride. 'He made a flush toilet in a lean-to on the side of the house, with the usual newspapers cut into squares on string. Our greatest treat was flushing it, and then running hell for leather down the back garden to watch our efforts come out in the beck.'

The winter evenings were generally spent making 'clip rugs' on a wooden frame. These were a variation of the peg rugs mentioned in Chapter One, and were mainly created using worn out clothes. As most old clothes at the farm would be made in sombre colours, black or navy, 'Granny,' she says, 'was really pleased to get red or blue for the centre diamond.'

In time, things began to change, not just the way of life for people in general who lived on

country estates, but for Molly's family in particular. Her grandfather died in the early 1930s, and her own parents now lived in Leeds, but at every opportunity her mother was drawn back to the estate for what she called 'a breath of fresh air'.

To reach the farm they would have to take the bus from Leeds to Harrogate. If it was Wednesday, Friday or Saturday, they were able to catch another bus to the village itself. Any other day of the week would entail a lengthy walk.

Molly Kinghorn (second from left), in the garden of Moor Park Hall, where her Uncle Dave was the head gardener. Also in the picture are (back row from left to right) Joan Tweed (adopted evacuee); Auntie Dora (Uncle Dave's wife); and Annie (Molly's mother). In the front are her cousin Michael and sister Joan.

When they arrived at the estate, the gamekeeper's cottage was the first they came to. 'It always smelled of the mash he brewed up for the game birds he was rearing in the woods,' she recollects. 'We would stop for a drink of water from the pump in his garden and sometimes for a chat. My dad used to tease my mum about talking to the gamekeeper and I used to wonder why she blushed? It wasn't till years later, when I read *Lady Chatterley's Lover* that I understood.'

In due course, her grandmother also fell seriously ill, so Molly and her mother spent even more time on the farm. 'When she died her funeral was very sad, as the car could not get up the farm track. The coffin had to go on the cart to the road – a very undignified ride.'

Now the farm had no one to manage it correctly and it fell into disrepair, so the estate took it back into their own hands. 'And that was the end of our visits,' she concludes with sadness, but she obviously delights in her memories of family, farm, and a vanished way of life.

Molly Kinghorn's grandparents were tenant farmers but more often than not, the Home Farm on country estates made them self-sufficient communities, providing the family and staff with most of their food. But with changing times, and the steady erosion of their income-producing assets, it became increasingly difficult for great houses to maintain their supporting estates. One way in which some estates have survived, is by the sale of estate produce. This at least maintains a level of employment in the local community and keeps alive a faint glimmer of the old lifestyle.

Uncle George leading a bull at Throstle Nest Farm on the Haverah Park Estate at Beckwithshaw near Harrogate.

The last load

Molly Kinghorn recalls the excitement of hay making time on the country estate in Yorkshire where her grandparents were tenant farmers. 'In the summer,' remembers Molly, 'there was traditional hay making, when it was all hands to the pump, turning the hay with big wooden rakes. Then, when it was dry, making haycocks ready to be collected on the farm cart. All the children were sent to bring the drinkings, cucumber sandwiches always spring to mind, and awful strong tea in big containers. For all our help we were allowed to ride on top of the last load back to the barn, one of life's great joys! Then there was a great big tea with grownups at one table and children at another. After a suitable rest there was the cricket match.' The photo shows Molly on the right and if you look carefully you can see the wheels of the hay cart on the left, almost hidden by the load.

To the manor born

Up to this point daily life has been observed and described from the perspective of those that lived in farms and cottages, or simply worked on country estates around the country. As a complete contrast, these are the thoughts and memories of Lord Digby, a representative of the gentry itself.

Lord and Lady Digby and their family at their home, Minterne House in Minterne Magna, Dorset circa 1960.

Edward, the present Lord Digby, was born in 1924 and grew up at Minterne House, between Sherborne and Dorchester, in the tiny Dorset village of Minterne Magna.

Sitting within a beautiful valley, the village of Minterne still retains much of its original charm, and Lord Digby says of it, 'Minterne is a tiny village consisting entirely of our own cottages, occupied by employees. Everyone worked in either the house, the garden, as a woodman or on the farm. It consists of the big house, and about 14 cottages, and used to have a Post Office but no shop. In the 1920s and 1930s, the carrier came once a week and the estate carpenter had a motorcycle and sidecar, but otherwise there was no transport in the village. Around the house were the stables, where the hunters were kept, and in the top yard, the farm horses and

the cowshed. The milk was brought down to the dairy near the house by a man with two churns fastened across a yoke over his shoulders. In the dairy, there were both separators to produce cream, and also large flat bowls so that you could skim off the cream. The estate carpenter always wore a stiff shirt, but no collar or tie.'

The gardens at Minterne are now open to the public, and have a chain of small lakes, waterfalls and streams. 'There was a very famous wild woodland garden,' notes Lord Digby, 'where all the Himalayas then rhododendrons and magnolias had been planted from the original seed, and also a kitchen garden with 16 greenhouses.'

All country estates were largely dependent on being self-sufficient, enabling them to feed both the family and the staff. 'Of course, you had to have a large kitchen garden,' he goes on to explain, 'as before the days of supermarkets or deep freezers, you had to provide all the food, and even if the family were away, they were still cooking for 21 every day. In the 1920s, my father used to show silent films to the staff in the servants' hall. My father reckoned he could have a peach from the greenhouse any time from March till October and the head gardener would go along, cupping his hands under a peach, and if it came off when it was just lifted up, then it was ripe to go into the dining room.'

The impression we're left with from the majority of contributors to this chapter is that in the main people living and working on these estates were happy and contented. When you consider how hard it was for many people living in rural areas, particularly through the 1930s, we can appreciate that the communities who lived within the shadow of the big house, were in a sense 'touched by grace'. There was work, accommodation, schooling, social activities, and everything else associated with a successful village. No doubt there was also a sense of security for those that lived there.

Lord Digby relates an incident that illustrates all of these points beautifully. 'The other day, I was asked by someone if his ashes could be spread near the keeper's cottage, as living there had been the happiest time of his life. He was one of nine children in this cottage, with two rooms up and two rooms down. Every time that the father returned happy from the pub in Cerne, another baby would appear, and in the 1920s my mother tried to get his wife birth control, which was just then starting, but all the Rector said was, "what they want is self control, not birth control". But you see it was the happiest time of his life. The older children had to look after the younger ones, and there is nothing children like more than a bit of responsibility.'

It must have been very much like having an extended family, with the lord and lady of the manor being the patriarchs. We've already heard how the gentry provided for the community in various ways, which they had no obligation to do, but they obviously felt a sense of responsibility towards those who worked for them, and towards the well-being of their families. Lord Digby says of his mother, 'other families my mother had to give actual shoes or clothes, because any money would have been spent on drink. Before the war, if anyone earned extra overtime, it all went into the pub. The thing that changed this culture was when, after the war, suddenly hire purchase came in and people started to realize that with a bit of extra money they could get household things and improve their homes for their wives.

Thus hire purchase did make a cultural difference although now I think everyone borrows far too much. Between the wars, landowners and farmers were not well off. It was very difficult to let a farm as they were so unprofitable, and a cottage would be let for three shillings per week, and it would cost far more to keep the roof on.'

But what about the people who actually worked at the big house itself, what are his memories of them? 'The lady's maid was one of the most important people and certainly ruled the roost, including my mother. They were very strong characters, together with the head housemaid. In the kitchen there was a cook, two kitchen maids and two scullery maids. My mother's big extravagance was that she always insisted on having two scullery maids washing the dishes, as she felt it was so unfair for these 14-year-old girls to be alone with all the other, much older servants. Then there was also a stillroom with a stillroom maid where all the sweet things, cakes,

A gardener rakes leaves away from the gate of a country house on Windlesham Moor, Surrey in 1947. After the war very few estates could afford large numbers of staff.

In this Raphael Tuck & Sons postcard, a footman finishes packing the car in the drive of a splendid looking house. The caption tells us that among the passengers are Lady Jeune, the Honourable Mrs St John Brodrick, and Alfred Austin the Poet Laureate. One assumes the poet to be the chap with grey hair, and the picture would therefore date to before 1913, when his term finished.

biscuits, drinks, sweets and toffee was made. It was certainly my haunt as a child, as the soft, crumbly toffee was marvellous.'

There was a social difference between senior and junior servants at the house, and everything operated according to a strict regime of etiquette. For instance, he explains that at lunchtime, the senior servants congregated in the housekeeper's room at 12 noon, whereas the junior servants would assemble in the servants' hall. The hallboy would then be dispatched to summon the senior

servants, who would come into the servants' hall, say Grace, cut the joint and eat their meat with the juniors. They would then retire to the housekeeper's room, where they would eat their puddings, leaving the junior staff to relax and enjoy themselves.

'There was a men servants wing,' he enlarges, 'and a maid servants wing. The cook had her own private room, and the butler his own room, which was next door to the brushing room, where all the muddy hunting coats and breeches would be

Young girls training to become domestic servants, about 1922.

scrubbed and dried.'

Lord Digby concludes by saying, 'you will see that it was in fact a happy community, despite the poverty. And of course the big object was to get your daughters into the big house, where they lived far better than in their homes.'

Several country estates, similar to Minterne, are now open to the public, and strolling around these big houses, their gardens and surrounding buildings, affords a tantalizing glimpse into a vanished world, echoing to the industry of the many people who lived, worked and played there, blissfully unaware that the life-style they enjoyed was quickly drawing to a close.

Beaurepaire Park House at Bramley in Hampshire, was the home of Sir Strati Ralli, owner of many racehorses and a big follower of the hunt. The estate also had a large pheasant shoot, the keeper being Jack Thatcher. Bill Johnson, who supplied the photograph, says, 'My grandfather Will Munday was the gardener at the big house, and lived in North Lodge, it is still lived in today.'

Chapter Four
Villages with a difference

Farming and the opportunities provided by big houses and estates around the United Kingdom played a major part in village life. But a few rural villages were in some way different from this generalization, or had something unique about them. In some places settlements evolved around a particular industry which employed the majority of their adult work force. There were also villages that were different for other reasons. During this period new settlements were built due to social or economic change, while others were destroyed, losing centuries of their history, thus bringing the communities that had developed within them over generations to a sad end.

Many varied industries

The term rural industry could apply to almost any activity that went on in country villages, which employed a large part of their community, and the following are two very different examples. For over 50 years a clog mill was a hive of activity until clogs went out of fashion and a rural mental asylum was the hub of a small community until it closed.

Charles Littlefair, lived on a farm in the small hamlet of Keverstone in County Durham. In 1921 a clog sole mill was established at Keverstone on the Raby Estate. The factory was owned by the Maude family who came from Ireland and it was established at Keverstone because of the great many large beech trees that existed, both on the estate and the surrounding countryside. Beech wood was considered to be the best for making clog soles and these splendid beech trees were 150-200 years old.

The new mill consisted of a large building constructed mainly out of iron sheeting, which housed the many types of saw benches used to shape the clog soles, ranging from bandsaws to finishing saws. There was also an engine shed and the steaming shed, where the finished clog soles were steam-heated before dispatch. The finished clog soles were at first taken by horse and cart to the nearest railway station at Winston but later lorries ferried them directly to the clog factory near Hebden Bridge.

The hamlet increased in size with the building of a few wooden houses, erected for families who

came from Ireland. The factory site itself also increased with the construction of repair and maintenance sheds.

'The mill became part of life for us, living through those years,' says Mr Littlefair. 'There was the gentle puffing from the smoke stack, the

Canals brought prosperity to many rural locations, and hamlets or villages appeared along their course to take advantage of the opportunities provided. This old postcard shows a canal barge being loaded at the village of Brimscombe in Gloucestershire.

Workers at the Keverstone clog sole mill in the 1930s, with the owner Jim Maude in the centre.

Munition Workers Lydbrook.

Women workers from a factory at the village of Lydbrook in Herefordshire that made munitions during World War I.

plume of white smoke, and the whine of the various saws from all the activity going on. Unfortunately it was not to last, for in 1973 the mill closed, as there was no longer any demand for clogs. The buildings and all the equipment were sold and the site cleared. The area is now once again planted with beech trees and no one can tell that a clog sole factory had ever existed on the site for over 50 years.'

A second, very different example is recalled by Bill Wilson, who grew up in Murthly in Perthshire, which during the war years had only a Post Office and a grocer's shop, but it was the large mental hospital which was by far the main source of employment, and where both his parents worked.

A rural asylum

Bill Wilson's father, a male mental nurse, had a favourite story. 'Two of the inmates were akin to Steinbeck's characters in The Grapes of Wrath, *and were absolutely devoted to each other. One of course, was the huge epileptic and his small mate had the brains. Well the little guy was devoted to his strong pal and cared for him every time he had a seizure. Now what the little chap said to my dad is really rather profound! He said, Mr Wilson (purely on account of their surnames, and I knew them all as a boy) we have a Taylor for a joiner, a Barber for a plumber, and a Mason for a cook – and we are the ones who are supposed to be daft! The hospital like so many others, is long-closed and converted to posh flats.'*

There were similar set ups all around the country, where these asylums, as they were known, were built in rural locations as far away from other settlements as possible, and the people who worked there often lived in self-contained villages, similar to those to be found on country estates.

Bill Wilson's father was an attendant, first appointed on a six-month probation at a salary of £50 per annum with board, lodging, laundry, and uniform included.

'I therefore as a young lad grew up in the company of paranoid schizophrenics,' says Bill Wilson, 'which gave me a life long understanding of the problems. One of them, allowed out because he was not dangerous, used to take me fishing. We used to guddle for trout (known as tickling in England) and catch sticklebacks.'

Eyam in the Derbyshire Peak District is known as the 'Plague Village', which went into voluntary quarantine in 1665. More recently, its main local industry was lead mining, and next to the village school there is still a mound which houses the shaft of a lead mine. From a postcard published by Raphael Tuck & Sons.

THE PLAGUE HOUSE, EYAM.

Fishing villages

Britain's coastline abounds with fishing villages, so numerous that they would require a book of their own to do them justice. Although next to the sea, they can still be regarded as country villages as they are often found in isolated and unspoiled locations, far away from the hustle and bustle of major towns and cities.

Avoch, pronounced as in 'loch', is a typical example. Found on the Black Isle, a peninsula north of Inverness, the industry at Avoch in the 1930s was predominantly fishing, but today there are few fishing boats to be seen in the harbour. Traditional fishing villages have changed as much as any other type of village, as since the 1950s their main industry has gone into continuous decline. There is still some demand for small fishing enterprises, but in the main, the people in these villages have had to adapt in order to survive, and in many places tourism and leisure have replaced fishing.

Donald Patience, born and raised in Avoch in the 1930s and 1940s, remembers several of the boats of that era in one of his many poems based on the area:

The Maggie MacLeman, Mizpah and The Betty leave the town,
  with the Budding Rose, Endeavour, The Elspeth and Renown.
The Lily and The Triumph and then The Pioneer,
The Eagle and Pathfinder cast off and leave the pier.
The Blossom's well out in the firth, The Nereid's on her way,
The Clever Lassie's next to go and then The Silver Spray.
The Heather Lea and Ormonde Hill are heading to the south,
The Cedar's punching through the swell outside the harbour mouth.
The drifter Castle Stuart, staying in today, rides gently at her
  moorings while the others cross the bay.
The water churns behind the yawls as they spread east and west,
  heading for the fishing grounds, Avoch men know the best.
Will they go down around the point or up towards The Stream,
  a hold of silver darlings is every Avochie's dream.'

Avoch from the west, a fishing village in Scotland. The photo is probably from the late 1940s, early 1950s. There are still some fishing boats visible in the harbour. Donald Patience, who supplied the photograph, was born in the cottage with the corrugated roof in the foreground.

Members of the Login family working in the cove around 1920. The family had been washed out of the fishing village of South Hallsands in January 1917, after it was swept into the sea during severe storms.

Today, nine or ten Avoch boats are still involved in the fishing industry but they work away from home, as there is no local fishing now. These boats fish for prawns, scallops or white fish, at ports from Mallaig round to Aberdeen. The herrings that once graced the tables of all the village folk are no longer brought to their harbour. From another of his verses Donald Patience reflects:

When I walk down the pier full of pleasure
    craft, I feel sad and tend to dream,
Of the days I watched the yawls go out, to
    'Try them up The Stream'.
The place was full of bustle then, that is so
    quiet today,
Things must change, but we can't allow our
    heritage slip away.

On the night of 26 January 1917, the small fishing village of South Hallsands on the South Devon coast was swept into the sea during severe storms. A large pebble ridge protected the village, but on the night in question, exceptionally high waves came pounding over this ridge, crashing into the houses. The village had become vulnerable because sand and gravel had been dredged from the seabed, reducing the shingle beaches, in order to extend the naval dockyards being built at Plymouth.

Among the families made homeless by the collapse of the village were the Trout family, a widow and her four daughters. But later in the year their luck was about to change. That summer World War 1 was still raging and offshore a German U boat sank an American ship. One of the daughters, Ella Trout, rowed out and managed to rescue one of the sailers and was awarded the OBE for her act of bravery. Later, a gift from the family of the rescued sailer enabled the sisters to build a guest house on the clifftop overlooking South Hallsands which is still there today. Walking the cliff path you can still see the ruins of the houses wedged up against the cliffs and pounded by the seas but who knows how long they will remain.

Some of the crab and lobster fishermen and their families, forced to leave their homes that night, went to live at the nearby village of East Prawle, which is situated on a high hill between

Fishing boats used by some of the South Devon crab fishermen in the 1920s and 1930s. They were 18 feet in length.

Wilfred Login and his father working at sea. They worked with the tide, often as far as four miles out and the best tide might have been at two in the morning.

including his father, went to East Prawle, but also fished from the cove.

Wilfred Login left school at 14 and went to work on a local farm, but this only lasted six months, as he explains: 'When my Dad's partner had to join up, there was no one else but me. One day on the farm, the next fishing, and it was the busiest time of the year – plenty of both she and he crabs.' Each day before work he had to walk a mile and a half from his home to the cove where the fishing boats were kept. As there was a war on, his father, as well as fishing, was the night-shift coastguard, and would sometimes sleep at the ex-coastguard house, so Wilfred had to walk to the cove on his own. The best tide might be at 2am, and he was not allowed to carry a light.

'Fishing was very hard work,' he explains. 'We had to work with the tide, work out about four miles, so it would take an hour to get back to shore. I fished for four years before receiving my call-up papers when I was 18. All fishermen had to go on the minesweepers, they were mostly fishing trawlers converted to the minesweeping role. I had a motorbike when I was 15, because I was tired of walking the one and a half miles to the cove each day, through fields and down a steep track. Worse than that was the climb home again at the end of a hard day's work. I didn't get my licence until I was 16, because the policeman was taken away when the war started. I took my motorbike to Plymouth to pass my medical, that being the first time in my life I'd been there. When I had my calling-up papers I worked the day before I left. I had made arrangements with the insurance man the week before to pick me

Start Point, which had a lighthouse, and Prawle Point, with its coastguard station. One such family was that of Wilfred Login, who was born at East Prawle in 1925. He was from a family of ten that had been washed out of Hallsands and his father was a crab fisherman.

As well as fishing, East Prawle was surrounded by farmland, so for the young men of the village there were two main options for employment. Mr Login recalls that at the time, the village consisted of some 40 cottages, seven farms, two inns, two shops, two wheelwrights, two carpenters, a blacksmith, chapel and the school.

Wilfred Login can trace his own family at South Hallsands back to 1758, and when the village was washed away, his grandfather and two of his sons bought three cottages at Ivy Cove, from where they continued to fish. Three other sons,

A scene on the banks of the river Dart at Dittisham in South Devon. From a postcard, published by F Frith & Co Ltd, Reigate.

Catching crabs

Crab fishermen from South Devon photographed in 1927. On the right of the photo is William Login, father of seven sons and two daughters. On the left is Bob Phillips, a fisherman from East Prawle. As well as mending nets, Wilfred Login, one of William's sons, remembers, 'We grew our own willows in plots on different farms. These would be cut in the winter and we would make about 80 crab pots each year.'

the village for them to live in, paying a mere £100. The last time it was sold as a holiday home in 1999, he states, 'it made £179,000.'

The farms themselves were built over springs, but for the ordinary village houses in the 1920s and 1930s, the only drinking water came from a well outside the ex-coastguard house. To emphasize how close-knit a community it must have been, Wilfred notes that there were 13 Logins attending the school at that time. Times were so hard, he can recall spending Saturday mornings catching up to 20 starlings in the refuse pit in the garden, which were then baked in a pie for Sunday.

Wilfred didn't like school much and left as soon as he could, explaining that the farmer's children went to the grammar school in Kingsbridge, while the children of the labourers and fishermen went to the council school in the village. 'Some got on well,' he admits, 'but the boys wanted to go and earn a few pennies to give to their mums for food. What was the use of education when we knew we had to work on the farm or go fishing when we left school?'

up at 3.30pm at home, to take me to Kingsbridge station. There I had to wait until 7pm for the train. It was the same train as the fishermen send their crabs to London arriving at 3.30am. I got to Lowestoft at 10.30pm. I can tell you it was very frightening.'

Much of the village of East Prawle itself was built around the village green, including the two shops and it was here that the public telephone could also be found. The village green is still there today, but other than that, the village is very different. Mr Login notes that only one of the farms is still in use, all the others have been made into private houses, many used as holiday homes. The largest farm was turned into 16 separate residences, both houses and flats.

To illustrate how things have changed, he recalls that when his father was given notice to leave their cottage in 1934, a farmer who his mother worked for, bought an empty cottage in

FISHING GEAR ON BEER BEACH

This old postcard published by The Dolphin Hotel in the village of Beer in south Devon, shows boats, pots, and other fishing gear on the beach.

The brickworks

Another type of industry that is found in many rural locations is the brickworks. They were built all over the country, wherever there was a clay soil suitable for making bricks. The industry was quite labour intensive and unusually both men and women were employed in the works.

One of the best examples of this kind of industry is found at Allandale on top of the Antonine Wall in Scotland. James Jamieson grew up in the village in the 1940s, when it was little more than two rows of red Dumfries sandstone houses, on either side of the road. To the north of the village was the Forth and Clyde Canal, and in the south the London, Midland, Scottish Railway. What was different about the village was the fact that every house belonged to the owners of the local brickworks, John G Stein & Co, and the householder had to be an employee of the works to live there.

At its peak the works employed around 600 people. Obviously, not all of these lived in the village of Allandale: others were bussed in from places like Airdrie, Kilsyth and Falkirk.

'Most of the brickworks in Scotland,' writes Mr Jamieson, 'were built on a line across the central belt as the clay seam ran along this. The larger firms would buy up smaller firms to get access to

their clay supplies. Women as well as men were employed in the works but they were only employed in certain areas such as taking the newly made bricks from the Bradley machines, laying them out on the floor to dry, and then working alongside the men in loading the dried bricks into the kilns for burning. Only men unloaded the kilns after burning. The hand moulders who made the more intricate shaped bricks were all men. All these operations, with the exception of the machine operators, were on piecework and they were usually finished by mid-afternoon. The factory hooter sounded at 6.30am and again at 6.55am. The hourly paid workers including all the tradesmen worked 44 hours per week in the 1940s and early 1950s. They started at 7am and finished at 5pm with 30 minutes off for breakfast at 9.30am and 40 minutes for lunch at 1pm. Many of the workers from Allandale went home for their meals.'

James Jamieson goes on to explain that you

Aerial view of the brickyard at Eastrington in the East Riding of Yorkshire. The brickyard was owned by Doreen Wilde's grandfather. When he died in 1940 her father took over the business and ran it until he retired. 'It was the only industry in the area,' notes Doreen.

Left: Archie Anderson, Jim Buchanan, and Jim Wilson – three lads from Allandale enjoying a drink.

Below left: James Jamieson's father, Company Sergeant Major David Jamieson of the Argyll & Sutherland Highlanders, who later worked at the brickworks. There were many accidents involving the loss of limbs at the Allandale brickworks but few fatalities, although sadly David Jamieson died from a head injury at the works in 1947.

Slate, brick and granite

Brickworks were found all over Britain, and Arthur William Henry Charles recalls the Pembrokeshire coastal village of Porthgain, with its little harbour. In earlier times it was known for its slate industry, but by the early 1900s this had given way to producing bricks, each of which had Porthgain proudly stamped on it. 'Later on came the granite works and for this it became most famous,' states Mr Charles. 'Huge stone crushers were installed to crush the stones to various sizes down to dust. It was reckoned to be the hardest granite in Great Britain and was transported by ship to all parts of the British Isles. Because of its hardness some buildings in London are faced with Porthgain granite. I can recall as many as six ships at one time, both in and outside the harbour waiting to be loaded.'

could normally identify long service employees by having one or more fingers missing. This was mainly caused when using the small brick presses which were kept moving all the time. 'One man put the block of clay in whilst his partner at the other side of the machine took the finished brick out. If the first man did not get the clay in quick enough, the next cycle of the press could catch his finger. Sometimes his partner knew of the accident first when he saw the finger pressed into the brick. The victim had not felt it coming off.'

Due to the fact that people were working with unguarded machines, others lost hands and even legs. There were few fatalities although, tragically, Mr Jamieson's own father was killed in the works in 1947, by an injury to his head.

The bricks were dispatched from the works by rail and Stein & Co exported them all over the world, usually shipping out of Grangemouth or Glasgow. For the people in the small village of Allandale, the brickworks was the main source of employment until the 1960s when the houses were passed over to the control of Stirling County Council, and the residents were no longer obliged to work for John G Stein & Co.

Mining

Throughout rural Britain, often situated in some of the most beautiful countryside, mining went on in its varied forms; from tin mining in Cornwall, to coal mining in the Mendip hills of Somerset. For those who lived in them, mining villages were very special places, and their communities were even more close-knit.

Ken Carruthers lived and worked in the coal mining community of Great Clifton in Cumbria and says: 'It was not an exciting village but when I was a child growing up there, and up to the moment they closed down our mine, the William Pit, in 1959, I knew every soul who lived there. We were a very close-knit community. We didn't lock our doors except at night time. Our doors were open to anyone who wished to call. You didn't need an invite to join with the household for tea and biscuits, you would enter and put the kettle on yourself.'

It's interesting to note that the pit at Great Clifton closed in 1959, the year before the one this book uses as its benchmark for change. After that date, things could never be the same again for the miners and their families, and since then, many of the cottages traditionally built for mine workers have been demolished.

But what was a mining village like? In truth, other than the fact that the pit replaced agriculture as the main source of employment, the village structure was much the same as everywhere else, with the same type of facilities and features. Ken Carruthers grew up in William Street, which consisted of two rows of miners' homes built prior to 1861. He describes the atmosphere of the street at the time.

'A little corner shop was part of the street, Henrietta's, where we bought our sweets and pop, and the menfolk purchased their fags and tobacco. To the left of the school stood Matty Campbell's grocery cum haberdashery store. His store faced Camerton Lane, at the top of which stood our coalmine and the coke ovens. Opposite this was a concrete terrace built around 1874 to accommodate the influx of miners. I lived in one of the two houses on the right of the school, a large garden and small orchard separating us. Another little shop, Joe Irving's stood right opposite the pit yard selling the same as Henrietta's. He had rows of cigarette packets lined across the mantelpiece that the colliers had bought. They couldn't smoke or take cigs down the pit, so they would take one cig from the packet when coming up from the pit. Mrs Graham had the Post Office next door.'

Like most other villages, as well as having shops, Clifton included pubs, a school, and

Salvage team in front of the William Pit coalmine at Great Clifton in Cumbria in 1959. This was the year the pit was finally closed. Back from left: Jonty Wilson, Norman McDonald, Tommy McKeating (in light shirt), Casson Wallace. Front from left: Dick Sloan, and Alf Byers. Other two unknown.

village hall. This was the Mechanics Hall, which at one time was the centre of village life. It was here that dances were held, with music provided by two men playing the melodeon and fiddle. 'If a girl refused to dance with any man she was not allowed to dance again until she relented,' notes Ken Carruthers.

Just below the hall were the only miners' homes in the village that are still in existence today. These were specially built for the men who ran the pit; manager, overmen, deputies, surface bosses, and the like. Built in 1895, they had the luxury of bathrooms, but still had outdoor toilets.

In 1926, with the pit community thriving, a miners' reading room was built, where the men could play snooker, billiards, or skittles. This included a little shop selling refreshments and cigarettes. A large iron stove provided the heating. In another room miners could play cards and dominoes in front of a warm glowing coal fire. Outside there was a bowling green. It was called the reading room because in the large hall there was a massive wooden table, upon which

every day would be the national daily papers, and a copy of *The London News*. To enjoy the facilities of the reading room you had to be a member, and a few coppers were deducted from your wages each week.

This old postcard published by *The Western Mail*, shows a colliery in South Wales. Keith Watkins lived in the village of Varteg in Gwent where he began work in the local colliery in 1939, when he was only 14 years old.

Clifton House in Cumbria, was built in 1824 by ship owner and magistrate Richard Watts. The house was built on soil shipped from Ireland, so that Mr Watts could see his ships sailing into Workington harbour. It was demolished in the 1930s but this picture was taken before 1900.

Some of the women who worked at the William Pit coalmine in the 1950s. Front row: Sarah Wallace, Ada Hidgson, Katy Irving, and Annie Grenwell. Centre: Florence Stephenson, Edith Wallace, Mrs Simpson, and Annie Jane Wallace. Back: Mary Wright, Jane Nutter, Mary Peart, Belle Parker, and Mrs Stephenson.

'Ten years later, in 1936, the Miners' Welfare Hall was built,' recalls Ken Carruthers. 'What a boon and exciting place that proved to be for the whole village, especially during the war years. I remember the opening when I was still a child.

Speeches, the first concert and the first dance held there. Activities of every kind happened in there. Every week we had a concert, proceeds for war charities. Tanner Hops as we called the twelve to four dances. It was also our wartime cinema. When the mine closed the reading room became derelict through lack of finance. Vandalized and robbed of anything useful it became unsafe, so in 1970 it was demolished. But not so the Welfare Hall. It was handed over to the village to become our village hall, run by a separate committee.'

When the pit closed in 1959, followed by the destruction of the miners' cottages, people sought work away from the village, and others dispersed around the region. 'Most of us miners were thrown on the dole,' admits Mr Carruthers, 'and some of us took quite a while to find work. There was no redundancy pay for us.'

Below: Miners' cottages in William Street, at Great Clifton in Cumbria, in the 1930s. This was the street in which Ken Carruthers grew up.

Another mining community was at Varteg in Gwent and 14-year-old Keith Watkins began work at the John Viponds Colliery at Lower Varteg in February 1939. He vividly remembers his first day. 'After collecting our miners' lamps,' he recalls, 'we had to wait at the entrance to the slope to be told where we were working and who with. There were 15 of us all from Varteg School. The only work available to us was at the colliery. I was to work with a man called Rowley Parry, I found him and we walked into the workplace. It was dark and so many things to watch out for. It was impossible to walk upright. We must have been about 200 men and boys going into work all

carrying our lamps like a column of gloworms.'

After walking for about half an hour, the group began to split up at various junctions, as parties went to different places to work. 'The rest of us carried on for another 20 minutes until we came to another junction, I was told that this was the "meadow vein". All the men and boys went into the coalface leaving Rowley Parry and me to carry on walking. About ten minutes later we arrived at our workplace. It transpired that he was a repairman, employed to keep the roadways and timber in good condition and I was to help him. We replaced some timber and cleaned the area, he then told me what to do next and said he

Miners' wives and children outside their cottages at Summerhill, Varteg around 1890.

Rows of cottages at the mining village of Varteg in Gwent.

Adapting to change

The success of some rural communities depended on their ability to accept change. A good illustration of this was found at Penybanc located between the villages of Fochriw and Deri in the county of Glamorgan. This purpose built village outlived its original use but had to be demolished when faults due to the nearby mines made the houses unsafe.

Penybanc had not originally been built as a village but as an isolation hospital, where the contagious diseases of the time were treated. The buildings formed a complex, in which the hospital was in the lower part and the accommodation for some of the staff, in the upper part. When its function as a hospital was discontinued, the buildings were converted into cottages for mine workers in the expanding coal industry in Wales.

So a new village was formed and it was here that Mr O F Evans lived. He recalls, 'As time passed a chapel, hotel and school were built and it became the village of Penybanc. The railways came and the Newport to Brecon line passed through the centre of the village, but the luxury of a station on that line was not to be, and if one wanted to use the railway train it was necessary to walk the one and a half miles to either Fochriw or Deri to board the train.'

Each of the newly converted cottages had two rooms downstairs and two bedrooms above, reached by a narrow twisting stone stairway. They also had a small lean-to at the rear for use as a coal-store and to house the primitive washing facilities. There was no piped water initially; a communal standpipe provided water for use by the families.

Each residence had a small garden at the rear with a toilet or 'ty bach' at the bottom, which means 'the small house', explains Mr Evans. Near the back door was a candle in a glass jam jar with a string handle attached and this was used to light one's way to the 'ty bach' if you were unlucky to be taken short at night.

This new village had no shops so daily requirements were provided by various travelling tradesmen, such as the baker, nicknamed 'Gilbert stale cakes'. He visited twice a week from Bargoed. His bread was delicious but his cakes left a lot to be desired. If due to bad winter snow he was unable to deliver his bread, he would place everything for the whole village into sacks and take the train from Deri to Fochriw, throwing out the sacks of bread as the train passed through Penybanc. Other groceries were delivered on Friday, from a shop in Fochriw. Milk was delivered by horse and cart, as was coal,

Although surrounded by a strong farming community, lead and copper were also mined near the village of Llanfair-Talhaiarn, but later tourism became its main industry as a centre for people wishing to explore the Welsh mountains. Reproduced from a postcard published by R. Griffith, of Llanfair-Talhaiarn.

which was dropped outside the front door, and carried to the coalhouse in buckets. As most households had a miner in them, coal was supplied at very low cost.

Overlooking the village was the Brithdir Level coalmine, and from its entrance horses would pull the drams of shining black coal. The coal was transported by tramway along the hillside to the nearby village of Pentwyn where it was loaded into railway wagons.

'My father was a miner and worked at nearby Ogilvie colliery,' explains Mr Evans. 'What a harsh job that was, because of the conditions he had to endure, hewing coal in a seam which was often only two feet six inches from the floor to roof. He would come home after his shift black with coal dust from head to foot, absolutely exhausted and would sometimes sit at the table and fall asleep with his knife and fork in his hands. There were no pithead baths in those days and he had to bath at home. We had for this purpose a large beer barrel, which had been sawn in half and was filled with hot water from a bucket that had been heated on our coal fire. As he washed, the abrasions became visible, some of them tattooed on his back by the coal dust.'

Mr Evans left the village of Penybanc when he got married, but his mother and father remained until his father's health gave out and he was forced to give up his job and move to a modern house at Fochriw. After a few years he died from the effects of the coal dust he had inhaled during his time working as a miner.

'Mam was never happy living in Fochriw and moved back to Penybanc with an elderly aunt who had lived with my parents for quite a few years. One evening in 1964 Mam was in bed and heard a loud rumbling and shaking and part of

the ceiling fell on to her bed. Large cracks appeared in the structure of the house, which had affected the whole village and rendered the houses uninhabitable. This was the death knell of Penybanc. All the residents were re-housed by the local council. Mam moved to a council flat at Gelligear. A wonderful community was thus broken up and it was with a heavy heart indeed and a tear in my eye that one day shortly after this event, I stood and watched the demolition of Penybanc.'

Every now and again Mr Evans still returns to the spot where Penybanc once stood, to enjoy the tranquility of the place and to re-live these and many other memories of his birthplace.

The village of Penybanc before its demolition, from an oil painting by O F Evans.

Night time frights

'Sometimes in the winter,' Mr Evans recalls, 'one would have to leave a warm bed to make the journey to the toilet at the bottom of the garden, only to find that the door had been left open and the shelf with a hole in was covered in snow. This had to be brushed away and one could spend a very uncomfortable few minutes there. I well remember the terror of one winter's night on one of these occasional visits, when through the small window behind me were two large pink eyes observing me. With a loud yell I ran back into the house and upon investigation by my father, the apparition was found not to be a "Bogey Bo" at all, just a large horse who was sheltering there. I have never forgotten the feeling of terror of that moment.'

A view across the rooftops of the mining village of Silverdale in Staffordshire. The houses in the foreground were called Brookside, and are where Joseph Cook, prime minister of Australia from 1913-14 lived as a child. The properties were originally thatched, and this photograph was taken in 1937 just prior to their demolition.

A railway village

Roggiett was a railway village where Glyn Dumphy was born, and where he joined the railway in 1937 as did most of the other school leavers of his age. Ninety-five per cent of the male population of the area was employed on the Great Western Railway, and sons followed their fathers.

Village life, until the outbreak of the 1939 war, was delightful, Glynn Dumphy recalls, with an annual carnival and village sports day usually held in the rectory grounds. The church and Methodist chapel were the focal points of village life. There was one pub, The Roggiett Hotel, and a non-political club, although ninety per cent of the village supported Labour.

Roggiett had been a rural village until the railway network expanded it. Nearby was the Severn Tunnel Junction, with its large marshalling yard that mainly handled coal from the South Wales pits.

Work times for railwaymen were varied, he remembers, and it was commonplace for the 'call boy' employed by the railway to wake the workers, to shout loud until acknowledged. This could happen at any time between midnight and 6am. Obviously, when the 'call boy' shouted for the 2.30am workers, it would wake the whole village. 'It mattered not,' he admits, 'It was life in those days.'

Glyn was of a musical disposition and recalls there being a local amateur operatic society

A train passing through the marshalling yards at East Ardsley in West Yorkshire.

This postcard published by G H Lake & Co Ltd shows Locomotive No 774, the Manchester to London express, near the village of Chinley in Derbyshire. Although a rural community, Chinley's agricultural economy was boosted, first by the arrival of the Peak Forest Canal, then a tramway, and finally several railway lines.

Members of the Roggiett and District Operatic Society posing after a performance of *HMS Pinafore* at the village of Caldicot in 1951.

formed in 1932, which is still performing today, although the name has changed from the Roggiett to the Caldicot Operatic Society – Caldicot being the larger town nearby. The brass/silver band, in existence from the early 1930s and made up mainly of railwaymen, is also still going strong. Glyn played the drums in the band at the regular dances held in the village hall, and he continued to do so regularly until his eightieth birthday.

Some things at Roggiett were similar to Penybanc. For instance, railway workers were able to buy coal at a special price. The coal merchant would deposit a ton of coal on the road from his horse-drawn cart and the householder had to transfer this to his coal shed, using buckets. Tradesmen would call at the village regularly and one day a week a van would sell soaps, paraffin for lamps, and general hardware. Another weekly visitor was the fishmonger, who had fish in boxes packed with ice. Then there was Henry Poretta, an Italian who travelled from Newport to sell ice cream from a cart, until he was interned during the war.

'We would have regular visits from unemployed men coming from the valleys,' Glyn states, 'who were members of a brass band in their area. This was possibly their only source of income, bearing in mind the villages of Ifton and Roggiett had full employment thanks to the railway. Drivers of

The Ifton Revellers

The band was from Roggiett in South Wales and mainly consisted of railway workers. As the only transport that they could afford was a bicycle, Glyn Dumphy remembers that it was normal to see anything up to 30 cycles outside the hall on dance nights. 'They would still be there when the dance finished,' he points out. 'How times have changed, you dare not leave your bicycle outside your own house now.' The picture was taken in 1938, and the band includes Glyn on drums, and brothers-in-law Gordon on violin and Johnnie on trumpet. The Roggiett village hall was in use most evenings and there were regular dances at which the band played. Glyn continued playing drums with bands in the area, until his 80th birthday, although the band in the picture finished shortly after the start of World War II. In 1938, his fee for playing in the band was five shillings and the music and dancing went on from 8pm until midnight.

The Peacock Hotel in Rowsley, Derbyshire, a 17th century country house set in beautiful gardens leading down to the river Derwent, which is still open to the public today. From a postcard by A P Co. At Rowsley there was a large railway marshalling yard and engine shed, and the village was very much constructed around the former Midland railway station.

steam locomotives were paid four pounds and ten shillings a week; and a guard three pounds and ten shillings. These were good wages in comparison to other means of employment.'

But apart from being a railway village with full employment, Roggiett was very much like any other village in the area. It had both football and cricket teams, with away matches being played anywhere up to 12 miles away. Although special buses were often laid on for supporters, such was their enthusiasm that it wasn't uncommon to see them cycling in all winds and weathers to the most distant fixtures.

In other ways, the village was similar to some of the more rural examples. The majority of the houses had large gardens plus allotments. Glyn explains, 'every type of vegetable and soft fruit was grown. Fifty per cent of the houses kept chickens, and quite a number pigs. So we were reasonably well fed, even during the food-rationing period.'

Glyn concludes by saying that, 'Village life didn't change much until about the mid-1950s, with the arrival of the car. Then of course, in 1962 Dr Beeching decided to close many railway stations.' The Severn Tunnel Junction was one of his victims, and the marshalling yards were closed. This meant that most of the men in the village had to find some kind of alternative employment elsewhere.

Plate layers at the marshalling yards at East Ardsley in West Yorkshire.

Homing pigeons

Once a week during summer, a train would arrive with a more unusual cargo, and 200 pigeon baskets would be shunted into the sidings. At 11am prompt a dozen or so men would release the pigeons from the baskets, which would race back to their homes in the South Wales valleys and sometimes even farther afield, as far as the north of England. For a few minutes each week the sky over Roggiett would be blackened with birds. The picture below, taken in November 1953, shows baskets filled with racing pigeons being loaded on to a train, from where they will be despatched to take part in the races which were held all over England.

Railway workers pose before the North Junction signal box at Lofthouse in West Yorkshire.

A new community

Today some villages are growing at a frightening speed but in the 1930s, with the effects of the recession still being felt, there was little growth in the countryside. This wasn't the case at Westbank, a few miles from Snaith in the East Riding of Yorkshire, one of the many communities established under the Land Settlement Association.

In 1937 the grandparents of Christine Arnold went to live at Westbank, along with 36 other families. Her grandparents came from Jarrow, her own father was eight years old at the time, his sister ten. 'The 37 houses were built by the government to provide work for families,' states Christine.

Nearly all of these people were relocated from the Jarrow area. They could no longer find employment in the northeast because the shipyards had closed down. The Jarrow March was still fresh in the memories of the government, so perhaps they decided that they should try and help some families to re-establish themselves and gain employment.

'My grandfather had been a carpenter in the shipyard and he was transported (not quite to Oz, but it must have seemed like it to them) to this new settlement called Westbank. All the families were given a house and approximately three

acres of land. They had to teach themselves to become market gardeners in order to survive. Everything they grew had to be sold exclusively through the Land Settlement Association. They were not allowed to sell anything to anyone else and the prices paid were very low.'

Some of these people had large families – it wasn't uncommon in those days for parents to have seven or eight children and that was a lot of mouths to fill. A new rural community was being created, where residents were expected to sustain a country existence, but it was established for people who had only known life in the towns and cities and had little idea of country matters. All were expected to leave behind their friends, relatives, place of birth and its associated traditions and history, in the quest to provide a living for their families.

In Westbank there were no shops, no school, no public transport, and no church or chapel. They were, in fact, completely isolated. None of the new community owned cars so they got around on bicycles. There was a tiny village close by that at least had a small school that all the children could attend.

Christine explains that at first, nobody in the area understood anything their new neighbours said, due to their Geordie accents. However, under very difficult circumstances, a community

In 1939, unemployed miner Nathan Turner and his wife bade farewell to friends in Durham, where they had both lived all their lives. They are moving to a cottage homestead in Reading, as part of the Land Settlement Association scheme run by the Ministry of Labour.

A young boy enjoying a tricycle ride on a clear broad road near his new home on a Land Settlement Association estate in Reading.

Men at work in one of the new greenhouses at the Boverton Land Settlement Scheme in Glamorgan, South Wales. They are transplanting tomato plants from pots.

spirit began to shine through. Christine's grandmother was instrumental in starting up a small chapel where she held Sunday-school. She also organized social evenings, gave dancing classes, ran whist drives and endeavored to make Westbank a sociable community.

'I spent a lot of my childhood at Westbank with my grandparents,' recalls Christine. 'They worked incredibly hard and, during the war, took evacuees in from Jarrow. My grandfather was excused war duties because he had to work the land. I cannot imagine anyone now having to leave their birthplace and being set in a 37 house community with no market garden experience and trying to survive by selling all produce back to the government. I suppose it was the government's way of gaining recompense for providing the families with a roof over their heads.'

Over the years Westbank has grown and most of the smallholdings are now privately owned. Many have been formed into a large commercial enterprise selling salads to supermarkets

Seasonal workers

Every year during the summer months the populations of some rural villages were bolstered by the influx of seasonal workers, who largely came from the cities. This was especially true of villages in Kent, where entire families who lived in the London slums would come to earn money hop picking, as shown in this postcard published by Salmon. This was a dirty, monotonous occupation, and very poorly paid. Many families stayed in purpose built wooden huts, which were often only about ten feet square. Conditions were extremely primitive, and it wasn't uncommon for a dozen or more people to be crammed into one hut. Other workers were bussed in daily, if the farms were close enough to the London suburbs where they lived. Although it was hard work, children often looked forward to hop picking, as it was the nearest thing to a holiday they were likely to get. From May onwards there would be great excitement and preparation for the approaching season.

A lost community

From a brand-new community, we turn our attentions to a lost community; the only evidence of which that now remains is the ghost village of Imber, on Salisbury Plain in Wiltshire, the story of which is not entirely unique. It is hard to imagine a whole village being emptied of its inhabitants in this way, today.

Doreen Charles was born in 1930, in what was then a lovely rural village. Salisbury Plain was owned by the Ministry of Defence, who had bought up the village of Imber in its entirety in 1933. In late October 1943, during World War II, all the inhabitants were called to a meeting in the village school only to be told that they all had to leave the village by 18 December. This gave the menfolk just six weeks to find new jobs and somewhere else to live.

'Thankfully everyone managed to do that,' writes Doreen, 'but we were all absolutely devastated. We were promised we could return after the war but they never kept their promise. There are not many of us left now and at the moment we are fighting to save the beautiful little church that is the only building left. There are a few shells of cottages but after 60 years it's all very sad to return. We learnt at a later date that troops were sent into the village soon after we left to train for street fighting for the D-Day landings. I have some wonderful memories of my years in Imber, which I shall cherish for the rest of my days, and then I shall return to Imber forever. It's the only way we can return. By breaking that promise in not letting us return they broke a lot

of hearts, especially my dear mum. She cried for days and days after leaving. She is now lying in the cemetery at her beloved Imber. It was her home, as she was born there.'

Life at Imber was very much like it was in any rural village at the time. There were 30 cottages and four farms providing much of the work. There was a pub called The Bell Inn, a Post Office and a beautiful little church. Most people in the village attended the evening service on Sunday and the children went to Sunday-school in the afternoon.

On summer evenings after church the whole family would go for a walk together; children, parents and grandparents. Then they would sit in their garden next to the inn, where the children would have lemonade and a bag of Smiths Crisps, and the adults something a little stronger.

Imber was quiet and peaceful, only disturbed by the occasional convoy of army vehicles that passed through. Being in the middle of Salisbury Plain the village people were used to the presence of the military, and then in 1943 when the MOD decided they needed the buildings for training the troops for street fighting in

The village of Imber on Salisbury Plain. In 1943 the inhabitants were given just six weeks to leave their homes, as the MOD required it to train soldiers for street fighting in Normandy.

Of the original village of Imber, the church is the only building which remains intact.

Normandy, the villagers were forced to go. They went with the promise that they could return after the war, but that promise was never kept.

A number of people have since fought very hard to get the village returned, but to no avail. The only way a resident can now be returned to Imber is to be laid to rest there. Doreen's grandfather was taken back only five or six weeks after he left, her grandmother was taken back in 1967, her mother in 1982 and her father in 1983.

Rabbit for the pot

Doreen has cherished memories of her grandfather, who had lived in Imber all his life, and was the blacksmith and village rabbit catcher in his spare time. 'We ate lots of rabbit; rabbit pie, roast rabbit, rabbit stew. I remember I always asked for the brains, which was lovely. When I tell my grandchildren they say "Oh gran! How could you?" I say, "That's why I am so alert at 74 years old." I remember he kept ferrets at the blacksmith's shop, and he took them with him on the downs.'

The imposing vicarage as it once stood in the village of Imber.

The village blacksmith

Before the era of the motorcar, most transport was by means of horse and cart, so the blacksmith was a very important figure in the village. But he was more than just a farrier, shoeing horses. Farm implements needed repairing, iron cartwheel tyres replacing and, if there was time, wrought iron gates and other decorative ironwork could be made.

Frank Stanford remembers when his father Douglas ran a blacksmith business in the village of St Margaret's at Cliffe, in Kent. The business was attached to their home, suitably called Forge House. The forge is the term used for the smith's furnace, and the shop itself was 'the smithy'. His father was the only blacksmith in a large rural area, so during the 1920s and 1930s, he was kept extremely busy shoeing the many horses belonging to local farmers, gentry and, of course, the village folk.

One of Mr Stanford's most illustrious customers was Lady Astor, whom his mother would entertain with tea and cakes while the blacksmith shod her horse. He made all his own horseshoes, which he would burn on to the hooves, to get a special fitting. When there were no horses to be shod, the blacksmith would spend his time manufacturing new horseshoes to replenish his stock.

Margaret Kirby, who lived in Burniston in North Yorkshire, was a keen horse-rider herself,

so she was constantly visiting the blacksmith, Edgar Readman, at nearby Cloughton, who she describes as, 'a real character who always had his braces fastened to his trousers with a couple of horse-nails.'

Margaret remembers that the smithy was divided into several areas. One section had stalls big enough to accommodate two horses. Another area housed the forge, anvil, bellows, a large water trough to cool the shaped iron, and so on. In the remainder of the shop, other work was carried out, such as making wrought iron gates, tools, and other items.

Bill McKay's father was a farrier and master blacksmith, who took over the tenancy of the 'smiddy' at Migvie in Aberdeenshire in the 1920s. Bill estimates that there were some 200 Shire and Clydesdale horses in the area, as well as travelling stallions, hill ponies and ponies belonging to the tinks (travelling folk). 'All found their way to the smiddy,' he writes, 'to have hooves pared, and new shoes made and fitted.' Ploughs were also brought to his father to be renewed, along with other farming equipment, 'coulters and socks to be made, harrows, grubbers, scythe blades, cart wheels to be rung, and so on.'

Above: Forge House at St Margaret's at Cliffe in Kent in 1930, where blacksmith Douglas Stanford lived with his family. Next to the house can be seen the smithy. Standing in the doorway is his wife, Mrs Edith Stanford, with their two sons, Frank aged three, and Arthur aged seven, holding a clockwork train.

Left: Douglas Stanford, the blacksmith at St Margaret's at Cliffe in the 1920s and 1930s, with his helper Alf.

Blacksmith and handyman

Iris Sanders' father, George Henry Longland was a village blacksmith for 52 years. He rented a shop at Hackleton in rural Northamptonshire, where he shod all sorts of horses, from Shetland ponies, to Shire horses. He even shod racehorses, one of which won the Derby. He served his blacksmith's apprenticeship before being conscripted into the Royal Engineers during World War I. 'He was regarded as a general handyman,' notes Iris, explaining that when the village pump broke down, or the hinges of a farm gate broke, the cry went up, 'fetch the blacksmith'. This picture shows George Henry Longland at work in his shop which appears to be well equipped with heavy machinery capable for a variety of tasks. Such a versatile workshop is sadly missed in today's villages.

Albert Nash, grandfather of Doreen Charles, was the blacksmith in the ill-fated village of Imber on Salisbury Plain. 'I spent long spells there watching Grandad making horseshoes,' she recalls. 'I remember the red glow of the embers, when Grandad placed a ready-cut piece of metal into the furnace. When it was red hot he would draw it out, take it to the anvil and make it into a horseshoe, which probably took him about ten to 15 minutes. He had to be quick, but if the metal got too cold, it was sometimes put back in the fire, to warm it through again. There was a large pair of bellows by the side of the forge, which every now and then he would pump to keep the fire aglow.'

When Imber was taken over by the army in 1943, Albert Nash was cruelly evicted from his smithy, which along with all the other houses and farms in the village became an area for training troops in street warfare. Albert, who had been

Left: Blacksmith, Edgar Readman, supervises his son Michael as he shoes Margaret Kirby's horse Lucky, outside the smithy in Cloughton, North Yorkshire in 1958.

the blacksmith for 44 years, was devastated and died a month after leaving his home. 'The doctor said of a broken heart,' recalls Doreen. 'He was taken back to his beloved Imber to lay to rest.'

Douglas Stanford also had the job of making iron tyres for wagons. The wheelwright would place his wheel on a stand in the yard, and when the metal tyre was hot and ready, it would be carried out with large tongs. Once in place, the blacksmith would hammer it tightly around the wheel. It was a big undertaking and he would often enlist the help of villagers to give a hand. These included the village policeman, the postmaster, the baker, the greengrocer, and occasionally even the vicar. 'At the end of the day, everyone got a slap-up meal supplied by mother,' says Frank Stanford.

Iris Sanders goes on to explain that after a certain amount of time the wooden wheels would shrink, and the iron tyre would become loose. 'The blacksmith then removed the tyre, heated it, and cut a small piece out, before re-fitting it. Being hot, it set fire to the wheel and two or three men would be standing around with buckets of water, which they threw at the wheel to douse the flames.'

The warm smithy was also a place for social gatherings. Bill McKay remembers the evenings when his father would prepare the carbide lamps and return to complete jobs required urgently. 'The ringing of the anvil and the dim light from the gas lamps would bring an array of chaps from their chamers (bothies). Discussions would centre around the next quoiting match, when the next ploughing match would take place, the next ball or the agricultural show.'

The village blacksmith was always known for his great strength, through years of wielding his heavy tools. Richard Shimmin remembers a certain blacksmith on the Isle of Man that proves this point. 'A gang of us youths, on our way home,' Douglas recalls, 'passed a local smithy and four

Mr Clift Consterdine, the blacksmith at Eaton village in Cheshire, busy at work on his anvil. The local hunt provided many opportunities for the blacksmith.

Mr Harry Pearce the saddler, pictured at work in his shop in Abingdon Lane, East Ilsley in Berkshire in 1951, with Rosa Hibbert. At the time the shop was a thriving concern. His grandfather and father had both been saddlers before him, but by 1950, the craft was already starting to die out, as fewer farmers used horses to work in their fields.

Blacksmith traditions

Several blacksmith shops are associated with local traditions, perhaps most famously at Gretna Green. Pre-wedding rituals also featured in the Scottish village of Migvie. 'Feet washing was a tradition played out at the smiddy, on more than one occasion,' notes Bill McKay. 'The prospective bride got a marginal feet washing, too, considered good luck before a wedding. Only the gallace (brace wearers) got a much more in-depth manhandling. The prospective groom, be it farm hand or farmer got his feet washed, he was blackened from head to toe in soot-black boot polish and cart grease. The belt and braces couldn't be held on to, and the custom usually ended in good humour and with someone going off to collect bottles of beer and maybe a bottle of whisky. This was a sort of stag night.'

or five of us carried his anvil weighing about 5cwt on to the roadside. We knocked on his door and hid in the bushes nearby. However, the last laugh was on us as the blacksmith simply picked up the anvil and carried it back inside on his own!'

As the motorcar became more and more prevalent, and farmers began to replace their horses with tractors, blacksmith businesses around the country went into decline. In order to survive, new opportunities were welcomed. In the case of Douglas Stanford he began to make wrought iron gates, including the 12-foot gates for the South Foreland lighthouse. 'On one occasion,' admits his son Frank with guilt, 'I noticed all these chalk marks on the floor. So I decided to sweep them up to please Father. Of course these chalk marks were the iron gate drawings and measurements. It must have taken him ages to plan. I had swept them up in a few minutes. But bless him, he never told me off or even gave me a slap.'

Marion Cooke, from Barbrook in Devon, recalls how the village wheelwright adapted to the changes. 'His name was Will but was always called "Wheel". He had the foresight to install petrol pumps next to his workshop, as he was not going to be outdone by motorized vehicles.'

Another craftsman associated with the blacksmith and a society where horses were indispensable, was the saddler. Jack Gee, who lived in the Isle of Ely near Thorney, remembers the wonderful smell of the saddler's shop where they made or repaired anything made of leather or canvas. 'I used to sit in the corner of the shop and see a hunter saddle or a pair of driving reins being made from the virgin leather.' Harvest time

Above: The Old Forge at Merrow in Surrey in the 1930s with its unusual horseshoe entrance.

Below: This old postcard from Raphael Tuck & Sons, shows a village blacksmith busy at work.

Bill Greatorex, the
village blacksmith and
beekeeper, at his smithy
in Malthouse Lane,
Barlaston. The smithy
is attached to the house
Bill shared with his sister
Leah Greatorex, who was
the school headmistress.

was particularly busy for the saddler, who would repair the canvas from corn binders, or broken leather harnesses.

There was also a wagon-builder in some villages, who made carts, wagons and traps from raw timber, carving the beautiful shapes with a plane and spokeshave. Often these carts would be brightly coloured, making him not only a skilled wood craftsman, but an accomplished artist as well.

Collectively, the blacksmith, wheelwright, saddler and wagon-builder, serviced an equestrian world in which the horse still maintained its indispensable role.

An atmospheric
photograph of the forge
in East Ilsley, Berkshire in
1910. On the left is Rosa
Hibbert's grandfather
William Field, who was
the village blacksmith,
her great grandfather
George Field, and her
uncle, Frank Field,
working on the right.

Baking the daily bread

One of the most wonderful aromas associated with bygone village life, was the smell of freshly baked bread wafting out of ovens on the early morning air. Today most people buy their bread in supermarkets, but not so long ago almost every village in the country could boast of having its own bakery.

Gordon Greenlaw served his time as a baker in the village of Kintore, 12 miles north of Aberdeen. His first pay as an apprentice baker in 1959 was three pounds, five shillings and one penny a week. As the apprentice, his first responsibility each morning at six, was to go round the village on the bakery bicycle, balancing a big basket of rolls, buns and butteries, which are a local Aberdeen speciality. The villagers would have pre-ordered their requirements and each day, with the exception of Sunday, their order would be delivered fresh to their doors.

'We worked on Christmas Day,' he recalls, 'as the baker's oven was a popular place for the villagers to get their turkeys cooked. We used to meet the locals coming from the Christmas Eve service at the kirk, as we went to work. We started baking Christmas cakes on the first week in October, so that they were in perfect condition for Christmas.'

A speciality of the Kintore bakery was shortbread, made with pure butter from New Zealand, which came in bulk, as a 56lb block. Many of the products were given local names; Paris buns were called Bennachie baps; fruit slices were Muckers or Muck Middens; and Russian sponges (a sponge on top of a short-crust pastry case, with jam and sultanas on the bottom) were known as Sputniks.

When Gordon first started at the bakery it employed eight bakers and three apprentices, serving a shop and five retail vans which went round other local villages and farms. Today, as with most villages, Kintore no longer has a bakery. The shop is now a pizza parlour and the bakery itself has been converted into flats.

The interior of Brown's Bakery in the village of Bramley in Hampshire, in 1916. In the picture are Mr Leslie Brown and Will Munday, Bill Johnson's grandfather, standing in front of the bread ovens. Note their long aprons and traditional bakers' hats.

Covered four-wheeled wagon belonging to W King and Sons bakery in Albury, Surrey, which was used to deliver bread to the local villages in the 1930s and 1940s. Photographed during the war years, it is being driven by Patricia Pyke.

Right: Scotch oven with peel used at the Kintore bakery in Aberdeenshire. The peel is a long pole for putting goods to be baked in and out of the oven.

Far right: The Divider from the old Kintore bakery. It was used to cut dough or pastry into equal segments.

Rosa Bowler remembers living next door to the village shop at East Ilsley in Berkshire, which was owned by her uncle, who also happened to be the village baker. It was a thriving business, and while her aunt served behind the counter, her uncle baked the bread in their bakehouse.

'As well as serving the bread and lovely, sticky lardy cakes in the shop,' she explains, 'he made daily deliveries in the village and on certain days he would make deliveries to the villages of West Ilsley and Compton, all in his old green Ford van. It always took him ages, as he was a welcome visitor at most homes, where he would be invited in for a chat and a cup of tea. In bad winters, when the snow cut off the villages, we carried the bread across the fields in baskets and sacks.'

The bakehouse she remembers as being a lovely, warm place in the early morning. The oven fire was lit early and her uncle would knead the dough and leave it to rise before baking the delicious bread. If she was lucky when she popped around to see him, there might have been sultanas left in the empty lardy cake tins, which she was allowed to eat.

For those villages that didn't have their own bakeries, fresh bread would be delivered from neighbouring settlements, usually by bicycle, or horse and cart. Irene Foster remembers how in the village of Bishopstone in Buckinghamshire in the early 1930s, the baker from Aylesbury would come to the village on Saturday with his horse-drawn bread van. 'The back doors of which would be opened wide,' she writes, 'to reveal fancy cakes of all kinds laid out neatly in trays. We girls could choose which one we wanted. Mine was always either a jam or cream

As well as a local bakery owned by Walter Hayes, the village of Stourton Caundle in Dorset had bread delivered by two other bakers, Arthur Ratley and Billy Dike, from nearby Stalbridge. Here Dike is delivering bread at Golden Hill in the 1920s. The cart was fitted with a semi-cylindrical canvas tilt, and on each side was displayed in bold lettering the owner's name and his trade. Competition between tradesmen was fierce, and when a new family moved into the village they would be greeted by a baker and butcher, both anxious to obtain the custom of the new residents.

Far left: The Brake, a machine used for rolling out pastry, from the old Kintore bakery.

Left: Specialities from the old Kintore bakery. Clockwise from top left are a Butterie, a Bennachie Bap, a Sputnik and a Muck Midden (Mucker).

doughnut, delicious! Mum would get her bread and we were allowed to feed the horse with a carrot or lump of sugar.'

Like all businessmen, bakers had to be astute when it came to earning a crust. William Moore from Tasburgh in Norfolk relates an amusing tale of Mr Funnell, who owned the bakery at nearby Newton Flotman. 'Mr Funnell was known to be a bit of a miser. Bread was four pence and three farthings a loaf, and should a customer only have four pence and a halfpenny, Mr Funnell would record them owing the farthing in his book before leaving the customer's house so he did not forget. A well known joke arose about his farthing book as follows: if Billy Funnell saw a farthing in a cows' tad he would not be satisfied with picking up the farthing, he would take the tad as well, (a tad being Norfolk for cow dung).'

During both world wars, many bakeries lost their male staff. Fred Gallacher's late wife Patricia was living with her family in the village of Farley Green in Surrey in 1942. Keen on horses, she approached the bakery, W King and Sons in Albury, with the offer of delivering the bread in one of their horse-drawn vans before she went to school. The bakery had three horses, Bill, Jumbo and Brownie, and two-wheel and four-wheel delivery vans. Patricia's daily tasks involved harnessing the horses up to the carts, collecting the bread, rolls and cakes and, with the help of a delivery list, completing the rounds.

'I remember her stories of the various characters,' says Fred. 'One horse would always stop at each house, even if no bread was required, and Patsy would have to pretend to deliver something to get him to move on. Another would take off as soon as her foot was on the cart; so some clever rein handling was necessary. When the Canadians arrived with their tanks, many a time the horse would bolt with Patsy hanging on like Boadicea, with bread and rolls shooting all over the countryside. Much of course to the amusement of the soldiers!'

As improbable as it might seem today, some villages had more than one bakery. At Corston near Bath, Peggy Shepherd remembers there were two. Adults and children alike loved the smell of freshly baked bread. 'If any dough was left over,' she reflects with pleasure, 'the baker would throw it into the oven and make little rolls for the children. We would follow the bread cart on its rounds, and the baker would stop and toss the rolls for us to catch. They were still warm, and went down well. We didn't need butter!'

Doing the bread round, Patricia Pyke delivering bread around Farley Green and other local villages for the W King and Sons bakery in Albury, Surrey, in their two-wheeled delivery van. She volunteered to do this as all of the men at the bakery had been called up for military service and delivered bread from August 1942 to February 1944.

The butcher's shop

In many remote villages people went into town once a week to do their shopping. This would include ordering the Sunday joint and any other meat the family might consume. The butcher would usually deliver these items out to the villages in his van or cart. However, although not as commonplace as the bakery, many villages had their own butcher's shop and slaughterhouse.

Charlie Harvey the butcher at Barlaston, with his sister on the left and his wife on the right. Charlie built the butcher's shop in about 1928.

Onchan village on the Isle of Man, where Richard Shimmin explains that traditionally, 'when the butcher bought a pig for slaughtering he would return a quarter to the farmer for the kitchen. It would be kept in the dairy along with the milk, butter and cheese, a very popular place when relatives called.' From a postcard.

Onchan Village I.O.M.

Ernest Hawkins recalls of Barlaston in Staffordshire, 'Charlie Harvey was the village butcher. He built a shop near The Plume of Feathers public house. He slaughtered animals down the canal side where Brookhouse Drive is now. The cattle used to come by train to Barlaston station and were driven down to the slaughterhouse by drovers.'

With the actual slaughtering of animals taking place in the village, everyone would be quite aware and perhaps immune to what was going on in their locality. The cries of beasts being killed were audible enough for all to hear. Pamela Gear lived in the village of Amberley in West Sussex, where the butcher had a slaughter yard near her school.

'We could hear the pigs squealing from the school,' she states. 'Then like blood-thirsty kids, we would cross the road, to watch the bloody water run down the stream.'

In rural villages everybody knew each other and many of the inhabitants were related. This resulted in a situation where certain customers received preferential treatment, not merely at the butcher's shop, but at the other local establishments as well.

'If the butcher liked you,' says Rosa Bowler, who lived at East Ilsley where there was a butcher's shop in the main street, 'you received

better cuts of meat than those he didn't like! The story is told that one lady went back with her joint one day, planted it down on the counter saying that, he would not give Mrs so-and-so meat like that, so she did not want it either!'

The butcher might purchase the livestock to slaughter by going to market in a nearby town, or by going direct to the local farmers. Richard Shimmin, who lived in Dalby on the Isle of Man, explains a tradition upheld locally, 'When the butcher bought a pig for slaughtering he would return a quarter to the farmer for the kitchen. It would be kept in the dairy along with the milk, butter and cheese, a very popular place when relatives called.'

Janet Burt lived in the Dorset village of Piddletrenthide in the Piddle Valley, where there were two butcher's shops, one of which also had its own slaughterhouse owned by Mr Wightman, (who was related to Ralph Wightman famous for his radio programmes during the 1950s). Mr Wightman also ran a farm, so Mr Legg managed the shop for him. 'This amused both villagers and visitors alike,' explains Janet, 'as we had a Mr Baker the baker and Mr Legg the butcher.' Nearby was the bakery, where the baker's name was indeed Mr Baker.

When the fact that there were numerous village outlets providing meat to the public is combined with the infancy of hygiene awareness, it's surprising that food poisoning wasn't more widespread. Marie Litchfield, from Ashcott in Somerset notes, 'The butcher and his assistant came round the village twice a week, delivering orders and selling things such as sausages and faggots. Today's standards of hygiene did not apply then. Meat was cut up on a wooden slab with grubby hands, occasionally wiped on a rag, as was the sharp knife. No one was bothered, and unless memory has gilded the truth the meat and sausages were delicious.'

The sale ring at Taunton Market in 1961 during a cow sale run by auctioneer Mr Dudley Hunt of F L Hunt & Sons. A dairy farmer would most likely have purchased this particular animal but local butchers also bought their meat by going to the market in their nearest town, or buying direct from the local farmers.

Wartime sausage specials

Mr V J Catt from Etchingham in East Sussex began work at the local butcher's shop at the end of 1939. He helped in the slaughterhouse, delivered meat, and made the sausages. At that time, with rationing in place, the making of sausages was governed by restrictions from the Ministry of Food. 'Only sausages containing one part beef, and three parts bread, were allowed,' he explains. Inspectors could descend on them at any time to test the sausages, and a heavy fine was liable if this mixture was not adhered to. However, twice a week they made 6lbs of pure pork sausages, and as soon as they were ready, he put 5lbs of them in a meat basket. His boss told him to cover the sausages with a cloth, so that nobody could see them. He then had to deliver 2lbs to the village squire, 1lb to two rich ladies who lived in the village, and 2lbs to the local public house. The remaining 1lb of sausages was also left at the public house, to be picked up later by the local policeman – thus keeping all the people that mattered, happy!

Delivering the milk

The countryside was still widely farmed by small independent farmers and many of these ran their own local dairies or simply provided milk as a commodity to the villagers in the area. In this instance, which was more often the case, the milk sometimes went straight from the cow to the customer, being delivered to the doorstep from a horse and cart.

In the late 1940s. Ethel Fisher was a milkmaid in the village of Seaton in West Cumberland. She worked at Buildings Farm, where after the milk was cooled it was poured into a ten-gallon steel churn, which was then lifted on to the back of a small four-wheeled truck. The truck was drawn by a black and white pony called Spotty, which Ethel would harness and yoke between the shafts, before setting off on her milk round.

At each house the customer would come to the door carrying the jug they wished to be filled with milk. Ethel carried a one-pint measure and a gill measure, made from tin, which was dipped into the churn, in order to fill the customer's jug with the required amount. If a customer was at work when she called, the jug was sometimes left on the doorstep. Quite often it would be inside the house itself, where she was welcome to enter, do the necessary delivery, before closing the door behind her. 'No one locked the back door in those days!' she says.

As private telephones were still rare in villages apart from the gentry, police house, and Post Office, Ethel was frequently asked to deliver messages from one family to another, who lived in different parts of the village. 'It was routine for me,' she says, 'to pick up a basket of dirty washing from more than one elderly parent, and deliver it to the daughter. When washed and ironed, the basket was returned a few days later. Quite often I was presented with a basket containing young pigeons, and asked to release them at the furthest point away from their loft – this was to train young birds to recognize their own home from above.'

'Everybody knew everyone else in the village at that time,' she continues, 'and I received many a friendly "good morning lass" from various people, including black-faced colliers returning home from the night shift. I travelled seven days a week, delivering milk at the princely cost of twopence halfpenny per pint.' For expectant mothers and children under five, it was only one and a halfpenny. 'Such was life in the slow lane, many years ago.' concludes Ethel.

Mrs J Peacock, who lived in Cayton, in North Yorkshire as a girl, remembers Audrey Pearson,

The daily pint

Leslie May was one of several people who delivered milk down the steep, cobbled streets of Clovelly in North Devon. He had his own cows and hand milked them every morning and evening. The most effective way he found of conducting a milk round in such a steep location, was to carry two milk pails swung from a yoke across his shoulders. He also carried half-pint and pint measures, with which he would fill up the jugs that waited for him on each village doorstep. He carried on the service until 1951, when regulations came in that milk should be supplied in bottles.

Two boys helping to deliver milk from a farmer's horse and cart around the village of Oving in Buckinghamshire, in about 1930.

who used to deliver the milk every morning on a hand-pulled cart. In the cart were two large churns of milk, with two metal pint cups. Her mother would take out a jug to be filled, and would then take it to the pantry, where there was a marble slab. This would help keep the milk cool, even in the summer. Sometimes the milk cart would double-up as a funeral conveyor. 'I remember poor Mr Willmore,' she writes, 'being pulled along the village to the cemetery in the milk-cart, because the family were too poor for anything else.'

Audrey Purser, who lived in Merrow in Surrey, has a more embarrassing reason to remember the milkman's horse. 'Every morning,' she recalls, 'after the milkman had been with his horse, my father would send me out with a bucket and shovel. I really didn't want to do it, but he said it was good for his roses. I can still see my sister Sheila smiling at what I had to do.'

Mr Burnett of Sutton in Elms, delivering milk in Leicestershire in the 1930s, by motorcycle.

Bringing the cows in for milking in the mid-1920s. Ron Foster worked at Crossroads Farm, Oving in Buckinghamshire between 1921–1961. The farm was owned by Mr Watts, who died in 1936, and the boy in the photo is his son Jim, who then took over the running of the farm. The milk was put into churns and the lorry took them to the Nestles milk factory in Aylesbury where it was bottled. On the farm they did the milking by hand until 1957, when they went over to machine milking.

Children were often drawn to the dairy farm, fascinated at the sight of the cows being milked. Geoffrey Charge would hang around the farmyard near his home at Eight Ash Green in Essex to watch the cows coming in for milking. Just as it still happens in some villages today, the herd would be brought along the road from a field, and all the traffic was held up for a few minutes. Unlike today though, there was very little traffic to be held up!

The cows were milked twice a day, once at nine in the morning and again at four in the afternoon. 'Two brothers and a sister owned the farm,' notes Mr Charge, 'and I used to watch the cows being milked into a big galvanized pail, from which the milk was poured into a churn. One of the brothers used to put the churn on a trailer and tow it round from door to door. He sold milk straight from the churn by using a small metal scoop. There were no crates of bottled milk in those days and no fridges to keep it cool. It was fresh from the cow every day.'

In some villages milk wasn't delivered to the doorstep, but was available from the farm by presenting your jug. Janet Beer, who lived in Dewlish in Dorset, was one of three children who

Leslie May milking his cows by hand on his North Devon farm in 1954. He carried on in this way until electricity was connected to the farm building in 1957.

were often sent to fetch the milk from a nearby farm, with a three-pint milk can. This proved to be a dangerous undertaking, as the back door of the farm was guarded by a fearsome gander who would put down his head, rush forward and hiss menacingly. Therefore Janet's older brother usually undertook this job. Children love to swing cans, and after a while he became quite proficient at swinging the can in a complete circle without spilling any of the milk. Inevitably, one day while he was performing this feat, the handle came off and all three pints of milk were lost. His mother was far from amused.

During the week, Dorothy Waters' Auntie Lily used to deliver milk round the village of Cassington in Oxfordshire, dispensing it from a three-gallon container on the handlebars of her bicycle. The one-pint and half-pint measures used to hang over a rail on the inside of the lidded container. 'If you wanted milk in the afternoon,' Dorothy explains, 'you had to walk up to the dairy at The Laurels, after Pop Waters had brought the afternoon milk from the farm. We had cans with lids and handles and it was quite a challenge to swing the cans over one's head without spilling the milk. Sometimes it was a treat to get beestings, locally known as cherrycurds. This was usually the second and third milking mixed together, after the birth of a calf and with a little sugar and nutmeg this made a delicious pudding similar to an egg custard.'

But as with all things in village life, changes were inevitable. Gertie May, the widow of Leslie May, who delivered his milk around Clovelly in Devon recalls, 'I think it was in 1951 that regulations came in, stating that milk had to be in bottles.' Leslie May was forced to discontinue his milk round and instead his milk was put into a churn and sent to a factory at Torrington. The age of the milk bottle and the large dairies had begun.

Above: Rita and Jennifer Parrish's pet goat jumps up to give the twins some help with the milk churns at Novelty Farm in Northamptonshire in 1940.

Milking Time.

Left: A typical cowshed where the cows would be brought in to feed while being hand milked into pails. Small three-legged milking stools can still be found in country antique shops. Some farmers in remote farms were still milking by hand until the late 1950s or early 1960s. From a postcard published by B B of London.

The village shop

Between 1900 and 1960, nearly every village in the country had its own shop. Some villages boasted several, selling everything imaginable. After all, where there were people, there was money to be made. And as the majority of village folk had limited access to transport, these shops had almost a monopoly on sales.

Large villages such as Cheddar in Somerset and Kingsteignton in Devon, maintained the appearance of small towns, with dozens of retail outlets, however, even in the smaller, more rural villages, most had some kind of general store. Sometimes these shops doubled up as a Post Office, which will be looked at more closely in the next chapter on public services.

A typical shop from the period would have been Agars in the village of Cayton, in North Yorkshire. It was here that Mrs J Peacock grew up, and she describes Agars as being 'the hub of Cayton'. 'There was nothing old Mr Agar didn't keep,' she says. 'Stock was hung from hooks in the beams, and every space was filled: shoe buttons, liberty bodices and large bloomers were intermingled with the flour, sugar, butter, and bread.'

Reputedly, old Mr Agar could sell anything. When she was a young girl, Mrs Peacock once ended up with a hideous pair of old ladies' shoes, simply because Mr Agar let her mother have them for a couple of shillings, pointing out how they would last. 'And last they did,' she says. 'I tried everything to wear the damned things out; climbing trees, walking through puddles, nothing worked – they lasted!'

At Tasburgh in Norfolk, William Moore remembers the village shop owned by Mr and Mrs Patrick. Mr Patrick was a Home Guard officer, who sadly died in the early part of World War II. His widow carried on the business, but without offering van deliveries to peoples' homes. Rationing made a big impact on shopkeepers, as they were limited in what they could sell. William Moore writes, '2oz of butter, 8oz of margarine, 4oz of sugar, 2oz of cheese, 4oz of sweets, per person weekly, just a few of the commodities allowed.'

Pre-packaging was unheard of, as everything came in bulk. Sugar was supplied in 1cwt sacks, and 28lb blocks of cheese were covered in hessian sacking. Butter arrived in 14lb blocks, and loose biscuits arrived in 14lb tins. Everything had to be weighed up and put into brown paper bags, according to the customer's requirements.

If life in general was slightly less hectic in

bygone days, shopping was an even more relaxing experience, unlike the stressful occupation it has become today. There was no point being in a hurry to get served, in order to rush on to the next part of a busy schedule. The shopkeeper took his time, weighing, measuring, cutting, and individually bagging up all the purchased goods. The shop was also a place for gossip, and you simply had to wait your turn until the shopkeeper's conversation with the customer in front was concluded. He knew everybody in the village, and everything that went on.

A young customer is served in one of the two shops which existed in Laxton, Nottinghamshire in 1952. The village was bought by the Civil Service when its previous owner, Earl Manvers was forced to sell because of death duties.

A typical rural village shop, the General Stores, at Draycott in Somerset. From the style of the signs in the windows, the picture was probably taken about 1930.

Carys Briddon's grandfather built and ran the shop in the little village of Bontgoch in Ceredigion, and she recalls that when she was growing up in the 1950s, a lot of people went to the shop to socialize, more than anything. 'Some housewives,' she says, 'would come two or three times a day, they would buy a small item, and then spend a lot of time chatting.'

During the war years, when their husbands were away at war, many village shops were run by their wives. 'Outside help was rarely allowed,' explains William Moore, 'as women had to work the land or in munitions factories.'

At one point in his life, Mr Moore rented a shop

Above: This humourous postcard published by Burlington, and postmarked 1931, gives a good impression of the inside of a village shop at the time.

Left: The village shop at Bontgoch in Ceredigion as it was in the 1950s. It was built and run by James Pearce Evans in 1905.

in Tasburgh himself, which he ran as a store and shoe-repairers until 1958, when it was badly damaged in a fire. Although the shop was restored, he didn't wish to reopen the business, and it was taken over by a local builder as their depot for storing thier building materials.

Janet Burt's parents ran the village shop called The Stores in Piddletrenthide in Dorset, from 1946 to 1971. 'They stocked a wide range of grocery items,' she says, 'but besides this they also sold wellington boots, plimsolls, knitting wool, patterns and needles, including sewing needles, cottons, embroidery threads, paraffin, chicken feed, vegetable and flower seeds, and all manner of other items.'

Janet's parents also ran a Christmas savings club into which customers could pay a small amount each week. When Christmas was imminent, they could use the money to buy presents and food. 'I remember going to the wholesalers in August,' she writes, 'where my parents would choose and order their Xmas stock, including cards, wrapping paper, gift tags, toys, puzzles, chocolates, and so on.'

She also remembers how the riding community in their corner of rural Dorset would stop to buy sweets or cigarettes. Her parents would either take their purchases out to them, or the riders would dismount and come into the shop still holding on to the reins, resulting in the horses heads being inside the shop doorway.

Mr Charles, who lived on a farm half way between the two Pembrokeshire villages of

Porthgain and Llanrhian, in which the shop in question was situated, relates an amusing wartime anecdote. Food rationing was at its height, but farmers could apply for a permit to obtain extra rations of sugar, margarine and cheese, to help feed the casual labour force required for harvesting.

'Once when my father went to the shop to collect these extra rations,' he recalls, 'the vicar's wife appeared. As every item was put into the cardboard box, she expressed her amazement, almost insinuating that my father should feel guilty for accepting the consignment. The shopkeeper also seemed to enjoy the situation. Father felt it was time to retaliate and told the vicar's wife, "Well if the vicar will come and give us a hand with the harvest he can have a share."

William Moore in front of the little shop he rented in Tasburgh, in Norfolk, and ran as a general store and shoe-repairers during the 1950s until it was burned.

Mrs Mary Perkins who owned this village shop at Little Addington in Northamptonshire during the 1920s. The shop was actually set up in the front room of her house.

Before packaging

At Stourton Caundle, Frank Palmer recalls the many items that arrived at the shop in bulk, and how they were packed. 'There were some tinned foods and jars on the shelves, but most of the provisions were delivered to the shop in bulk, and were weighed up to the customer's requirements. Foodstuffs, such as sugar, rice, lentils, and dried fruit were delivered in hessian sacks, and other products including margarine, and lard were delivered in wooden boxes of varying sizes, tea came in three-ply chests. A small room to the rear of the grocery section served as a store for such items

as a barrel of malt vinegar, and seven-pound tins of corned beef, which was sliced with a sharp carving knife to the customer's wishes. Cheese was cut by means of a wire with wooden handles attached to each end, and metal scoops were used to weigh up other items such as rice, which were then placed in a brown paper bag. Sometimes dried fish could be purchased. The fish arrived at the shop in a wooden barrel, and had the appearance of a piece of leather. However after an overnight soaking in a bowl of water, it provided a nutritious meal when cooked.'

There was complete silence as he left the shop!'

Then of course, as well as shops selling all manner of goods, each week the villages would be visited by various travelling traders. William Moore notes that at Tasburgh, fresh fish was sold weekly from a four-wheeled cart with pneumatic tyres, horse driven by E Morley of Norwich, who also sold culled rabbits.

'The Ice Cream Man also came from Norwich,' he says, 'on a three-wheeled bike, with a container on the front. He always came on Thursdays and Sundays, assuming that he had not sold out on the way. However, this service quickly ceased at the beginning of the war, and it wasn't until about 1950 when an Italian man from Norwich started a similar round on Sundays. He drove a motor cycle, with a sidecar container,

and you could take a large pudding basin out to him and have it filled for a shilling. The first ice cream available after the war was made of vanilla custard powder.'

William Moore has good reason to remember that Mr Patrick the village shopkeeper, would also bring paraffin around the village in his van. 'Being clever one day,' he says, 'I turned the tap on and could not turn it off as it had a special locking key. How many gallons lost I don't know. I do know how the buckle end of the leather belt felt, however.'

During the war of course, the ability to shop was harder for every one, as many items, not just food were being rationed, including clothes and bed linen. For their purchase, books were issued, from which coupons were detached every time an

A smiling boy, surrounded by jars of sweets, as he celebrates the end of sweet rationing.

As there was little access to manmade fibres in those days, wool was commonly used for many things. However, wool was vital for the needs of the armed forces, and was difficult to get hold of. So if wool was purchased, it meant going without something else, as clothing coupons had to be used. These coupons had to be used with great thought, as the more scarce the item, the more coupons one had to hand over. This was particularly true of ladies nylon stockings, though cloth by the yard was less expensive and cost fewer coupons.

Another way of buying things during the war years, was to have the local tallyman call. He would come once a fortnight, and would issue a book into which you would pay installments, very similar to modern HP. Most women usually did this to purchase linen items or clothes for Sunday best. The difference was that each fortnight you paid the tallyman a certain amount in advance, and he only provided the goods once you had accumulated enough money to pay for them. It was, therefore, a cash purchase, but the tallyman had the ability to bank the money and draw interest on it, long before the housewife ever saw her linen or clothes.

'Few tallymen had cars,' writes Mr Moore. 'A trade cycle would be used with two suitcases holding samples in one and saleable items in the other.' They were much appreciated in the villages. They had pride in their job and wore highly polished boots and buskins, which were leggings made of leather approximately twelve inches deep, and buttoned up on the outside. They also wore corduroy plus (similar to riding breeches), a tweed jacket and cloth cap. Like all men they always raised their hats to a lady, or touched their peak when addressing a man.

Geoffrey Charge from Eight Ash Green in Essex also remembers the ice cream man coming at weekends and some evenings from Colchester. It was Walls ice cream and he would cycle out to the villages on a tricycle that had a coolbox on the front. The traditional sign on it read 'Stop me and buy one.'

'He sold the most delicious ice-cream called a Snofrute,' recalls Mr Charge nostalgically, 'which was actually a water ice in a triangular cardboard packet and it was in different fruit flavours and cost one penny. At the village garage there was a tiny shop that sold sweets and cigarettes and Smiths crisps which had a little blue bag of salt in them and they were about two pence a bag. Another favourite of mine was a bar of milk chocolate the size of a Mars bar filled with soft cream in different flavours, it was made by Fullers and I have never seen them anywhere since the war ended.'

item was bought. 'A man would probably be able to buy a jacket, vest, pants and two pairs of socks, in a twelve-month period,' notes William Moore. 'A lady similar, around one pair of sheets and pillow cases, or a blanket would be allowed, if you had not used the coupons to buy towels, etc.'

A schoolboy might normally possess three pairs of short trousers, one pair for school, one for Sunday best, and the third for playing in. Mr Moore remembers the embarrassment this caused for boys who were starting school, or even older ones of a nervous disposition. If they wet their trousers, although their mothers would dry them out by the fireside at night, they would be humiliated at school the next day, as their body heat combined with the heat of the room, caused a reaction to the acidity of the urine. Girls were in a better situation he states, as their knickers were easily and readily changed. 'My personal humiliation,' he recalls, 'was having to wear nurses' cut down thick black stockings when I had no socks.'

The mill house

When we think of mills, many of us might automatically draw a mental picture of large industrial towns in the Midlands and the north of England, which were known as mill towns. In the country a mill was more likely to be one which ground corn and was powered either by wind or water.

These buildings produced everything from textiles to metalwork. But in its basic form as defined by the dictionary, a mill is a building fitted with mechanical apparatus for grinding corn, and mills like this could be found in villages throughout Britain. Some employed several local people while others were run by a solitary miller who often lived on the premises with his family.

William Moore, from Tasburgh in Norfolk has good reason to remember his local mill, Duffields Mill, which was out in the countryside in the tiny village of Saxlingham Thorpe, about two miles from his home. This was where he had his very first job, at the age of 15. Duffields was a provender mill, producing animal feed. It was run by a foreman, and as well as employing young William Moore, the staff included another senior miller.

They started work each day at seven in the morning and usually finished around six in the

evening. During the day they mixed eight tons of cattle feed, and loaded the lorries. Quite often he worked till nine in the evening, and occasionally right up till midnight. 'We still had to be on time next morning,' he points out. The mill, which is still working today, also employed a lady who mended sacks, four office workers and, of course, the boss himself.

Many mills were situated near a river, particularly those employing a waterwheel. The area around Saxlingham Thorpe would often flood so in order to protect the mill from flooding, bricks and rubble were collected from an old World War II airfield nearby, which were used to fill in a void right up to the river edge. William Moore would accompany the lorry as driver's mate and recalls, 'It was cruel heavy work and my hands were raw with blisters. My wage was £4-£5 a week, this included overtime averaging about 20 hours a week. Once I did 44 hours

Duffields provender mill in Saxlingham Thorpe, Norfolk, Christmas 1950. Lined up outside are the boss's car and the lorries used to transport the cattle feed. It was here that William Moore began his working life aged 15.

The Old Mill, Rye, Sussex.

The old mill

The corn mill at Buttercrambe in North Yorkshire was run by Ken Rennison's father. He recalls, 'The farmers brought the grain to the mill – barley, wheat and oats. It was weighed. The barley and wheat were ground for beef cattle and pigs, and the oats were rolled for horse food. My brother and I used to help Dad pull the sacks to the top of the mill and tip them into the hopper to be ground and rolled ready for the farmers to collect.' The Buttercrambe mill was leased from the Darley Estate, and it was also used to pump water into storage tanks at the top of Aldby Hall. Ken Rennison's father had to check the water levels daily, and it was there he met his mother, who was nanny for the family at the Hall.

Windmills like this one in Sussex, shown on an old postcard published by A H Homewood of Burgess Hill, were once a common sight in villages in many parts of Britain.

overtime, equal to a full week's work. We had to work Saturday mornings as well.'

At one time Tasburgh also had a provender mill, which in Victorian and Edwardian days was driven by a wooden waterwheel and a steam engine. William Moore remembers the mill, although by his time it had already closed down. 'The owner went bankrupt,' he explains, 'as he seemingly spent more time in the pub than the

mill.' At the time though, it must have been quite a major concern, as opposite the mill, there were three cottages for the men who worked there.

At Melbourne in Yorkshire, there were two mills. Walbut Mill was a watermill driven by Pocklington Beck. The second mill was housed in a large timber building that belonged to a local builder and was driven by a large hot-bulb petrol engine that was started with a blowlamp.

Hemingford Grey Mill on the Ouse.

Hemingford Grey Mill, on the river Ouse near St Ives. From a coloured postcard published by Langsdorff & Co.

The Old Mill at the village of Bathampton, near Bath in Somerset from an old postcard.

Ken Sleight, who lived at Melbourne says, 'these mills were used to grind and roll the farmers own grain for animal feed. The builder of the mill was also one of the village undertakers, and he also sold petrol from two pumps at the side of the road.'

In the beautiful village of Cattistock in Dorset, Marie Langford still lives in the cottage adjoining the mill house that has been in her family since the 1700s. The mill stands on the River Frome, which meanders through the water meadows on its way to the coast at Poole. 'The mill ceased to work about 1927,' she explains, 'and I remember my brother and I, as children, going down to the underground part of the mill where the main machinery was. We would turn a wheel which started the whole building shuddering and rumbling like an angry giant, while the water would start thrashing and pounding and the big

iron wheel would start turning and everything would settle down to a steady drumming sound. I never cease to wonder how we escaped being crushed to death, drowned in the millpond, or decapitated by the circular saw, which was driven by the machinery. At the outbreak of World War II, all the machinery and the millwheel were removed to help the war effort and the mill was left as an empty shell used for storing hay and cattle feed.'

Today most rural village mills have been turned into private houses, and a few have made rather splendid restaurants, where we can relax and watch the waterwheel slowly turn, as we drink and eat, helping to remind us of the important place these buildings once had in the overall scheme of village life. Some others have been lovingly restored to their original use and are still used to grind corn as a tourist attraction.

The windmill in Reedness Road, at the Yorkshire village of Swinefleet, about 1939–40.

Chapter Six

Public servants

Like any city or town, a rural village needed public services and professional people to be able to function effectively. There were, of course, rural, district and parish councils, where community representatives helped to make decisions governing the welfare of the village. A local Member of Parliament also represented the village. But there is a group of people who up until 1959 were still very evident in the community, though largely missing today.

If someone was ill, they needed the doctor or district nurse; the post didn't deliver itself; the roads had to be maintained; and of course, all communities needed law and order, and an authority figure telling them what they could or couldn't do.

The village bobby

The duties of a rural policeman covered a range of activities from the supervision of agricultural procedures and attending traffic accidents to apprehending local villains. During the Second World War they were joined by the Home Guard, Special Constables and Air Raid Wardens for added security.

John Radford Cartwright became the police constable in the village of Shenstone Wood End, five miles south of Lichfield in 1936. His usual working day went from 9am to 1pm, and then 7pm to 11pm. Night patrols were essential and included 'conference points', where he would liaise with his opposite numbers from adjoining beats. These meetings could take place at any time from midnight to 5am, and were an opportunity to exchange information regarding village security and local crime. As few of these conference points were within easy walking distance of the police house, a bicycle would have to be used. Constable Cartwright had to purchase his own bicycle, but he was given one shilling and sixpence a month 'cycle allowance' to keep the cycle in good repair.

Police Constable John Radford Cartwright, pictured in 1942, was the village bobby for Shenstone Wood End in Staffordshire for 26 years.

Being the village bobby was a full time occupation. Reports were required on all road accidents involving humans and dogs. Stray dogs were kept at the police house, and an allowance of threepence a day was paid for their food. But if the animal was not claimed or sold, the fee being a standard price of seven shillings and sixpence, it had to be destroyed. Threepence was also allowed for the cost of the poison and a further threepence for digging the necessary hole to bury the unfortunate creature.

As a village constable John had to become conversant with animal and veterinary law. He had to attend the sheep dipping, at which farmers cleansed their animals of various diseases and parasites. It was his responsibility to superintend the destruction of any infected animals. He also had to know the game laws, as much of his beat consisted of agricultural land and woodland.

But what sort of crime went on in rural Staffordshire in the late 1930s? His first prosecution came soon after his arrival, when he saw a man on a motorbike and sidecar, who failed to stop at a halt sign. On apprehending the culprit, he discovered him to be his new neighbour, and despite the prosecution, they were friends for the next 40 years.

Another example of crime on his patch, happened on a winter's night, when he was cycling to Footherley, and noticed a van parked in a field near the side of the road. The van was empty, so he covered the lamp on his bicycle and continued along the road. A short while later, a light flashing near a poultry farm alerted him to the presence of two men, who were busy killing the fowls. He caught one of the men red-handed and marched him back to the van, where he handcuffed him through the window to the steering wheel. He notified the farmer and then found and arrested the second man.

In 1939 war was declared, and many police officers with previous military service were immediately called up by the armed forces. To help John Cartwright and other village

In this comic postcard published by W B, and posted in 1927, a bobby in a typical uniform of the day, with buttoned up tunic, shows concern for an open door on his beat.

An accident in June 1952 in Birmingham Road, Shenstone Wood End. Three people died in the car when an army vehicle hit it. It was the worst road traffic accident that PC Cartwright could remember.

policemen around the country, air raid personnel and Special Constables were recruited and, of course, in many villages, there was a Home Guard platoon to add extra security.

In the autumn of 1940, when the bombing of the Midlands commenced, the second bomb to be dropped in the area landed at Moor Lane, Footherley, and the third at Crown Lane, Four Oaks. The only fatalities were two sheep, grazing in a field on Footherley Farm. After this, night time air raids and the wailing of sirens became more and more frequent.

As a member of the Staffordshire Police Mutual Aid Squad, when Coventry was badly bombed, Cartwright was sent to the city with about 20 other officers. Coventry had been devastated, whole buildings destroyed, and the water and electric supplies largely out of action. They were billeted at Central Hall near the bombed cathedral, and their job was to prevent looting

A bobby poses with a Home Guard platoon at Wykeham in Yorkshire. During the war years, the work of the village policeman was assisted by the recruitment of Special Constables, ARP (Air Raid Precaution) wardens, and even the Home Guard.

decided to drop its final bomb on Cartwright's beat. He heard the sound of the falling bomb, which exploded on – you've guessed it – Boghole Lane. Cartwright got up, dusted himself off, and raced to the scene. Coming the other way, he noticed the car he had earlier directed to Boghole Lane, in order to find peace and tranquility. The driver didn't stop to thank him.

About half a mile from the village of Shenstone Wood End, the MOD built a decoy factory, which was reached along a dirt track almost opposite the police house. The decoy was manned by two employees of the Ministry, and they lived in a specially built blast-proof building on the site. The idea of such decoys was that once a bombing raid was in progress, bonfires at the site would be lit, in order to confuse the enemy into thinking that their target was below them and on fire. Of course, if the plan worked well, the bombers would attack the decoy site, instead of their real targets. This was the reason for the blast-proof shelter, so the two men who lit the fires, were afforded protection. However, even though during raids the decoy was set alight, the bombers ignored it, and it was soon decided that enemy intelligence was aware of its existence, and it was abandoned.

Early in the war several searchlights were set up in the area, including one on a farm along Lynn Lane in Shenstone, but two of the searchlight crew were killed when raiders fired shots down the course of the searchlight beam. A little later these searchlights were abandoned.

In January 1948, Cartwright received a

Above left: PC Harold Hoile of the Somerset Constabulary, shortly after joining the Police Force in 1926.

Above right: PC Hoile shortly before his retirement in 1954. Note how the uniform style had changed from the buttoned-up collar of the 1920s.

and to help at bombsites, where victims were being recovered dead or alive

Sometime after his arrival back at the village of Shenstone, he was on patrol one evening when a car approached, in which a man was travelling with his entire family. Exhausted by the nightly bombing of Birmingham, the man was trying to find somewhere quiet to spend the night. Constable Cartwright recommended Boghole Lane, at Little Hay.

At about midnight, when he was visiting Little Hay himself, an air raid on Birmingham was in progress. An enemy aircraft returning home,

Retirement day, August 1962. The villagers of Shenstone Wood End present John Cartwright with a writing bureau in gratitude for his 26 years as their village bobby.

commendation from the Chief Constable of Staffordshire, following the apprehension of a war refugee, who had murdered his wife on a farm near Kidderminster. The whole of the Midland Police Force was out searching, when Cartwright, on patrol, noticed a man walking along the road. He stopped the man, who couldn't speak a word of English, and his suspicions were immediately aroused. Pointing to the man he asked, 'Are you Omeljanchuck?' which was the name of the wanted man and he replied 'Me Andy,' which happened to be the wanted man's Christian name. Cartwright took him to the home of Mr Woolley, the nearest Special Constable, telephoned Lichfield police station and a car was sent to fetch him. Andy Omeljanchuck was tried, found guilty and sentenced to life imprisonment.

John Cartwright and his family loved their life in the village so much, that when John came up for promotion to sergeant and a posting to Uttoxeter, he turned it down. He decided that the increase in wages of ten shillings per week, to become a probationary sergeant, was not worth the upheaval. Consequently, he remained the village bobby until his retirement in August 1962, after 31 years in the police force, 26 of them spent at Shenstone Wood End.

Harold Hoile of the Somerset Constabulary joined the police in July 1926. His son Maurice tells us a little about his father who started his career in Frome, before being moved to the village of Pill, near Bristol. It was while he was stationed in Pill that he met Maurice's mother. 'Before they could marry,' explains Maurice, 'my mother was interviewed by the Chief Constable to make sure she was suitable to become a policeman's wife.'

Flooded out

In 1957 and 1958 there was severe flooding in the Kent marshes, which caused a lot of problems for villagers in some remote locations. With the ground floor of many cottages flooded, several people were forced into living upstairs. The only way to get supplies to them was by boat, so PC Ted Tudor enlisted the help of the gamekeeper at Stodmarsh and together they would row around the area visiting stranded families. In other cases, they were able to visit and supply people using a tractor with a very high trailer borrowed from a farmer, or help them move out as seen here..

After a period in the village of Coleford, PC Hoile finally moved to Midsomer Norton, where he retired in 1954. Although he ended his career in town, his jurisdiction still covered several outlying villages, hamlets and farms. The police station at that time was an austere place with cold

PC Ted Tudor, the village bobby at Littlebourne in Kent, on a Norman 'Nippy' auto cycle which was used by police during 1958–1959.

cells and an exercise yard. One day the young Maurice heard peculiar noises coming from one of the cells and closer investigation revealed a large pig making himself at home on the other side of the bars. His father explained that this was a gift from a local farmer, which he was going to fatten up for Christmas. Maurice stayed away from the cells after that, until the day the poor pig had a ring inserted in its nose to prevent it from digging up the floor of the cell.

PC Hoile's normal routine was to cycle from one village to another, and wait at the phone box at each, in case the sergeant rang. 'It was quite amazing what dad brought home with him. My mother found a length of rope with a noose on the end of it. It was lying on the sofa where dad had left it. Apparently someone had hanged themselves the night before and he needed the rope for evidence.'

Another village bobby was Ted Tudor, the policeman at Littlebourne in rural Kent, a few miles east of Canterbury. He and his wife moved into the village police house in 1956. All his reports had to be typed, and as he didn't have a typewriter, he had to get one and was paid 25p per week for its use. His means of transport for getting around was a bicycle, for which he was also paid 25p per week.

Rural policework often involved animals and the area had a few cases of foot and mouth that had to be dealt with, and one case of anthrax. In this instance, with no help from Ministry officials as there is today, the local policeman had to

provide the coal and wood to burn the affected animal himself and claim the costs incurred for material and labour.

Poaching was always a problem in rural communities. In Ted Tudor's area, there were three gamekeepers and most of the poaching was done on Sunday mornings. So he made a point of turning out at the crossroads in the middle of the woods near Littlebourne, with the

Stand and deliver!

Of all the characters that lived in his area of responsibility, the one that PC Ted Tudor remembers most fondly was Bill, who lived at Wickhambreaux. Bill was also the strangest! He was a large swan that wandered around the village and lanes. The postmistress would always come out in the morning and call 'Bill! Bill! Bill!' the swan would come running and she would feed him with bread. However, Bill objected to all the coaches that came to his village, carrying the fruit pickers and tourists, and he would lie down in the middle of the road to stop them going through. The drivers didn't know what was going on and, of course, didn't understand his peculiar ways. The police house had many a call from drivers, asking if he could move the swan. PC Tudor's advice to them was always the same, when they came to the village they should bring a bit of bread and stand on the village green calling 'Bill! Bill! Bill!' Bill would then follow them on to the green, which was what he appeared to be hoping for in the first place, and the coach could pass. This behaviour went on for several years.

Above: 'Excuse me! There's no rain.' A rural bobby offers a courting couple some friendly advice in this old postcard published by Bamforth & Co.

Left: 'On my Noddy Bike,' says Ted Tudor, pictured on a Velocette police motor cycle in 1963.

gamekeeper. They stopped and searched every car or vehicle that went by, announcing that they were looking for any signs of poaching. The message soon got around the area, particularly in the mining village of Aylesham, which was where most of the poachers were believed to have come from. After this incident poaching in the area dropped off quite dramatically.

There were six pubs in the area, which rarely caused any problems for the police but he remembers one bit of trouble that Dickie Mayes had. Mayes, who was the landlord of the Volunteer (now the Haywain) at Bramling was very worried because there was a group of gypsies living out near Wingham that would call into his pub and booze heavily. At closing time they refused to go and he found it difficult to get rid of them. So he had a quiet word with PC Tudor and between them they came up with a plan. The next Saturday night, when the gypsies were in the pub, the policeman arrived ten minutes after closing time. He pointed to Dickie Mayes and demanded to see him privately in the back room straight away. The couple stamped next door, and sat down for ten minutes, having a drink and a bit of pleasant conversation. When they eventually returned to the bar, the gypsies had gone. When they next visited the pub, Mr Mayes said to them, 'I'm going to lose my licence

through you', and he told them to get out. They all went quietly elsewhere, and he never saw them again.

Perhaps the most unusual piece of police work that Ted Tudor was involved with during his time stationed at Littlebourne, was when a bear escaped from Howletts, the zoological park a few miles to the south. About six local policemen, armed with stakes, were called out to deal with the situation and they eventually located the animal. The inspector then turned up with his gun, but before he was able to use it the veterinary surgeon tranquilized the beast with a dart, which was then dragged back to Howletts by the keepers.

Four village policemen from rural Staffordshire. From left to right, back: PC B Ison (Whittington), PC J Ball (Shenstone); front: Sergeant G Haycock (Whittington), PC J R Cartwright (Shenstone Wood End).

Tickling trout

Of course there were always a few local poachers but many of these were farm workers, and if they took the odd rabbit or pheasant it was considered a perk of the job, and a blind eye would be turned to it. Fish poaching on the other hand did cause a bit of concern. The River Stour at Wickhambreaux was stocked with trout and the Ickham Flycatchers Association would fish there. They were frequently complaining about fish poachers, so the local policeman had to keep an eye on the situation. Sometimes a fishing line would be tied to the bridge late at night, and the poacher would return in the morning for his catch. One culprit known to PC Tudor was a twelve-year-old local lad, who was an expert at tickling trout. One day he observed the boy from across the river, as he slowly and patiently leaned in to the water, and eventually flipped a trout on to the bank. PC Tudor appeared and asked the boy what he was doing, to which he cheekily suggested that he was merely playing with the trout, and was going to put it back in the river again. So the constable left him to it.

This postcard published by Davidson Bros, is titled 'A Country Girl'. You will have to draw your own conclusions as to why the policeman is moving her on, with such a stern expression to his face.

The Fire Brigade

As well as having their own bobby, a few rural villages, but certainly not all, were blessed with having their own fire engine as well. It was during the Second World War, with the added danger of fires from enemy action that rural fire services expanded, many of them manned by volunteers from the local community.

One such village was Thorney in the Isle of Ely, where Jack Gee and his family lived on a nearby farm. On the way to and from school he would pass the Thorney council offices that were situated inside the main gate of the Tank Yard which was an enclosed area, with a six-foot high wall around it. It was named the Tank Yard because the village water tank was within it, at the top of a 100-foot high brick tower. The water was pumped to the tank at the top of this tower, from the river opposite, by a great steam driven beam engine housed in the base of the tower. It was also the home of the Shand Mason steam fire engine that was the pride of the village.

'It was a four-wheel, horse-drawn vehicle,' writes Jack Gee, 'with a highly polished coffee-pot boiler. The firemen were all local men who made up the crew on a voluntary basis and when the siren wailed like a banshee from the top of the tower, the nearest volunteers would race to the yard on their bike, or motorcycle if they owned one. At the same time the baker or butcher would get their horses to the engine house, I think other horse keepers would be available on stand-by. The boiler would be lit as soon as the siren sounded by anyone nearby, usually the engineer running the beam engine. When all was ready and the horses raring to go, the big brass bell that hung above the driver would be rung and the excited horses would leap into action with smoke billowing from the boiler.'

Only once was Jack Gee lucky enough to see this splendid fire engine charge through the entrance of the Tank Yard, and lurch into the road. 'By the time we kids got to the scene,' he admits, 'the engine was taking water from the river and forcing a jet of water into the air across the river, it was just another practise call.'

In wartime, of course, with the possibility of bombing, more and more villages were equipped with some form of fire service, and the Auxiliary Fire Service (AFS) was formed, later to become the National Fire Service (NFS).

At Barlaston in Staffordshire, Ernest Hawkins recalls that the local AFS unit trained with a two-wheel trailer fire pump towed behind a car, which was stored in the garage of The Mount, home of Mrs Warner.

'The only time its services were required in Barlaston,' admits Mr Hawkins, 'I was told by Bill Johnson, is when a silo caught fire at Billy Pointon's Lea Farm. Bill and another man attended with the pump and put out the fire before the Stone Fire Brigade arrived.'

And in Burniston in North Yorkshire, Margaret Kirby relates the story of her paternal grandfather, local wartime firefighter Fred Wood, whose own father had been a firefighter before him. Mr Wood was the proprietor of a local garage, and when war erupted, he decided that the best way for him to serve his neighbours was

'Fighting the flames', this Raphael Tuck & Sons postcard shows an unidentified Fire Brigade at work, connecting their water hoses.

to follow in his father's firefighting footsteps.

Realizing that there was little chance of their village being equipped with any firefighting equipment at Home Office expense, he took it upon himself to form his own Fire Brigade and supplied all the equipment. He experimented with old oil drums for tanks, acquired a hand rotary pump, lengths of hose, a few fire buckets, chemical extinguishers and an extension ladder.

Fred's Fire Brigade HQ was set up in an old shop in Burniston High Street, which was equipped with a telephone. Volunteer firemen were placed on a rota, with two or three on duty each night. They passed the time playing dominoes and other such games.

Margaret says that Fred Wood's Fire Brigade trailer was called out to the first stick of bombs to be dropped in the Scarborough area, which happened to be on Burniston, as a result of which many houses in the village were damaged. Her father, Thomas Wood, was on duty that night and pulled one chap from the rubble. Fred's Fire Brigade is a wonderful example of how in a bygone age people cared enough about their community to invest so much of their own time and money for the benefit of others.

The Fire Brigade was there to put out fires, while the ARP existed in most villages to make sure that no lights could attract enemy bombs during the hours of darkness, thus causing fires in the first place. This photograph is from Holbeton in Devon. Shown here are (top row) Jack Rogers, Mrs Jarret, Jack Williams, Fred Rogers, Mr Wilson, Mrs Williams, and William Masters; (middle row) Mrs Brown, Joan Steer, Mrs Light, not known, Mrs Steer, Miss Warren, and Joan Squire; (bottom row) Mr King, not known, not known, Mr Hammon, and Jack Ackland.

Fred's Fire Engine

Wartime firefighter Fred Wood made his own fire engine using a two-wheeled trailer that could be connected to a motorcar. In the centre of the trailer he installed a 50-gallon tank, at the rear of which was a stirrup pump. He also fitted several brackets, and a superstructure able to carry the 20-foot extension ladder. Six buckets of sand were conveniently arranged in the trailer and room was found for various tools, such as saws and an axe. He completed the unit by painting the buckets and tank in fire engine red, and the trailer in battleship grey.

Village volunteers

For people who wanted to take a more active role in village life, there were various groups that they could become involved with. Decisions about the way in which rural people lived their lives, their facilities and services, were often made by strangers in distant places, but there were bodies which offered a voice to local people.

Previously, the church itself had taken an active role in the business of the village, and decision makers were normally the local squire, the parson, and sometimes the school master, with church wardens carrying out many civil tasks. However, the Local Government Act of 1894, removed the church itself from formal participation in local government, so that during the 20th century, parish councillors were all volunteers, and could come from any walk of life, within the community itself.

The parish council was often the most important of these, as it was concerned with the day to day running of the village. It had responsibility for things like the playing field and the children's play area, if the village had one. It could also allocate allotments and make consideration of the many planning applications for new buildings and modifications to old.

Typically, a parish council would meet in the church or village hall, one evening every fortnight. A notice of the meeting would be displayed on the council notice board because, although the council was an elected body, the meetings were normally open to the public. The public would not be allowed to speak unless invited to do so, and if an elector wished the council to discuss a subject, the clerk would have to be notified in advance. There was nothing secretive about the meetings, and the minutes would be available to anybody who wished to see them. Parish councillors also had some say over the finances of village projects, so it was a responsible position to take on.

There were several different organizations like these with which the adult population of the village could become involved if they wished to take part in village life.

Three members of Bishop Itchington parish council at a meeting in 1951. The women's dresses are typical of the period.

The Post Office and postmen

In very rural communities the postman provided an invaluable service. In the most remote reaches of a parish, where even the horse and cart of the butcher and baker might not venture, the postman was often the only regular link to the outside world. From the early 1900s most villages had their own Post Office.

The penny post first began in 1840 and during the decades that followed people took out contracts, often those who already ran a village shop, enabling their premises to double up as the Post Office. In this period the number of village Post Offices was at its peak, and even though there have been numerous rounds of closures since 1959, Post Offices still survive in a great number of villages.

Dorothy Waters who lived in Cassington in Oxfordshire recalls the Post Office, which was kept by two sisters, Miss Hutchins and Mrs Ferrett, and like the majority of village Post Offices was also a general store. 'There was a hinged counter on the sweets and grocery side and wire mesh on the Post Office side. There was also a black telephone with a separate earpiece on the wall just inside the door. You turned the handle and waited for the operator to answer. She was based at Eynsham and she always knew any number you needed.'

Rosa Bowler has particularly pleasant memories while growing up of the Post Office at East Ilsley in Berkshire, which she describes as, 'another meeting place for gossip'. She continues, 'The postman was local and delivered the mail, which arrived from Newbury, on his bicycle. I lived opposite the Post Office and played with Jill who

A postman pushing his bicycle up a hill in the village of Parracombe in Devon. The picture was taken in 1954.

lived there. There were wonderful hiding places in the Post Office – huge cupboards under the counters and lots of dark corners. The rooms in the house were large and mostly empty. There were frogs in the cellars!'

Before 1935 the mail was brought from Hungerford to Woodlands St Mary in Berkshire, the home of David Andrews. 'The postman's name was Mr Haines,' he recalls. 'At that time all postmen wore helmets, with a navy blue serge uniform. About 1935 the mail delivery was changed over to Newbury and a van brought the letters and parcels out to Shefford Woodlands Post Office. From there it was delivered by two postmen, Mr J Marshall – who was also the postmaster – and Mr L Rivers.'

The Post Office, at the village of Ombersley in Worcestershire. From a postcard, published by E Baylis & Son.

Both of these men delivered the mail on bicycles, and although the village was remote, with lots of outlying farms and cottages, it had two deliveries each day, including Saturdays. The two postmen alternated their shifts weekly, from morning to afternoon. Their post round covered a distance of 18 miles every day, and before starting deliveries, Mr Rivers had already cycled up from Eastbury, which was quite an ordeal for him explains David Andrews, 'as he had lost an arm during World War I.'

Tom Thomas, known locally at Twm Bach, was the postman serving the Pembrokeshire village of Mathri (also spelt Mathry), which is about two and a half miles from the home of Mr Charles, who lived on a farm between the villages of Porthgain and Llanrhian. Mr Charles has several memories of the man he describes as being, 'small of stature but having a huge character'.

'Twm was a law unto himself. He would judge the importance of the mail to be delivered, and if it was a sales catalogue, or in his view some other unimportant document, he would not bother making the long journey to some remote cottage or farmhouse, especially in bad weather. Instead he would hold on to the letters until the next day, or maybe longer, but would always deliver them in the end.' I wonder what Twm would do with all the junk mail that comes by post today?

Apparently Twm was very fond of his pint and

on one Christmas Day, when the post still had to be delivered, he had accepted rather too many festive drinks during the course of his rounds. This resulted in many late deliveries. By the time he got to the vicarage, the vicar's wife was in the doorway waiting for him. Twm was struggling up the drive, weighed down with a large number of parcels he still had to deliver, when he happened to look up.

'When Twm saw her,' says Mr Charles, 'he stopped in his tracks and cried out, "When will the buggers come to their senses?" obviously referring to the people who had sent the parcels. I can add that this outburst delivered in Welsh was far more effective than any translation I could ever make!'

As well as maintaining links with the wider community, the postman might also provide other neighbourly services. For instance, in the village of Netley Abbey in Hampshire, Lynda Crotty notes that their postman, Dick Rowe, would ask her mother if she needed any shopping when he

Good Tidings from Cambridge

In this Photochrom Co Ltd postcard, a postman delivers a letter from Cambridge to a rural cottage.

Postman Alec Roberts from Stalbridge had a bicycle for his morning delivery round. He is seen outside the Post Office at Stourton Caundle in Dorset.

delivered their first post in the morning, and if she did, he would return with it, when he delivered the second post.

As well as delivering the mail, the Post Office also carried telegrams, which by their very nature were required more urgently than other letters and parcels. There was no point waiting for the postman, and to provide this service, the postmaster might enlist the help of a local lad. One such telegram boy was Frank Stanford, from St Margaret's at Cliffe in Kent. During the 1930s, he recalls how the postmaster, Mr Gould, would call upon him and pay threepence for each delivery. The young boy had to earn his money though, occasionally having to cycle many miles to way out locations.

Donkey mail

Over the years, particularly before the advent of motor transport, postmen employed several methods of delivering the mail, from bicycles to ponies. Perhaps one of the most unusual was the donkey Roy Fisher used to negotiate the famously steep, and painfully cobbled streets of Clovelly in North Devon. Gertie May remembers him using his donkey to take the mail up and down the hill, to where the mail van would be parked ready to collect it. She's not absolutely sure when this was discontinued, but Mr Fisher's donkey was certainly still going strong, carrying the mail, during the 1950s.

The famously steep High Street of Clovelly in North Devon, along which Postman Roy Fisher would take the mail by donkey well into the 1950s. From a postcard, published by F Frith & Co Ltd, Reigate.

The Post Office at Bramley in Hampshire in 1937, known as Benhams Stores. Outside is a postman wearing the typical uniform of the day. From a postcard by the Vandyke Studio, Basingstoke.

Maintaining the roads

It is difficult to imagine that at one time each council employed local people to look after the lanes in their own vicinity, on a permanent basis. At a time when there was still little traffic in evidence, other than by horse and cart, these roadmen, or 'lengthmen' as they were known, were a common sight.

In Dorset, around Stourton Caundle and Stalbridge where Frank Palmer lived, the Rural District Council maintained the road system in the parish until 1924, when responsibility transferred to the Dorset County Council.

'The stone used for road building was excavated from a quarry at Garvey,' wrote Frank Palmer, 'using iron bars and sledgehammers to break out the rock. The quarrymen were paid on piecework rates for every square yard of stone excavated, they were also paid a day work rate for removal of topsoil prior to commencement of quarrying. The stone was loaded by shovel into horse-drawn putts, and hauled to the location where it was required for road building purposes. The stone was then cracked to the required size, and placed in position on the road surface for compaction by means of a steamroller.'

In those days, once the steamroller had finished pressing it, that section of road was finished, and there was no surface dressing in the form of tarmac. This is perhaps the main reason why the roads required constant attention.

Mr Palmer goes on to explain that surface dressing of the roads did not start until the 1930s. He describes the operation as follows, 'Liquid tar was forced through a lance spray by means of a hand pump requiring two men to operate it. The liquid tar was transported in barrels, which were collected by horse and cart from Stalbridge station. During the spraying operations the barrel was hauled by a purpose built horse putt, with a coal fire underneath to heat and emulsify the liquid tar prior to spraying. The putt was constructed with quick release shafts, to enable speedy release of the horses should the tar catch on fire.' After it had been sprayed, the liquid tar was covered with gravel, which came from a quarry at Warmwell. This was done by the men using hand shovels.

The weekly wage for men working on the roads during the 1930s was about one pound and twelve shillings, and there was an additional allowance of a shilling a week, for the provision of a pedal cycle to ride to work.

Tarmac was introduced as a surfacing material to this part of rural Dorset in the late 1940s, and was delivered from quarries on the Mendip Hills. It was dropped off in heaps along the sides of the roads, for spreading by hand shovels, followed by compaction by a steamroller.

As well as gangs of men constantly maintaining the road surface, usually accompanied by their steamroller, there were individual lengthmen with the responsibility of administering to the aesthetics of a particular area. At Woodlands St

A typical road gang, working near Church Knowle in Dorset. Apparently the steamroller ran over the foot of one of these local roadmen, after he was coming out of the public house. Afterwards, the man had a cork foot fitted in its place.

Mary near Newbury in Berkshire, David Andrews remembers the local men who were employed to look after the roads in their neck of the woods, and goes into a little more detail about their duties and the way they operated.

'The sides of the main road were kept tidy by roadmen, they were called lengthmen, and Mr Chuggie Smith was the local one. He kept the drainage ditches clear and all through the summer he cut the grass verges by hand, using a riphook and scythe. He worked from the county boundary at Baydon, and another lengthman, Mr F Annetts from Eastbury, was responsible for the length of Eastbury Lane, Goodings Lane and Poughley Lane, also from the B4000 down to Old Hayward Bottom. They were the last two men that I can remember seeing using a scythe. Although the traffic was sparse the roadmen flew a red flag. It was mounted on a stick, which was pushed into the grass verge as a warning to approaching vehicles, that work was in progress. Farmers were able to drive herds of cattle or a flock of sheep on the roads in complete safety, and we schoolchildren crossed the main road from the school to the meadow opposite for our playground. It would be unthinkable to even try this, with today's traffic. We used to run out to the road to see a car go by, we might not see another until the next day.'

And Marie Litchfield from Ashcott in Somerset also recalls the men who swept the lanes and trimmed the verges for the local council. 'They worked their way round the village at a leisurely pace with a wheelbarrow, spades and brooms, tidying up as they went along. Somehow they managed to appear at the best vantage point when anything was going on in the village – near the church when there was a wedding or funeral, near the pubs when some function was on. They didn't miss much, but it was a poorly paid job and was looked on as being rather a comedown by most people. Yet the lanes were beautifully kept, indeed often far better than they are today.'

Sturminster Newton District Council roadmen who looked after the country roads and lanes in this corner of rural Dorset. The steamroller was used to compact the road surfaces.

Out of control

It caused a great sensation at Church Knowle in Dorset in about 1936 when a steamroller ran down a hill road and broke in half. Mr Cleall was working there at the time, but luckily no one was injured. These men seem to be inspecting the damage.

Medical services

One area of life that has improved for rural people since the early part of the 20th century is the quality and availability of health care. Having said that, many rural communities are still without immediate access to a doctor, nurse, or hospital, and some people have to travel several miles for assistance.

A doctor from the emergency call service treats an infirm patient in 1957. After the introduction of the National Health Service people were less reluctant to call out the doctor.

There would rarely have been a permanent surgery in rural villages, and normally a doctor would visit from elsewhere, maybe once or twice a week. Jim Dunlop who lived in Auchengray in Lanarkshire notes that up until 1948, you had to pay every time you went to see the doctor. Consequently, the only people who did go were those with a serious illness. From 1948, a doctor visited the area twice weekly, and if you wanted him to make a house call, you had to register this at the village Post Office.

In Barlaston in Staffordshire, Ernest Hawkins remembers that there were two visiting doctors, Dr Dawes and Dr Oliver. They held a surgery in a

cottage in the village every Tuesday and Friday from 2pm to 4pm, and although they were only ever there for four hours a week, he recalls that they had their names on a brass plate by the front door. In those days, before National Insurance, which was introduced in 1946, helped towards your health care, people often paid a few pence a week into a variety of schemes run by local doctors, which would normally cover the cost of their requirements.

At Eastrington in the East Riding of Yorkshire, Doreen Wilde has an unpleasant memory of a doctor's house call. When she was three years old, he came and took her tonsils out on the dining room table, which cost her parents three

The next generation

Mothers with babies and small children pictured outside West Ayton village hall in 1944. These children were taken to the hall from the outlying areas, to be weighed at the clinic set up there. The nurses issued them with orange juice, cod liver oil, and tins of dried milk. There was still rationing on, so the oil and orange juice were intended to make up for the lack of vitamins in their diet. Mrs J Peacock's husband Ron is being held by his mother Mary, second from right in the back row. 'I think the photograph must have been for the records of the time,' she suggests, 'for people to see the new generation coming along, after the terrible losses in the war.'

guineas. Before the advent of the National Health, this seems to have been the usual way of dealing with tonsils. Others have also told horrifying tales of similar extractions made at home, and quite often the only aftercare was a bowl of ice cream.

In the 1930s, Marie Litchfield recalls that the village of Ashcott in Somerset was medically well served, with two doctors from Street and Glastonbury each running a surgery in a private house in the village two days a week.

'But doctors had to be paid,' she reaffirms, 'and were only called on in great need. The main source of help, healing and comfort for all and sundry was that unforgettable woman, the District Nurse. She lived right at the centre of the village beside the village green. It was called The Batch, and the huge tree that stood in the middle was reputed to mark the central spot of Somerset. In our early days she rode a bicycle, but quite soon, to everyone's delight and approval, she acquired a little car. Nurse was available whenever she was wanted, day or night, rain or shine. Everyone began to feel better the moment she greeted them with her kindly smile. She was called out to all the births and all the dyings, to helpless old men or to little children with measles. Nothing was too much trouble. In theory, she had a day off each week, when she put on ordinary clothes instead of her familiar navy uniform. Everyone did their best to observe this day, which they felt she should have, yet if there was a sudden emergency no one feared to go along and knock on the door. Hers was truly a vocation. She loved all her patients, rejoiced with them in their return to health, and helped them in their anxieties. She saw the younger members of our family into the world, assisting the doctor from Street, and found time to enter into the play of the older children on her way in or out of the home. Everyone loved Nurse.'

It appears that the District Nurse had a special place in all communities. This was certainly so at the hamlet of Doddycross in Cornwall in the 1950s, where Martin Skin remembers Nurse Cowling, who lived in a house on Minehill in Menheniot. Nurse Cowling worked or cycled around the area, tending to all the medical nursing needs of those in the community. There were also two local GPs working out of a practice in Liskeard. Although they were on call 24 hours a day, seven days a week, people would only bother

A district nurse from the remote Scottish Highlands sitting outside a house with a child. She is wearing the uniform provided in 1955.

'It's a girl!' Postcard published by Bamforth & Co of Holmfirth.

them in dire emergencies. More often not, Nurse Cowling would be approached first.

Martin Skin has good reason to remember Nurse Cowling, as he was the victim of an unusual accident that happened when he was fetching water from the communal hand pump, which in those days provided the only water to the inhabitants of Doddycross.

'To get water,' he explains, 'one would have to release the chain holding the iron handle and then pump. One evening I decided to pump water, but as soon as I started to release the chain, the pump handle flew up and the hook holding the chain went right through my left hand, I still have the scar today. I was rushed to Nurse Cowling, who eventually put my hand into something that looked like a goldfish bowl full of golden sand, it really hurt, but she insisted that despite my having a gaping hole in my hand I would not need hospital attention. Over the next two weeks, and after she had given a couple of inspections to my hand, it regained its full mobility and has never given me any problems.'

As well as doctors and nurses, some communities had a midwife, although in earlier times these were often totally untrained people. Quite often a woman in the village would take on this responsibility, and would be on call if needed. She might have been a farmer's wife, or a shopkeeper, but would have been trusted by all in the local community.

In 1955 in the village of Hernhill in Kent, Allan and Iris George recall that parents still accepted the responsibility of making their own arrangements for the birth of their children. On

Left: Mrs Iris George and her daughter Linda nine weeks after the difficult journey described by her husband Allan.

one memorable occasion Allan's sister Daphne, who lived three miles away in the old market town of Faversham, kindly offered the use of her home for the birth of their second child. At that time, like most people in the village, they didn't own a car, so Allan had noted in the Faversham News that a taxi firm offered an all-night service. An adventure was about to unfold.

'Early on 3 August at 2.30am Iris said that we should now make the journey to sister Daphne's house,' he relates. 'I hurriedly dressed and cycled up to the village green to telephone for the taxi. Although explaining the urgency to the taxi operator he refused to come out to Hernhill. I returned home saying, Sorry, dear no taxi.'

The only four-wheeled transport in their home was their son Clifford's perambulator, so the pram it had to be. Before departing they made sure that Clifford was sound asleep and then set off on their journey to Faversham. 'The night was clear,' he continues, 'with an almost full moon and the first two miles was along typical country lanes with no footpaths. When we reached the Thanet Way, the last mile gave us a footpath although at that time of the morning we did not meet a living soul until we approached the last half-mile. As we passed the Smedley Canning Factory on the outskirts of Faversham, the site

was busy washing down the elevators for the coming day's intake of fresh peas.'

An hour after leaving their home they eventually arrived at his sister's house. She hastily removed her two sons from their bedroom and also called out Nurse Hayes the local midwife to prepare Iris for the birth. In the meantime Allan himself made a speedy journey back to Hernhill on his sister's bicycle, to find that Clifford was thankfully still fast asleep. At about 8.30am a near neighbour called the new father to say that mother and daughter Linda were both doing well.

After the hardships of World War II, the nation's medical health became a political priority and remains so. This led to the creation of the National Health Service, in July 1948. This was set up to provide healthcare for all citizens, based on their medical needs, rather than their ability to pay.

The NHS was funded by the taxpayer and managed by the Department of Health. So from 1948 onwards, the most-up-to-date healthcare, was becoming available to everybody, from those who lived in the cities to the inhabitants of the most remote country villages.

In conclusion, thank goodness for modern doctors, nurses, and the ambulance service!

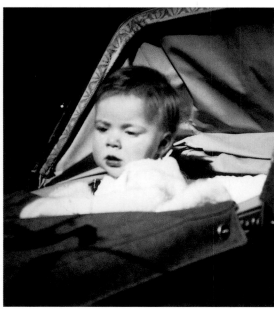

Left: Baby Clifford's perambulator in which his father, Allan George, trundled his wife Iris on the long journey to his sister's house for the birth of their daughter Linda. A friend poses for a picture with the pram.

Below: Baby Linda, pictured in March 1956, unaffected by the unconventional transport used to get her to the midwife.

Burying the dead

Having heard about the facilities for giving birth, this chapter ends with a look at what happened to people in rural villages when they died. Once again there was seldom an official person who took responsibility for the handling of corpses, and the laying out, as it was known, was often done by the same woman who acted as the community midwife.

At Barlaston in Staffordshire, Ernest Hawkins remembers Mrs Clewes, who lived in a cottage in the village, who was always called upon to assist as midwife whenever there was a birth, and she would also be asked to lay out the body, when there was a death. Whether she received any payment for this service, Mr Hawkins doesn't know, and indeed thinks it was highly unlikely that she did, instead receiving gifts in lieu, such as fresh eggs or vegetables.

Like everything else funerals cost money, so in former times very few ordinary people could afford anything elaborate. Undertakers did exist, but mainly to administer to the needs of the gentry or members of the business community.

Ernest Hawkins was born in 1916, and writes that when he was young, 'In the event of death, for most village people the deceased was left in a coffin in the front room or parlour on two chairs. Neighbours and friends were invited to visit and pay their respects; the coffin would remain open until about an hour before the funeral. The bier would be fetched from the cemetery chapel, it was like a stretcher on four wheels and the mourners would follow the cortege on foot to the old church and then to the cemetery chapel. The cemetery bell would toll throughout the journey. Sometimes the funeral service would be held in the cemetery chapel, where there was an altar and pews.'

The old chapel at Barlaston closed down in the early 1930s, and Mr Hawkins remembers attending its final funeral service, when he was in his teens. It was for Mr Fowell, the husband of Mrs Martha Fowell of the telephone exchange in Vicarage Lane, who died young, leaving his widow with two young children.

'Something that may be found eerie and hard to believe,' he says, 'is that the cockerels seemed to crow more than usual when there was a death in the village.'

As there were very few funeral businesses as we know them today, a local wheelwright, carpenter or joiner would normally make coffins for the ordinary folk of the village. As part of his duties, the verger would dig the graves, and there were no wreaths, merely bunches of seasonal flowers picked from the garden.

The names on the headstones in peaceful graveyards around rural churches, such as at Mylor in Kent, record the history of the village. From a postcard, published in the Argall's Series

Mylor Church

In 1912 Bramley in Hampshire had a population of approximately 500. There was also a military garrison and during World War I, German prisoners were taken to the garrison to help build ammunition sheds. Several prisoners died while at Bramley and were buried in the churchyard.

'When children were stillborn,' Ernest Hawkins continues, 'I have known the father make the small coffin himself and carry it to the cemetery under his arm or on his shoulders, with family and friends following.'

If a baby or small child should die before being christened, they would be buried in a remote part of the churchyard, which would quite probably be unconsecrated ground.

The father of Stanley Church from Yardley Gobion in Northamptonshire, was a skilled signwriter, and performed many duties in the village, which included painting the shield-shaped plates that were fastened on to coffins. The Yardley Gobion undertaker was the village carpenter and he would make the coffins in his workshop and fix the plates on after Mr Church had painted them according to the wishes of the family. The carpenter paid him a shilling for each of these plates, 'unofficially of course,' says Mr Church, 'I don't know what the undertaker charged the mourning families.'

Similar to many establishments around the country at that time, the Yardley Gobion chapel had no graveyard, and Congregationalists would not dream of being buried in the parish church graveyard. 'The only way round that little problem,' Stanley Church explains, 'was for the undertaker/carpenter to place the coffin on his little hand-cart and push it to the next village at Potterspury, with the bereaved family walking slowly behind. Bad enough in the summer, of course, but not very pleasant sitting through a long service wet through and then going into the graveyard for another 15 minutes last respects. I don't need to mention the walk back.'

A village funeral

Marie Langford, who grew up in Cattistock in Dorset, remembers another local character no longer found in rural villages today, 'Another aspect in the change of village life is the missing village undertaker. He was the village carpenter and builder and made the coffins in his workshop. When needed, the coffin would be taken by a hand-cart to the home of the deceased, who would be placed in it, and perhaps left on a table in the parlour for neighbours to pay their respects, until being loaded again on the hand-cart and taken to the church, with mourners walking behind – no funeral cars in those days. The blinds in the windows on the way would be drawn until the cortege had passed by, and the church bell would be tolling. If the death had occurred some way out of the village a farm cart would be used to carry the coffin to the church. The sexton would have dug the grave and local men were always used as bearers. After the funeral the mourners would go back to the deceased person's house for what was often a splendid high tea.' No doubt the deceased's past life would be the topic of conversation.

Behind the gates in this old postcard published by The Stores, Ombersley, is the impressive mausoleum, which stands in the grounds of St Andrew's Church, in the village of Ombersley in Worcestershire.

Chapter Seven

Getting around

Village transport can be put into three main categories, personal, public, and working. Personal transport is the means by which people have ferried themselves, over the years, from place to place. It might have been for recreational purposes, to visit family and friends, to go shopping, or to get to work in the morning and was restricted to the better off members of the community. Public transport such as horse-drawn carriages, trams, trains or buses refers to vehicles provided by someone else to take people to their destination for a fee. The reasons for using them may have been the same as above. Finally, working transport includes vehicles operated by those doing their job, such as a milkman or lorry driver.

Horse power

In the early part of the 20th century, very few people needed to leave their village on a regular basis. Most found employment within the community, and the village shop and all the other amenities previously described, meant that they were able to acquire most of the things they needed for their daily lives without travelling too far away.

For ordinary working people, walking was the preferred form of transport, but for the wealthy who could afford to keep them, the horse has been used for centuries either as an individual mode of transport, or to pull various carts. In former times the stagecoach was once a common sight in Britain, but by 1920 it had been replaced by trains and buses. However, during the period covered by this book the horse was still widely used as a personal form of transport and also, as we have already seen, used for pulling the baker's cart, milk float and a variety of agricultural equipment.

In rural locations around the country, it wasn't uncommon for someone owning a pony and trap, to run this as a taxi or bus service. In the village of Fivehead in Somerset, Dot Hunt remembers two spinster ladies, Kate and Alice Talbot, who lived opposite her family farmhouse in a neat, stone, detached cottage. The two sisters ran a laundry service for a big country mansion nearby, but every Saturday morning Alice Talbot augmented

their income by hitching up her strong cob to a wagonette that had seats all round the sides. She then drove any villagers that wanted to do their weekly shopping, the eight miles to the county town of Taunton and back.

'For this service I believe they paid eight pence return,' recalls Mrs Hunt. 'At about five o'clock the returning wagonette would be full of boxes and baskets and the shoppers would be shouting their farewells outside our windows.'

At Cattistock in Dorset in the 1930s, before a railway halt was built at Chilfrome Lane, the nearest railway station was some miles away at Maiden Newton. Marie Langford recalls that before the days of motorcars, if anybody wanted to go to Maiden Newton station, especially if they had luggage, they could hire Mrs Burch's spring wagon to take or fetch them. A magnificent chestnut horse drew the wagon and when it died of old age it was buried in a local field and appropriately a chestnut tree was planted over its grave. The tree, incidentally, although

Coach travel was rather exposed in South Yorkshire around 1910.

Going visiting

Not all traps were intended for public use, many people owned one for their own personal means of getting around, such as the family of Marion Cooke, who lived in Barbrook on the Devon side of Exmoor. Her grandfather's trap was pulled by a pony called Kitty shown here in the photograph on the right. 'My memories go back to a happy childhood,' she writes. 'The earliest I recall was being taken in my grandfather's pony trap. We would go to Lynton station to collect friends and family from the train and on shopping trips with my grandmother.'

But of course, for country people the horse was much more than just a means of transport. They were part of daily life and riding was almost an essential skill. 'I was taught to ride by my father,' recalls Marion Cooke, 'who ran along leading the pony. Eventually he got fed up with so much exertion and arranged for me to go to the riding stables at Lynton. Soon I was able to go on moorland rides, often to Ilkerton Ridge taking various routes back to the stables. Cheriton Ridge was a favourite place where we had a good gallop.

There were many wonderful rides, quite the best way to see the moors. In later years I rode over Brendon Common and the surrounding areas. I do not remember seeing as many Exmoor ponies as we see these days. Certainly my long-lasting love of Exmoor was from those frequent riding trips in all weathers. I never went hunting – even though the hunt met in front of Barbrook Post Office, opposite the end of our garden.'

flourishing well for some years, has sadly died.

Horses have served man faithfully for centuries in many different ways. In today's Britain they are seldom used as working animals, although you might catch a ride in an old-fashioned trap at a country fete or fair. Today they are still enjoyed by country people, but mainly as a form of recreation. There is no doubt that riding around remote places like Exmoor helps us to keep in tune with the countryside and appreciate how people must have travelled in bygone days.

The legacy of a time when the horse was the principle mode of transport can be seen in the network of ancient bridleways across the country. These public rights of way give us access to the countryside, and enable us to enjoy walking, cycling or riding on routes devoid of speeding motor traffic.

Around 1910, horse-drawn carriages were still a familiar sight, as at this wedding in the village of Cottingham in Leicestershire.

Pedal power

Between 1900 and 1960, the bicycle had its heyday, and it seems that in rural villages almost everybody owned one. They were relatively cheap to buy and inexpensive to run. As a mode of transport some people only used their bicycle to get them to work, others such as the village bobby or the postman used them to aid their employment.

One such lad was Ivor John who delivered Post Office telegrams around the Pembrokeshire villages of Porthgain and Llanrhian, an area that included the farm owned by the family of Mr Charles set halfway between the two. Mr Charles recalls that bicycles were the most common form of transport in that corner of south-west Wales in the 1930s, and that nearly everyone possessed one. Like all transport, bicycles were safe in careful hands, but as with motorbikes and sports cars today, put a young lad behind the wheel and you might have trouble.

On the subject of Ivor John he notes, 'He boasted that he could ride a bike faster than anyone in the whole area. He once rode his bike from Llanrhian village straight through Porthgain at terrific speed, but it was too late when he realized that his brakes had failed and he ended up in the harbour. Luck was on his side however – the tide was in and although he could not swim, he was rescued no worse for his ordeal. Although he was not delivering a telegram at the time, the shock must have affected him, because he was seen searching frantically in his soaking wet pockets for one. Obviously afraid of losing his job.'

The bicycle was also used for personal recreation, or in conjunction with other modes of

Blessing the bikes

An annual cyclists service was held at Coxwold church. Mrs J Peacock recalls that Mr Shakleton, who attended these services, would cycle every year from Lancashire to Yorkshire to stay with her husband's parents in Wykeham village. He did this well into his late 80s, and lived well into his 90s. A good advertisement for getting on your bike. The service of blessing is still held in the village today.

transport. In those days people didn't think twice about using several kinds of transport to reach their destination. They might cycle to the train station, catch a train, and then get on a bus at the other end to reach their final goal.

At the Sedge Fen estate in Suffolk, Hilary Price notes that the local railway station was about a mile and a half away from their house at the end of a very straight exposed road. The railway line ran parallel to the road so you were able to see the train coming from some distance. If they wished to travel on the train they would cycle to

Riding in tandem. Ernest Hawkins admits to knowing very little about this reverend gentleman and his lady, other than the fact that they were friends of his mother's, who would visit her in Barlaston around 1910. But this photograph illustrates another example of how people might have pedalled for pleasure – note the guard over the chain to prevent a long skirt catching in it.

a nearby house, where they would leave their bicycles before going on to the platform. She remembers that it was advisable to leave in plenty of time, as being exposed, the road was always windy, which made the journey a real struggle.

David Andrews and his friends at Woodlands St Mary in Berkshire used various means of transport. 'Sometimes we cycled to Newbury on Saturday afternoons, and left our cycles at Stradlings yard,' he recalls, 'which is now part of the Vodaphone complex. Or we might leave them at Peter's Bakery, in Oxford Street. We were charged sixpence for this service.'

If they wanted to go to Newbury by bus, the bus stop was in the next village of Shefford Woodlands, so they had to cycle there to catch the 2.10pm Newbury and District bus. 'This bus company was run by the Durnford family in Newbury,' he notes, 'and the last bus back to Shefford Woodlands left the Wharf at 9.10pm.'

If they had gone to the cinema in Newbury this meant that they would miss the end of the film. So, if it were a good film, they would stay until the end and catch the 10.10pm bus from the Wharf, which only ran as far as Wickham. Of course, this would mean walking back to Shefford Woodlands to pick up their bicycles, before pedalling the final part of the journey back to Woodlands St Mary.

Similarly, Shirley Payne, who lived in the village of Sway on the edge of the New Forest, would go to New Milton on the bus to visit the cinema. Once again the last bus would leave before the end of the evening film. Her answer to this problem was to watch the end of the afternoon matinee first, and then see the start of the evening showing – thus seeing the entire picture, out of sequence.

Top: These two separate groups of cyclists progressing through the village of Hockley Heath in Warwickshire, give a good indication of how important bicycles were on an otherwise deserted road. From a postcard, published by Scott, Russell & Co.

Above: This hand-painted illustration is taken from a personalized card, and clearly shows the dangers one could expect when cycling on a country road. But did the pig or the stick, cause the accident? The card was sent to Ede, who would appear to be unwell at the time. Had she experienced something similar, I wonder?

Of course bicycles have always been a popular way for children to get to school, particularly in the days when the traffic was not as heavy as it is today. In rural Oxfordshire this proved to be a logistical headache, not to mention being the catalyst for several adventures for Dorothy Waters, who lived at Cassington between Oxford and Eynsham.

'In 1943 I went to Witney Grammar School,' she relates. 'Those who went to Gosford Hill school had a school bus from the village, but the few of us who went to Witney had to cycle to Eynsham and there get a bus to Witney. In winter it was dark when we started out in the morning and once, when everyone else had flu, I had to go on my own and was frightened when a ghostly shape appeared beside me. It was a barn owl and it glided alongside me for quite some distance. On that occasion I had the consolation prize, because I eventually went down with flu during the week that the end of term exams were held. On another occasion Monica French and her brother Edward were with us. Edward was quite a lot younger and was on a small bicycle. We looked round to see him some way back, dragging his bicycle out of the ditch.'

Rosa Hibbert being held on a penny farthing by her mother, at the bottom of their garden in East Ilsley in Berkshire in the late 1930s.

Glastonbury were well served, and there were
village stops all the way to the coast. These lines
connected with the Great Western Railway, which
enabled you to travel even farther afield, in what
was unquestionably the greatest and most
comprehensive public transport system this
country has ever seen.

Marie Litchfield who lived in Ashcott at the
time notes, 'My father was able to be in London by
11am, providing that he had made an early start
by cycling to the station. It was a tiny station – just
a single track with its little platform,
stationmaster's house, level-crossing gates and
signal box. We thought it very exciting, although

it was rare indeed that we used it.'

The level crossing is a feature that many are
still familiar with, but obviously when there were
more railway lines, there were more crossings. In
the early days, level-crossing gates were operated
by hand. If the crossing was situated some
distance from towns or villages, they required
someone to look after them and sometimes a
gatekeeper's cottage would be specially built for
this purpose. Mr V J Catt from Etchingham in
East Sussex remembers that on the way to school,
as steam trains passed through the village, the
children would have to wait at the line gates while
one of the old couple who lived in the little

THE MANX ELECTRIC RAILWAY. GROUDLE STATION.

In some rural locations, railways were used for pleasure purposes, as well as for transport. In this old postcard of the Manx Electric Railway, at Groudle station near the village of Onchan on the Isle of Man, as one group of tourists leave, another group waits in the carriages for their train ride to begin.

gatekeeper's cottage by the road, would pull the gates open or shut.

'The signal box,' he says, 'had no large wheel to open the gates at that time. Later the old couple passed on, so a wheel was installed in the signal box, and the little cottage demolished. I remember standing by the gates with my friends as the trains pulled into the station. Mostly the engines would be by the gates, and we would be enveloped in warm steam accompanied by an ear-piercing screech as surplus steam was released from the bottom of the engine.'

For several years Mr Catt did wiring and lighting for large pantomimes held at nearby Robertsbridge, and he recalls that in the late 1940s the railway ticket cost one shilling and ten pence for the distance of two and a half miles.

During the war years the railways were used as a vital line of communication and for transporting munitions and goods in aid of the war effort. Inevitably, therefore, the enemy sometimes targeted them. Jim Dunlop lived at Auchengray in Lanarkshire, 25 miles west of Edinburgh and 40 miles east of Glasgow. Even though in 1939 the village only consisted of 18 houses, and a few outlying farms, it still had its own train station, and was once the target of a German attack, as Mr Dunlop describes.

'Being far from industrial sites, personal safety was not a major concern during the war. Nevertheless a bomb was dropped within a mile of the village. It was believed that the Germans' target was Carstairs rail junction, which was a main artery for transporting steel and munitions

to the south. However the rail line between Carstairs and Edinburgh runs within 800 yards of the village and it is thought that the pilot had seen a train and believed he had reached his target.'

The year 1968 may well have seen the end of Britain's steam trains, but in truth closures had begun long before that date, as Marion Cooke, who lived at Barbrook on Exmoor, describes. 'In 1935 the Lynton to Barnstaple Railway was closed. On the day the last train went out, all the Barbrook schoolchildren waved farewell from outside the school as the train pulled its way through the woods on the hillside opposite. A very sad day! After the track was demolished, we would walk the line and pick wild strawberries.'

A train passing through Kerne Bridge, near Ross-on-Wye, Herefordshire. As the rails have already been removed from one side of the track, the photograph must have been taken during the demolition of this part of the line, probably in the early 1960s.

The bus service

The bus service has always been a vital lifeline for rural communities both to get to work or school on time and in the context of going shopping. Most villages had a general store and Post Office, which could supply the basic needs. But for more choice a trip into town by bus was possible, even if sometimes logistically difficult.

Carys Briddon lived in the little village of Bontgoch (or Elerch as it is called on the map) in Ceredigion. 'When I was a child,' she says, 'it was small and rather remote, with no regular bus service – only one bus at 10am every Monday morning to take passengers to the nearest town of Aberystwyth, seven miles away, and returning at 6pm that evening.'

Irene Foster remembers the bus service to Bishopstone in Buckinghamshire in the late 1920s and early 1930s, which also illustrates this point. 'There was one small general store situated in what had been the front room of a cottage. Here basic goods were sold, but for a family shop we went to Aylesbury. There was a bus service on Wednesdays and Saturdays – market days – these buses ran twice into town and twice back. If you missed the bus to come home, you could catch the bus going to Oxford but this meant a long walk from the main road to home, a distance of about two miles, laden with shopping and my younger sister in a pushchair. But we children loved going to the market as we were allowed to have an ice cream from Mr Plested who made his own. There was a choice of colours, white, pink

and green. I think these cost one or maybe two pence each.'

Jack Gee has already described his school trip to the seaside and in many places around the country, the village outing became an annual occurrence, especially for children. It might have involved several forms of transport, particularly buses and trains, yet in Stourton Caundle in rural

The people of East Ilsley in Berkshire go on an outing to the seaside, around 1920.

A typical rural bus service from the 1950s.

Dorset, Frank Palmer recalls outings that began aboard a horse-drawn cart, and then during the 1920s, the coming of the famous charabanc.

'During the early years of the last century,' he writes, 'the annual day's outing to the seaside was the highlight of the year for village children. The parents and their children would assemble in the roadway at the Pound, which was situated opposite the school entrance. They would then climb excitedly aboard the horse-drawn farm wagons, and make themselves comfortable on bundles of clean straw for the journey to Stalbridge station to await the arrival of the steam train to take them on their journey to the seaside.' During the 1920s the mode of transport used for these outings changed, as a fleet of charabancs were hired from a Mr Seager of Sherborne.

He also points out that for both the men and women of the village, these annual outings to the seaside were a temporary release from the harshness of their everyday working lives. It's difficult for us today to appreciate the importance they had on the morale of the community. Children looked forward to them so much, they found it difficult to concentrate on schoolwork during the preceding weeks.

'The outings restarted again post-war,' Frank Palmer concluded, 'with a fleet of Bere Regis coaches transporting families to the seaside

A charabanc outing

There was an annual outing to the seaside for the parents and children of Stourton Caundle in Dorset. Frank Palmer remembers how, 'The children would take a few coppers to school during the course of the year, for the headmistress to hold in safe keeping for them as spending money for the annual outing. The children would also help to raise money for their fares by taking part in a Christmas concert held in the hut. The young men of the village would also contribute to the collection from their Good Friday football match.' Their yearly destination was Weymouth, and the route would always take the charabancs slowly down the Piddle valley. Packed lunches would be taken, and the only treats the children could expect were an ice cream and a ride on a donkey. For afternoon tea, the entire party would meet up at a chosen restaurant. Children might return home with a bucketful of sand, with their mothers clutching a handful of seaweed, which they apparently used in place of a barometer. There was light hearted banter, 'especially when passing the Cerne Giant,' noted Frank Palmer. Anyone who is aware of this particular Dorset landmark, carved out of the chalky hillside, will know what he means!

destinations of either Weymouth or Swanage. By the late 1950s increasing car ownership, and the introduction of a statutory paid week's holiday for farm workers, sadly meant that there was no longer sufficient support for the annual outing.'

Unlike today, where one person does it all, the early buses had both a driver and a conductor who took your money in exchange for a ticket. These men are fondly remembered for being friendly and helpful; they would help children

Motor transport flourishes

The variety of public motor transport included charabancs and buses, but inevitably, as the wealth and living standards of people improved in rural areas, personal motorized transport became everybody's preference. The nation's subsequent obsession with the motorcar ultimately brought about the end for many rural train and bus services.

In the beginning, of course, motor transport in its many forms could only be afforded by the gentry and wealthy businessmen. But by the 1920s, more and more people were acquiring some form of personal transport, especially those who needed it for their work.

Bill McKay's father was the blacksmith in the village of Migvie in Aberdeenshire and as such, he also worked in several other nearby smiddys. To do this he required transport, and although in earlier times a horse and carriage of some sort might have sufficed, by the 1920s he was the owner of both a motorcar and a motorbike.

'Father had a motorbike and sidecar,' he explains, 'and a bull-nosed Morris Cowley. It was very necessary for him to have transport as he still worked the smiddys at Corgaff and Strathdon. Mother had her own motorbike and a 16 hands high shalt (horse) and trap. We children had a Shetland pony and small float. Later we all cycled. Father's car was like a charabanc. Other local young buddies crowded in with us for an outing, as the youngsters of that day, say and remind me, had it not been for my father and his Morris Cowley, they would never have been from home, it was fun for all of us.'

As in the case of Mr McKay, those who were lucky enough to own their own transport were quite often happy to offer it for the benefit of others in the village. Elizabeth Stodart from

This Raphael Tuck & Sons postcard gives an idea of the smoke, noise, and disruption that early motorcars brought to rural locations. The old man is saying, 'I'm certainly not so deaf as people make out. I hear a little bee humming quite plainly!'

Skirling in the Borders Region recalls that in the 1940s, a haulage business was begun in the village, with one lorry taking milk churns to a milk processing plant in Edinburgh. The churns were collected from the road ends of local farms and on the return journey the lorry would bring back and deliver parcels, and anything else destined for people living in the area. In snowy winters, of which there were many in the Borders

Workmen waiting for transport in Avoch, Scotland, in the early 1950s. Donald Patience, seen in the long coat in the centre of the photo making a snowball, notes that this was probably held up by the snow.

in those days, she notes that this lorry often made the journey when buses could not, carrying as many passengers as possible. 'Village people tend to be resourceful and determined,' she points out.

Mr L A Reed came to the village of Swinefleet in the East Riding of Yorkshire in 1936. He started a haulage business, L A Reed & Son, with one lorry, which was a five-ton Bedford. The business he started is still going strong and he now has 18 heavy-goods vehicles, and 54 trailers. 'I used to carry farm produce, mainly sugar beet, grain and oilseed rape. Now it is mainly steel coils and flat plates.' His son, who he took into partnership in 1957, now mainly runs the business and over the years it has provided a lot of jobs for the community, including drivers, mechanics and office staff.

Lorries were also a feature in the daily lives of children in the Pembrokeshire villages of Porthgain and Llanrhian, but for more dangerous reasons. Mr Charles who lived in the area recalls that lorries were constantly transporting stones from Porthgain and on the return journey they were forced to slow down when passing through the crossroads at Llanrhian. Schoolboys would jump on to the tailboards of the lorries and hang on until they reached Porthgain. It certainly saved having to walk home from school, he admits, although I am sure today's parents would have a fit. 'Strangely,' he says in defence of the practice, 'there was never a single accident.'

Gradually taxis became more available as a way of moving around. At Chipstable in West

Moving sheep from a farm in Buckinghamshire in August 1938. By this time lorries were widely used both on farms and by hauliers.

Somerset, Frank Hind remembers that the husband of the village storekeeper ran a taxi business. This was quite necessary as the bus only came up to the village once a week. He had two vehicles; one was an ex-US army 4-wheel drive scout car, which Frank says was useful in the winter snows to get to the railway station at Venn Cross on the old Taunton-Barnstaple line. The other vehicle was a smart Chevrolet sedan.

There had always been blacksmiths and wheelwrights in villages to look after the needs of people with horse-drawn transport, but the age of

FOREST ROAD, CUDDINGTON.

It's the 1930s, and the cars parked at the side of Forest Road in the Cheshire village of Cuddington, illustrated in this postcard, begin to show how the look of village streets were about to change for ever.

the motorcar saw the advent of a new type of business – the garage. Margaret Kirby's family in Burniston in North Yorkshire began a garage and caravan business before World War II, during which her father had been a civilian aero-mechanic at RAF Silloth. In 1945 he returned to the business, which was also a filling station.

'The garage had been built in 1933,' she explains, 'when a whole tanker load of petrol could be bought for £200. Originally it had five hand-operated Wayne petrol pumps. One was kept for decorative purposes and the last two operational pumps were removed in 1947 to make way for electric pumps.

In 1974 a 50p coin operated pump was installed which meant petrol was available on a self service basis 24 hours a day. I can only recall it being broken into on one occasion. The shop also sold sweets and cigarettes as well as the usual garage accessories. With a small caravan field at the rear of the garage, we also kept a few groceries. Retired men from the village would often linger here, after buying their tobacco, for a chat. When my own children were young, these chaps would like a game of dominoes in the winter, and thus taught my two girls to play and count before they reached school age!'

Margaret claims that her father and his Burniston garage, have left the world with a special legacy. as she goes on to explain. 'An up and coming young comedian used to come to the garage and was tickled to see Dad swivel his peaked cap to one side before sliding on a wheeled board under a car to repair it. He was

Norman Wisdom, and he would peer down through the engine at Dad. From this he adopted wearing his own cap at the same angle. Right up to the death of my father in 1979 Norman would call in at the garage to see Dad if he was appearing in the Scarborough area.'

Duncan Lucas, who grew up in Wigston Magna recalls the time when many village people preferred the use of motorbikes and sidecars. 'Chipper Vann used a motorbike for his rabbit and game shop, as did Mr Bradshaw of the hardware shop. My own combination was known in the village for the collie I owned who would stand in my sidecar. My first motorbike was a 1927 AJS and when the cylinder head gasket kept blowing, I got fed up and ran it without one. It was rather noisy

Above: By the time this postcard was sent, motor cars had evidently become so common in the village of Hornby in Lancashire, that only the dog in the foreground gives this one a second glance.

Below: Model T Fords, owned by Thomas Bar, lined up for a day trip to Cleethorpes for the people of Swinefleet in Yorkshire in the late 1920s or early 1930s.

Patrol on duty

The AA (Automobile Association) box at the crossroads near Gaydon in Warwickshire can just be seen at the left of this photograph. Judith Nedderman says that an AA man would often be on duty here, just as he is in the photograph. Today, just one box remains in a rural setting at Eardsland in Herefordshire. Enthusiasts have renovated it using tins of the original black and yellow paint.

but still remarkably efficient. I would come down the street, the dog barking, and the motorbike pop, popping, and they said they always knew when Duncan was coming!'

In Britain today, the car is an essential part of our lives. But if we stand in the centre of a village and count the vehicles that pass, their numbers are the measure of one of the profoundest changes that have taken place in village life. If we try and remember what it was like on that same spot when we were children, we would be surprised – even disturbed – by the difference.

Margaret Wilce's father Charlie in football kit, and Uncle Fred on bike, with their friend Ivo Evans. The motorbike belonged to Charlie, and Fred was merely posing for the photograph. Both worked for the village builder, and Charlie married the boss's daughter. Similar to village lads today, football and bikes were popular interests.

Frank Hind, who grew up at Chipstable in the Brendon Hills of West Somerset, shows off his very first car, a 1938 Ford 8. Just the thing for all country lads of the day! He bought the car in about 1959 from Silver Street Motors in Taunton, just after passing his driving test, for which he had only taken four lessons.

Chapter Eight

Village institutions

Other than the houses and farms in which people lived, and the shops and businesses which provided for their needs, most villages also had a number of other establishments that catered for the educational, spiritual, and social requirements of the community. These buildings included the village school, the church or chapel, the village hall and the local public house. In some villages, all of these have now disappeared.

In today's changing world village children often travel to town to attend school. Churches have closed, village halls have become neglected and pubs find it hard to compete with smarter venues in town.

The village school

Most villages, except for tiny hamlets, had their own elementary school where children began to feel part of their community and started to be aware of the wider world and the opportunities that were available to them in life. As their name implies, these elementary schools taught the basic three Rs, of reading, writing and arithmetic.

Class 1 at Varteg Infants School in 1933. The picture shows the type of desk used in rural schools at the time. After leaving school at 14, most of the boys in this class would have worked as miners in the local coal mine.

At Yardley Gobion in Northamptonshire, Stanley Church notes that the infants were in one class from ages 4-8; junior or middle from 8-12; and senior from 12-14. Most children left school at 14 in those days.

Over the years there have been many changes in the educational system in Britain, but at one time it was the 11+ examination that everybody had to take. This however caused problems. Those that passed the exam were rewarded with a certificate. 'That's where the reality began to show through,' says Mr Church. 'If you passed the 11+ you were entitled to move on to a grammar school. The snag was, only one or two from our school were fortunate enough to have parents who could afford to buy the required uniform and sports gear and the result was that pupils like myself, although achieving pass rates had to leave the village school at 14 and go out to work, mainly to help our parents afford the bare minimum standards of life.'

At Skirling in the Borders, things were even more basic. Here the school had only one classroom and only one teacher for all seven classes. The children were aged from 5 to 12 and the maximum school roll was only 25. Elizabeth Stodart explains that even this number was constantly changing, as families came and went from farm cottages.

In the 1920s, Kathleen White attended a strict village school at Bratton in Wiltshire, where she still lives today. The school was called 'The British

Children enjoy country dancing at Barbrook School on Empire Day, 1938. The school, which is on the Devon side of Exmoor, has commanding views of the surrounding countryside.

The school stove

Junior and senior classes at The British School in Bratton in Wiltshire. Kathleen White is seated on the form to the left of the two teachers. Kathleen recalls that, 'Heating in the winter months was by Tortoise stove which the teacher had to feed every few hours with coke. When the wind was in a certain direction the smoke and fumes came belching out across the classroom making eyes water, and breathing difficult. It was very useful though, as a drying area when children (some of whom had walked four or five miles to school) arrived wet through and cold. The room was then very steamy and there was a strong smell of drying wet clothes and shoes. There was always a supply of clean clothes in the cupboard in case of accidents or bad weather.'

School' and twice a week drill sessions were held after prayers, when arm flinging, toe touching, stretching up, and running on the spot took place.

The school was lit by gas and the toilet was in a shed, a short walk across a rough patch of grass. There was no running water, and drinking water was taken from a bucket in the cloakroom, where an enamel mug hung on a hook for this purpose.

'School started at a much younger age than it does today,' Kathleen continues. 'I was three years old, and a few children were even younger.' The school day went from 9am-4pm. There were no breaks during the morning and afternoon sessions, but there was a midday break from 12.30pm-1pm.

Discipline was very strict at The British School, and punishments included caning, which was administered for misdemeanors such as disobedience, lying, cheating and bullying. Children arriving late would be given lines to write out, usually after school. For copying, talking, being cheeky, fidgeting, or having inkblots on written work, you were made to stand in a corner for ten minutes with your hands on your head. For extremely bad behaviour, children were made to wash out the inkwells on a Friday afternoon with cold water that was fetched in a bucket from a spring across the road. Kathleen White describes this as being 'extremely messy',

as powdered ink was used which tended to go lumpy in the inkwells.

If children played truant from school at Woodlands St Mary in Berkshire, the school attendance officer would be sent to their homes to sound them out. David Andrews explains that he always cycled to the village school on Monday mornings from Hungerford. He would check the school register and if any pupils had been absent

The junior class at The British School at Bratton in Wiltshire, in 1926. Kathleen White is seen to the right of the teacher in the back row.

with no written explanation from their parents, he would visit their homes to find out if there was a genuine reason. As the school catchment covered a large area, he cycled many miles over the years doing his job.

In severe winters whole schools would be sent home. Such was the case throughout the United Kingdom during the famously bad winter of 1947. Valerie Blackburn was at school at Wrenbury in Cheshire and recalls being sent home for several happy weeks because of frozen or burst pipes. The snowplough took days to cut its way through and for at least six weeks the snow lay higher than the hedges. During this time she remembers skating on the river, where the ice was eighteen inches thick, and being pulled along the canal while sitting on a sack.

For village schoolchildren in the UK, one of the most unusual times was during World War II. This was particularly true in the eastern counties, which being closer to London were in the front line during the Battle of Britain and were later the home of numerous American air force bases.

At Eight Ash Green in Essex, Geoffrey Charge remembers two big air-raid shelters being built in the playground in the spring of 1940. They had a full-size entrance door set in an L-shape and an emergency exit via a small concrete tunnel at the far end. 'I never felt safe in there,' he says, 'all I could think of was the reinforced concrete roof coming down on top of us if we got hit by a bomb. We had to practise going out of the classroom into the shelter, and one day the air-

raid siren went off, and we went into shelter for real this time. We heard German bombers overhead on their way to Colchester to bomb the factories and the riverside docks. There was a lot of anti-aircraft fire but no aircraft got shot down.'

Air-raid shelters were only one of several affects that the war had on schoolchildren. Others included gas masks, rationing, and for children in rural areas the appearance of evacuees from towns and cities.

In the main, people seem to have happy memories of village schools in a bygone age, and

Children of Bow Brickhill admiring the school's sports shield.

Some of the junior class making puppets at Bow Brickhill County Primary School in Buckinghamshire. Sheila Fullman, whose sister Muriel is second from the right, notes, 'I believe the puppets were made out of clay, dressed, and then used to perform a play in the puppet theatre – probably for a parents evening.'

Peggy Shepherd, who lived at Corston near Bath couldn't wait to start. Her father died soon after she was born, so her mother had to find work. She got a job as a housekeeper and had to live-in. Peggy was sent to live with her grandparents in their two-bedroom cottage, and her sister was taken to live with an aunt. She was three at the time, and as she had no picture books to look at, one day she went upstairs, sat in the window seat and then decided it was time to go to school like the other children.

'I opened the window and jumped out,' she recalls, 'still with little red slippers on. Fortunately in those days there were very few cars about, so I crossed what is now a very busy road and made my way to school. I tapped for some time on the front door. Then Mrs Okey the headmistress came to the door, she did look surprised. I said I wanted to come in. "I am sorry, you are much too young but stay there, and sit on the mat," she replied. This I did and she came back with a board and a couple of lumps of clay. I played there until lunch time when someone took me home.'

Her anticipation was rewarded by the fact that when she did eventually go to school, she loved it. As well as running the village school, her headmistress coached a team of country dancers and Peggy joined them. 'We won every cup and shield in 1936,' she proudly claims, 'and represented our country at the Royal Albert Hall. Some poor families couldn't afford new daps for their child, so the headmistress would buy them herself, so that we all looked smartly turned out. The discipline did us good, and we loved her!' Quite a suitable epitaph to end on, for those much lamented days when almost every village had its own school. Today, many from rural villages now have to travel to their nearest town.

School milk

Another thing that everybody remembers about yesterday's school days was the daily bottle of milk. At Cassington in Oxfordshire, Dorothy Waters remembers having to take two and a half pence to school on Monday mornings to pay for her mid-morning milk, which was brought to the school by Mr Perrin in one-third of a pint bottles. The milk was drunk through a straw, and in those days the bottles had cardboard tops, which Dorothy recalls taking home to use for making balls to hang on babies' prams, or for kittens to play with. Later, when foil tops came in the tops were strung across gardens to scare birds. The picture below, taken in 1931, shows rows of well-behaved and orderly children seated in rows, drinking their free school milk during their morning break.

Church and chapel

The village church or chapel provided a gathering place for people to meet and interact. As well as offering facilities for worship, it was the location for events such as weddings, christenings, or funeral services. Even the smallest village might have had several churches or chapels – Catholic, Baptist, Methodist, Pentecostal – as well as the Church of England parish church.

The church and chapels are rich sources of village history, and the graves, monuments, plaques, windows and documents provide a record of the people who lived and worked there.

Like many other villages, Barlaston in Staffordshire lost its 15th century church many years ago and Ernest Hawkins considers that the decline of the church is one of the saddest aspects of present day life. 'Many things are blamed for the decline in church attendance,' he states, 'chief of which appears to be television and the motorcar. At a local level the loss of our old church in its idyllic setting was a deciding factor for many of my age in abandoning a way of life to which we had become accustomed over decades. We had contributed so much both physically and financially over the years. We were told that the church was unsafe, but never remember being consulted for our views. It was a sore point, which still rankles to this day. We could not understand why the hall, next door to the church could be saved by underpinning, but not the church.'

Having its own church usually meant that the village also had a vicarage, and of course the vicar's responsibility to his parishioners went far beyond Sunday services. So perhaps the best person to ask about the church's role in village life would be somebody who lived in a rural vicarage at the time.

Judith Nedderman's father, Thomas Edward Mayo, was vicar of Gaydon in Warwickshire, and he moved into the vicarage with his wife, Monica Mary Boultbee, their daughter and maid Kathleen in the 1920s. Judith was only four when they settled in, but she vividly recalls how important a role the vicar and indeed his wife had in village life. 'My mother was always a great organizer,' she said, 'and had everything in order in no time and we were ready for the callers.' In those days the vicar's wife was the chief organizer of almost everything in the village.

The usual procedure she explains would be for neighbouring clergy and the elite of village society to leave their visiting cards. But her father considered it just as important to visit everyone in the village, regardless of social position or what religion they might be. He kept a record of these visits and updated the details each time he went.

He had two churches to man, those at Gaydon and nearby Chadshunt, and Judith remembers Sundays and festivals being anything but days of

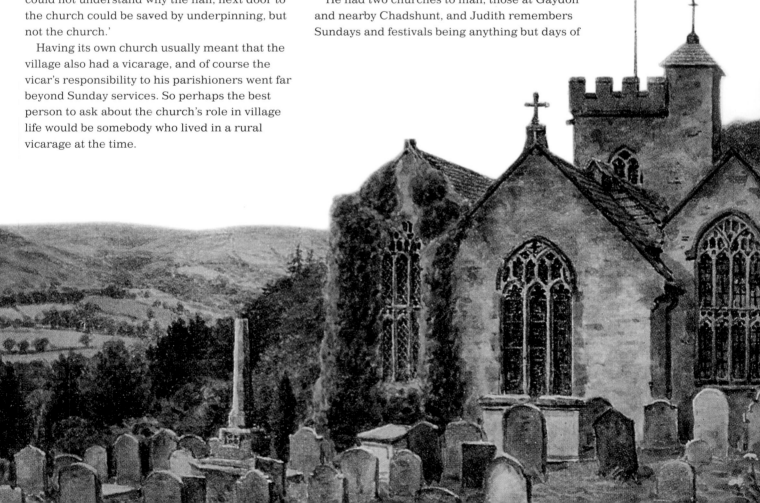

The beautiful church at Selworthy must surely boast one of the finest views in England, as it looks out across Exmoor in Somerset. From a postcard published by J. Salmon.

rest for the family and recalls their busy routine.

'Since my mother was the only one who drove the car, the two of them had to set out for Chadshunt soon after 6am to light the paraffin stoves and candles, and ring the bell for the 7am service.' The chalice and other items used for the service were kept at Chadshunt Hall, and they had to be collected, if someone did not bring them over. After the service the process was reversed as her parents quickly drove back to Gaydon for the 8am service. It was then home to the vicarage for breakfast, but they were back at Gaydon for 11am, with an occasional 10am service at Chadshunt. After lunch there was a children's service at 2.30pm, for which her mother played the harmonium, and finally evensong at 6.30pm.

Diana Phillips, who lived in Winterbourne Abbas in Dorset remembers when their new vicar, Dr Don, arrived among them. He was full of energy and life and in no time at all had set up a youth club, but in order to join you would also have to join the church choir and attend church services regularly.

Dr Don was slightly unconventional, and several years before he had been appointed padre to the circus world, and he maintained his interest in all things theatrical. Diana recalls that every time Billy Smart's, or any other circus was in the area, Dr Don would arrange for a

Barlaston Church.

coachload of villagers to journey to the show, getting the best seats in the house and being treated like royalty.

'If a new baby had been born in the last year,' she recalls, 'a portable font was set up in the ring, and a christening service conducted, with the stars in their best costumes; clowns, trapeze artists, lion tamers, and ringmaster all gathered around the baby. After the performance, we would troop backstage to see the animals, and were invited inside the gaily-decorated caravans to meet the families of the stars.'

As Dr Don was familiar with many show-business personalities, when there was a show on at the Alexander Gardens Theatre in Weymouth, he would invite people to stay at the vicarage for a restful weekend. While at the village, they attended church and join the kids at youth club.

Diana particularly remembers when Charlie Drake came to the vicarage and was talked into conducting the village flitch trial to find the couple that had lasted a year and a day without a cross word. Several couples took part, amid much fun and laughter, and eventually an elderly couple Mr and Mrs Chipp, were chosen. 'I shall always have a high regard for Charlie Drake,' admits Diana, 'as Mrs Chipp had an awful affliction. Her face and body were covered in

A view of St Swithun's church in Woodbury, Devon, where there is a chapel dedicated to the family of Sir Francis Drake who frequented the parish. From a postcard, published by F Frith & Co.

Travelling preachers

The Bucks Gospel Car visiting Oving, Buckinghamshire, on 18 August 1914, bringing their message to a rural community. Bernard Foster notes that the man in the back row third from left is Mr Horace Elmer, an Oving farmer. The lady beside him in the big white hat is his wife. The girl right in the centre is Mr Foster's Aunt Daisy, then aged 12.

The old Rectory shown in this postcard published by Valentine's, is one of a small group of beautiful buildings which made up the village of Gawsworth, including the church of St James and Gawsworth Hall. The village, near Macclesfield is said to be one of the true gems of Cheshire.

large wart-like lumps, but Charlie gave her a big hug and kiss, to the great delight of everyone present, and the lady glowed with pleasure.'

Diana also recalls how Dr Don became the victim of a local custom. 'If anyone fell into the village stream, they would automatically become mayor of the village, until the next unlucky person got a soaking. One winter night, as the youth club toured singing carols, Dr Don stepped back and fell into the cold water with a splash, much to the amusement of us youngsters. The regulars of the local pub invited the vicar to join them for the mayor-making ceremony and the Reverend agreed, on condition that the drinkers joined him first at evensong. We all enjoyed the sight of hardened non-church goers filing from the pub to the church and back to the pub. For many it was their one and only view of the inside of the holy building, between their christening and funeral.'

After his wife Mabel died, Dr Don moved to another parish. 'Some years later,' Diana explains, 'we were without a vicar, so he was invited back to perform my wedding service. Not long after, he passed away, and I am sure he is up in heaven, organizing the angels into giving concerts for the new arrivals and getting up outings for the cherubs to enjoy a show at the circus in the sky.'

One thing associated with church is the sound of bells and in the Borders region at the village of Skirling, Elizabeth Stodart recalls that her father, an elder for nearly 50 years, rang the bell every Sunday before the service. She also remembers a blind organist who came from Peebles each week on the red SMT (Scottish Motor Traction) bus. She brought her black Labrador guidedog called Jill, who would lie peacefully by the organ throughout the service, only occasionally having a good scratch.

On the subject of music, Denys Damen recalls being a reluctant member of the church choir at St Simon and St Jude in Milton-on-Stour in Dorset. Choir practice was held on a Thursday evening at the church, and Denys and his brother would try to avoid it. However the choirmaster who was also the curate, the Reverend Walker, would hunt around the village on a Thursday evening in his three-wheeled Morgan car attempting to force people to attend the choir practices. 'We could hear his old Morgan car coming,' says Denys, 'and would hop over a gate or hedge into a field to avoid him. I remember on one occasion the Reverend Walker complained to my father about our conduct, only to be told by my father that he should attempt to encourage the boys in a more humane manner.'

Blessing the horses

A local tradition at the village of Scalby in North Yorkshire, recalled by Margaret Kirby, was the annual horseman's service conducted by Reverend Christopher Tubbs. An altar would be erected by the stream, with a small tent over it, and the horses and riders would line up on the other side. After the short service all the horses would cross the bridge and go up to the vicar to receive a handful of oats, before fording the stream back to their own side. At the time this was one of only three such horseman's services in England.

The bell-ringers outing in about 1950. Members came from Amberley, Chiltington, and Thakeham, in Sussex, and would ring bells in several villages, usually on Bank Holidays.

At the village of Bilton in Yorkshire, the aptly named Don Bilton recalls that the local vicar was the prime motivator in most village activities. 'Reverend J D Tytler was a large florid man, much loved by all,' he says. 'He managed to recruit a sufficiently large gang of young school lads into a choir. Under his eye this unwilling bunch were transformed into a group of singing angels – complete with soloists and all the descants and harmonies of professionals. I was also trained to be a server at the Communion services. This proved to be no sinecure, as it meant attendance at the 8am service. It took some effort to get out of a warm bed on those cold, dark, winter mornings. Another of my church duties involved me in periods of prolonged physical effort: I had to pump the old manual organ, while the Vicar pounded out the hymns and the psalms with great gusto, singing at maximum decibels. To carry out my part in this performance I was hidden from view at the back of the instrument, and pumped a large handle up and down. If I didn't keep on pumping at a fast rate, the music wound down to a stony silence. I found this out one night at evensong. The Vicar was not amused.'

Of course the church or chapel was involved with special occasions throughout the year, which brought the community together. Sheila Andrew from Chartridge attended the local Baptist chapel and was particularly fond of Harvest Festival, when she would help to decorate the chapel on the Saturday afternoon, and display all the vegetables. 'The smell of all that lovely fruit and veg,' she recalls, 'will remain with me forever. It was so fresh when you went in on the

The Methodist chapel at Oving in Buckinghamshire during Edwardian times. The chapel was built in 1869, and it is still open and functioning to this day unlike many similar chapels that have since closed.

The Bishop of Peterborough attends confirmation day at the village of Cottingham, Leicestershire in 1939.

Sunday, you just had to stand and sniff the air.'

At Christmas there would be a party, and in the school summer holidays the chapel would arrange an outing to a farm, where there would be races in the fields, tea in the barn, and the enjoyment of seeing and playing with all the farm animals.

In bygone days a place of worship was very important to villages, and that's why, even in quite small settlements you often saw several chapels and a church. Ken Sleight, who came from Melbourne in Yorkshire, recalls that his village – as far as he is aware – never had a proper stone or brick built church. 'It did have a corrugated zinc one,' he explains, 'built in the mid 19th century.' The village also had Methodist and Wesleyan chapels and there was a reading room, with a full-size billiard table, situated next to the Wesleyan chapel. 'Could it be that the chapelgoers wished to offer somewhere for the men of the village other than the public houses?' suggests Ken Sleight.

Over the years there have been many amusing anecdotes told about village clergy and their drinking habits. Whether or not this reputation is deserved, this section ends with a memory from John Wood who lived at Shipton-under-Wychwood in Oxfordshire. In 1958 the then vicar, Reverend Cundell, had the habit of always ending the Sunday morning service in time to walk across the village green to arrive at the Shaven Crown pub exactly at opening time. 'On one occasion,' recalls Mr Wood, 'his sermon went on a bit longer than usual and several of us exchanged glances expressing the feeling that he had blown it this time. Then he finished his sermon and announced "and now we'll sing the final hymn – just the last verse". We made it to the pub dead on time.'

The spire or tower of the church is often the first thing you see when approaching a quiet country village. Towering over fields and hedges, it gives an immediate indication of the important part religion always played in village life.

Rebuilding the church tower in Cattistock, Dorset in 1875. Marie Langford who still lives in the village today, says of the photo, 'It shows my great uncle on the parapet leaning on his elbow, and my uncle with his hat on a stick – he was later headmaster of the College Choir School, Winchester for 45 years.'

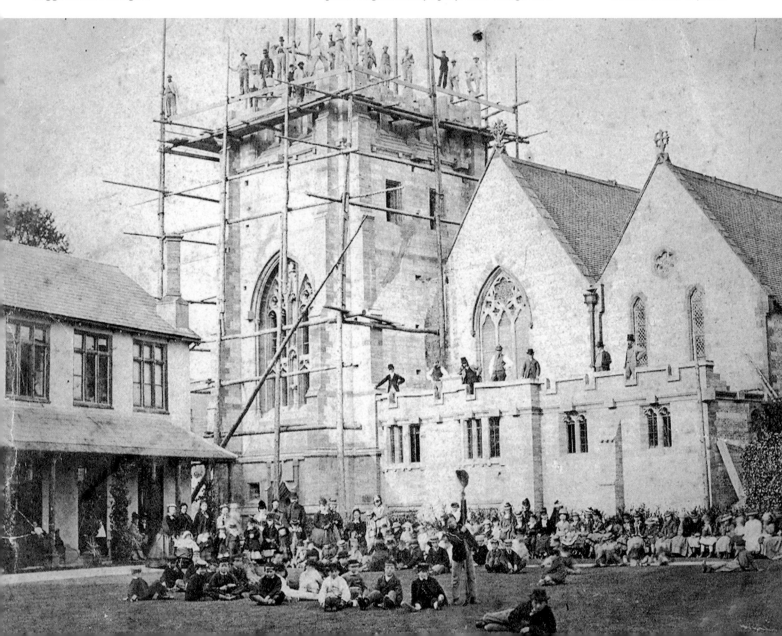

The village hall

The village hall has always been, and still is, the centre of the community. The hall provided the setting for events such as flower shows, birthday parties, wedding receptions, dances, concerts and plays by the local drama society, and so on. This was also where clubs met once a week, such as the Women's Institute, the Brownies, or the Youth Club.

Back in 1923, at Eamont Bridge near Penrith in Cumbria, Audrey Battersby remembers when the villagers decided it was time they had a village hall of their own. They set up a committee and started to raise funds, but they soon realized there was no suitable site for a hall in the village, so the plans were shelved.

'In 1932,' she says, 'the idea surfaced again and the plan was to build it on the site of the Mission Hall which was owned by the Church Commissioners and the land on which it stood was owned by Major Geoffrey Carleton Cowper, this was offered to the village and accepted.'

The plans were for a timber-framed and weather-boarded building with a roof of felt slates. Once the go-ahead was given this building was soon completed and she recalls that the total cost of the hall, which included the plans, the building, lighting, heating, plumbing, billiard table, chairs, tables and a piano, came to £771.67.

The Earl of Lonsdale officially opened the Eamont Bridge village hall on 5 October 1933. The hall was used extensively in those days for dances, whist drives, children's parties, concerts and many other activities.

Marie Langford tells us about a building in the village of Cattistock in Dorset, known as the Savill Hall, which is without doubt one of the most impressive village halls in the south-west of England. The village didn't really have a hall as such, and in the early 1900s, a barn at Prospect Farm was used for dances and social gatherings. After World War I, the school was used for village activities and it wasn't until 1926 that the Savill Hall was built and the community had its own hall to house its activities.

'This imposing building is probably one of the best village halls in Dorset,' writes Marie. 'It was built on the site of old farm buildings opposite the Pound House in memory of Mr Savill of Chantmarle who died of his wounds after World War I. He left a large sum of money to a friend living in the village, and this money was used to perpetuate his memory by building the hall in the same Tudor design as Chantmarle Manor. An energetic hall committee have looked after it over the years and modernized it. A new ceiling was put in, also a new floor, which I believe was

The opening of the new village hall at Swinefleet in Yorkshire, about 1926. Many village halls were also church halls and the presence of the vicar and choir in this picture suggests this may have been the case here.

The Waifs and Strays Club at Stourton Caundle, 16 June 1923. This church-sponsored Youth Club met once a week at the village hut during the 1920s and the club leader was a Miss Starr. Games and fancy dress competitions were organized with each child paying a halfpenny to attend. The money raised was donated to Dr Barnardo's children's homes.

paid for by a local benefactor. The kitchens and cloakrooms have also been modernized and electric heating installed instead of a large coke fire, which heated one end of the hall, but those unfortunate to be sitting at the other end, froze!'

In the late 1920s the hall provided the venue for regular concerts by the Cattistock Concert Party. One of its popular turns was a local farmer called Ernest Dewdney who, dressed in a smock and gaiters, sang country songs such as 'The fly be on the turnips!' 'If anything was risqué,' Marie points out, 'we didn't understand it.'

In the final days of silent movies, film shows were also put on in the village hall and the children delighted to the adventures of Charlie Chaplin and Pearl White. Marie recalls that the captions appeared under the picture, and the children would read them out in one loud chorus. Since then the Savill Hall has continued to be the scene of the annual harvest supper, wedding receptions, whist drives, village pantomimes and plays put on by the local drama society.

Sid Green remembers when the movies came to his village hall at Donington in Lincolnshire. 'The village hall was used by the film owners. They visited other villages during the week. Saturday was our turn; youngsters in the afternoon and adults at night. The operator used one reel at a time, so lights came on till part two was in action, and the previous reel was rewound. All black and white; often silent.'

At Cayton in North Yorkshire, Mrs J Peacock also remembers the silent movies, with Laurel and Hardy, Charlie Chaplin and of course Buster Keaton. Her memories include the youth club at the village hall and also everything ranging from garden produce shows to bonny baby competitions, which her brother once won. When it was her turn, she disgraced herself just at the point of judging and her mother had to take her outside before everyone expired with the smell.

One of the most notable events at the village hall at Woodlands St Mary in Berkshire, was the annual Fur and Feather whist drive. So called, David Andrews explains, because the prizes were pheasants, partridges, hares, and other game. 'There was also a whist drive called a qualifying whist drive,' he says. 'This took place in village halls all through the district and the winners of these events went to the grand final in the Newbury Corn Exchange.'

Although village halls are community buildings, and were sometimes financed by the local council, this certainly wasn't always the case. Instead, the community itself often paid for their construction and maintenance. They did this by holding fund-raising events. This was the case at Skirling in the Borders region where Elizabeth

A village wedding

'This is the wedding meal of my husband's mother and father,' says Mrs Peacock. They were married at St John's church, Cayton in Yorkshire, in 1939, and then walked to the reception at the village hall, where this photo was taken. All the village ladies helped with the catering, by making cakes and sandwiches and although there was rationing it doesn't look like a bad spread. 'The Peacock family weren't too badly off,' she says, 'but it wasn't the lavish affair that brides expect today.' The couple were married for 52 years.

Stodart lived. 'The finance was raised,' she explains, 'by valiant efforts of fund-raising in the village.' As there was no council help for the hall, fund-raising for the heating, lighting and maintenance were ongoing projects.

At Greenodd, the village hall was called The Institute and it, 'played a large part in village life,' says Elizabeth Crowe. There were dances, hot-pot suppers at harvest time, horticultural shows, baby shows, and her favourite, the Christmas party. 'At Halloween,' she remembers, 'we went to the Institute for Duck Apple Night, ducking for apples in a tub of water, also trying to catch a bun on a string covered in syrup. Very messy but good fun.'

The annual Youth Club May Queen celebrations at East Ilsley, which were held in the old village hall. June Woodage, on the left, was crowned May Queen in 1952, and is here with Phyllis Dew and Rosa Hibbert, both previous May Queens.

The village green

An area of common pasture round which is set a collection of cottages, pub and church describes the green, and a duckpond and a pair of stocks completes this picture-book image of a country village. In reality, not all villages had a green and very few still exist today but they were certainly well used, even up to the recent past.

Above: As well as the village green, the village duck pond was another common feature of rural villages. This Raphael Tuck & Sons postcard, posted in 1923, shows a particularly fine example at Runton, near Cromer in Norfolk.

Another institution that was common to rural villages, would have been the village green and, in some places, the village pond.

The green was usually a central feature of the village, and around it would be the church and any other important community buildings. In ancient times it was a place of common pasture, where markets and fairs would be held. By the start of the 20th century, the importance of the village green was already beginning to decline, but many were still widely used for a variety of different reasons.

At Barlaston in Staffordshire Ernest Hawkins remembers that the village green was particularly busy on Saturdays when he was growing up. It was a popular destination for schoolchildren from the Potteries and on most Saturdays, trains and canal boats came to the village, loaded with children and their parents for a day in the country.

'The focal point was the village green where sports were organized,' he writes. 'Our own local village children used to take part and join in the fun. Sometimes we were banned because we were much fitter than their children and we were winning too many of the prizes. Teas were organized for them in the Parish Room. A tearoom was also built behind Russell's Bakery, which was situated behind the present Post Office, and quite a few villagers used to do a

Below: Cottages surround the village green at the Norfolk coastal village of Heacham.

roaring trade in pots of tea. Oram's shop used to take their horse and wagon down, loaded with oranges and apples and sweets. There were Okey Pokey carts from the Potteries selling delicious ice-cream. They were drawn by donkeys that were allowed to graze on the green and seemed to enjoy the day as much as we did. There was very little motor traffic in those days and I never remember any child getting hurt.'

Another occasion that he remembers the village green being used was for the annual Barlaston Wakes which were held every year in August. This was a colourful occasion, well attended by gypsies in their caravans and always enjoyed by the villagers, especially the children.

'The village green was used more in the pre-war days,' he admits, 'not only for sport and festivities but also by local farmers who would occasionally tether their horses and cattle to graze.'

The green was quite often the location for a community monument, such as a statue, plaque, or bench, but most significantly perhaps, the cenotaph or war memorial.

At Barlaston, a well-known local hero was Billy Lowe who lost an arm and an eye in World War I; his mother was the cook for the Wedgwood family. Billy was given the honour of unveiling the newly built war memorial on Barlaston Green in 1926. At that time it recorded the names of 18 men from the village who had given their lives for their country. Only 21 years later a further seven names of men from the village were added after World War II.

A fair on the village green at West Burton, Yorkshire, in 1904. It seems to be a combination of farm animals, rides and sideshows.

Remembering the dead

War memorials proudly stand on village greens all around the country, listing the names of a generation of young men who left their homes to fight for their country and never returned. The carnage of World War I saw one of the most significant changes in rural life, as afterwards many farms and country estates found their workforce decimated, and many village families never fully recovered from the effect. Here, the Reverend Fincher dedicates the war memorial at Stourton Caundle in 1922.

The public house

The public house has always been a colourful central facility in the village. Not frequented by everybody, it still provides the village with its most available focal point for socializing. It also provides a place for certain clubs to meet, and sports to take place. And in some rural areas it might be a contact place for the emergency services.

The Navigation Inn at Kilby Bridge, Wigston Magna in Leicestershire.

In the period covered by this book, and particularly in the earlier days, it is evident that the pub was male territory only, where a lady never ventured if she wished to keep her reputation intact.

Janet Beer says of the village pub at Dewlish in Dorset, 'the only places of entertainment were the pub and the village hall. The pub was purely for male drinking and the only entertainment was on Friday nights when my grandfather and a short chap with a cloth cap and one leg shorter than the other named Charlie Slade, played the accordion and tambourine. Obviously I was never part of the audience, but it was pretty popular. Women only entered the off licence – and that was for strictly medicinal purposes, of course.'

As a boy Fred Simpson remembers the brewery delivering the beer to the pub at Church Knowle in Dorset on Wednesdays. It was transported in a steam wagon that had a chimney like a railway engine. He recalls that burning coals kept falling

out of the firebox and all down the street the boys would kick them like tiny footballs.

Dorothy Waters from Cassington in Oxfordshire remembers the patriotic part played by landlord Ernie Pancott, who ran The Bell during the war years. 'Mr Pancott,' she says, 'was the senior air-raid warden. Eventually he had a manually operated siren fixed on to the side of The Bell. However, the first time there was an air-raid warning he went round the village sounding a klaxon horn as no other arrangements had been made. It was early one Saturday morning and Mum hauled me out of bed, shoved a gas mask on me, which promptly steamed up from where I was crying.'

Some pubs at this time were still very basic, such as The Pheasant at Shefford Woodlands in Berkshire, which David Andrews recalls.

'It was a Simmonds House, tied to the old brewery at Reading. It was not licensed to sell wine or spirits, and was known as an alehouse. It

sold beer, ales and stout, some of which was in bottles, but most of it was served straight from the wooden barrel in which it was delivered. The barrels were put on a low trestle in hot weather, and a wet sack was draped over them to keep the beer cool. Lager and canned beer was still a long way off. Today The Pheasant is a smart restaurant. The tap-room where old men played dominoes or shove-halfpenny is long gone.'

In Scotland pubs would appear to have been even more rustic. Jim Dunlop who lived in Auchengray in Lanarkshire points out that, 'Pubs in Scotland were – unlike in England – used for one purpose only and that was to drink alcohol. They were never seen as social venues and the presence of a female, if they wished to have a good reputation, was unheard of. Sawdust covered the floor and it was the only public house within a radius of six miles, so many customers made long walks or cycle runs to have a drink.'

In deepest Dorset at Stourton Caundle, Frank Palmer writes about The Trooper Inn, the freehold of which was purchased by Wykes Brewery of Gillingham in 1894. The first tenant was a Mr Walter Green, who, apart from

Four village characters having a lunchtime drink at The Trooper Inn in 1960. From left to right are Bill Lane, Shep Knight, Bill Brown and Joe Walden. Joe was a professional photographer who transported his equipment in a motorbike and sidecar.

The Swan Hotel, East Ilsley in Berkshire around 1920. Note the wording on the front and side, whereas today it might say 'car parking at rear', instead it offers, 'good stabling, and loose boxes'.

This old postcard shows The White Horse Inn at Curdworth, a Warwickshire village that at one time was larger than its neighbour, Birmingham.

running the pub, owned a pony and trap and provided a local taxi service. He was also the local coal merchant, the coal being collected by horse and cart from Stalbridge station, and stored in the yard at the rear of The Trooper.

'Home-produced cider was the pub's speciality during the early years of the century,' says Mr Palmer. The cider making took place in the stables at the rear of the inn during the autumn evenings. There was always a band of willing helpers as cider making was looked on as an annual social occasion.

'There were many apple orchards in the village and the apples were sold as a standing crop to either a cider factory, or a local cider maker. The apples were knocked down from the trees with long poles and young boys were recruited to pick up the fallen apples and load them on to horse-drawn putts for transportation back to the stable block at the rear of the inn. Hurricane lamps were suspended from the rafters as the men built up the cheese under the press, with apples and layers of straw. Pressure was applied to the cheese by screwing down the press, causing the apple juice to gush out into a wooden tub placed beneath it. The apple juice was then stored in wooden barrels, and left to ferment. The squeezed dry pulp that remained was known as pummy.'

It cost four pence for a pint of cider in the 1930s, and men working in the fields would call at the back door of The Trooper Inn early in the morning, and buy flagons of cider to take with them to work. It was thirsty work toiling in the fields all day.

Gypsies were a more common sight in those days, and many would camp around the village. Those that did would invariably visit the pub, and often they would sing and dance long into the night. However, they were also known for causing a disturbance by fighting.

The local hunt regularly met outside public houses, where drinks would be served to the riders before they set off. In England the pub was also the venue for several traditional games such as shove-halfpenny, table skittles, darts and dominoes. Card games were also very popular; crib usually. And of course gambling took place. William Moore from Tasburgh remembers a game called Pokey Die, played with dice, which

THE WHITE HORSE INN, CURDWORTH

for some reason was illegal. Whenever it was played, a lookout was posted in case the village bobby interrupted them. But in those days people put bets on all manner of things.

'At the age of 18,' says William Moore, 'I accepted a challenge bet by nearly everyone in the pub one Christmas Eve that after closing time I could consume the vinegar in the pickled onion jar (a large jar which originally held sweets). I drank every drop, over a pint, and put about £20 in my pocket, but promptly crashed to the floor.'

But pubs are, perhaps, best known for the people who frequent them and the characters you find there. At Porthgain in Pembrokeshire Mr Charles recalls a certain local who would entertain visiting drinkers for profit in the 1950s. By this time women were more commonly seen in licensed premises, and Pembrokeshire was already becoming a summer holiday destination.

'One old chap was a bit of an orator,' says Mr Charles. 'One of his favourite episodes was recalling the occasion he was out fishing in his engine-driven boat when the weather turned against him. "I was coming round Carreg Gwylan Rocks (seagull rocks), in a force nine gale on two and a half plugs." He would then stand up and with intense emotion prayed in Welsh exactly as he did on that terrible night. His prayers were answered and that was how he was able to get back to harbour. His audience were mesmerized and the drinks came pouring in.'

There were other storytellers as well and they, too, were rewarded with drinks – more than they could possibly consume. This went on all through the summer because there were always new visitors around ready to hear the tales. So they devised a system whereby the visitors would pay the landlady and she would keep a drinks account. This kept the old fellows going well into the winter months! Some of the stories were true, some were half-true and some were not true at all, but the holidaymakers loved them.

Chapter Nine

Sporting times

Sport has always played an important part in village life giving people a sense of belonging and promoting a healthy rivalry between neighbouring villages and a chance for people to socialize outside their immediate community. The main village team sports were cricket and football, but there were other sporting activities and many people have memories of village sports days when people took part in the various events, some of which were highly competitive, while others were just for fun.

There are also sports that are unique to different areas of Britain, most notably perhaps the Highland Games in Scotland. Also included in the sporting calendar is the controversial subject of field sports, as well as other related country pursuits.

The cricket club

There are thousands of village cricket clubs around the country and it would be impossible to mention each of them, so the memories of Albert Constable from the village of Balcombe in the fine cricketing county of Sussex are pretty universal and will have to represent them all.

A lbert's memories of Balcombe Cricket Club really begin after World War II. Cricket had been abandoned at Balcombe during the war years, as it was in many other places, and the cricket ground had reverted to a farm field in order to help dig for victory. There had been an attractive pavilion with a thatched roof on the site but this unfortunately burnt down in 1939. Luckily the club's equipment, which included tables, deckchairs and the all-important mower, was rescued from the blaze by the newly formed Turners Hill Fire Brigade.

In April 1946 the first post-war meeting was held at Balcombe Men's Club, to discuss the future of the cricket club. The mower was inspected to see if it was still serviceable, and all members were required to attend the ground the following Sunday to help with renovation. Mr Miller of the Paddockhurst Estate donated a Nissen hut to the club, which had been left at Monks Farm after the war. The only proviso was that the members dismantled it, transported it to the cricket ground and re-erected it there. Mrs

Malthouse was asked if she would provide the teas for home matches.

Plans were then put forward for the construction of a pavilion to replace the one that had burnt down. Cuckfield Rural District Council approved them, as long as no building materials were required. This apparently meant that there should be no concrete foundations, brickwork or tiled roof, so it was eventually built of timber framing with shiplap sides and a corrugated iron roof. An insurance policy was drafted for £1.00 a year, and this covered the hut, kit, mower and general liability. At the end of the 1946 season, three tons of marl, a red limey clay compound, was purchased to spread on the square. The accounts also show that the club purchased four dozen caps from Selfridges, which were blue and had a white shield with BCC in gold lettering, at a cost of £31.16.0.

Albert's first involvement with the club was to take a collecting box around the spectators, the proceeds of which helped to boost club funds.

In 1947 Merton College Oxford was offered an all-day game against Balcombe Cricket Club during their tour of Sussex, provided they arranged their own lunch. They accepted and this fixture continued on a home and away basis for over ten years.

As happened in most villages, other groups also used the facilities of the cricket ground. In the case of Balcombe, the stoolball club was

Above: The 1954 team of the Balcombe Cricket Club. Back row left to right: 'Vine' Hayler (umpire), Phil Secretan, Noel Wells, 'Drummer' Robins, 'Dicker' Botting, Harry Thomason, Fred Stevens, and Harry Thompson (scorer). Front row left to right: Harry Thompson (Junior), Tony Baldwin, Reg Kenward, Cyril Hayler, and Albert Constable who has shared his memories of the club in the 1940s and 1950s.

Left: Balcombe cricket ground in 1916, with Will Botting (left) and Charlie Finch (right) mowing the square. The rope enabled one man to pull while the other pushed the mower.

granted use of the ground on Tuesday and Thursday evenings, and it was agreed that the British Legion could hold a fete there in August. The social highlight of Balcombe's cricket season was the annual August Bank Holiday dance held at the Victory Hall.

Sanitary arrangements at the ground were extremely basic. The mens' toilet was a trench surrounded by upright sheets of corrugated iron, with no door. Periodically the trench would be filled in with grass mowings. Later it was decided that some form of lavatory facilities should be made available for women as well, and a further 12 sheets of corrugated iron were purchased for a toilet of similar design. In 1950, after requests by the stoolball club, a proper toilet hut was provided with a lockable door and an Elsan chemical toilet.

The year 1948 was to prove particularly memorable for Albert, as he started playing in the junior side. As there weren't many villages nearby that were able to raise a side, they tended to play against Cuckfield, Lindfield and Brook

Street on a fairly regular basis. The only stipulation for becoming a junior was that you were under 16!

There was always a problem with transport to away matches and the club applied to the Regional Fuel Office for a petrol grant for members who were willing to use their own vehicles. The other problem was water, and Mr Porter of the Old Rectory, agreed that Mid-Sussex Water Company should bring a supply into his grounds and install a meter for joint use. He would pay two-thirds the cost of consumption, and the club the other third.

One of the players that Albert remembers from that period was 'Dicker' Botting, who could

A postcard illustrating an amusing incident at The Village Cricket Match.

Three young people relax in the shade to watch a typical summer afternoon's cricket on the village pitch. The date is 1959 when scooters were a popular form of transport.

Team photograph

The Bramley cricket team from Hampshire in 1906, posing before the old pavilion at Beaurepaire Park, which is still standing today. Beaurepaire Park House was the home of Sir Strati Ralli and the team's mixture of clothes suggests it was made up of members of the gentry, farmers and estate workers.

hit the ball harder than anyone he has ever seen before or after. Albert suggests, 'this may have been helped by the fact he was a woodman at Paddockhurst Estate then and during the war, when every day was spent swinging an axe cutting down trees, which naturally gave him very powerful arms, a cricket bat must have seemed so light to him. During the season he scored over a thousand runs and the club recognized the achievement by presenting him with a clock with the inscription – Presented to L J Botting by Balcombe CC and supporters, on scoring 1,063 runs, season 1948.'

By 1949 the fixture list was full, with two teams playing on Saturdays, plus the Sunday side. During this period the cricket ground or Braky Mead to give its correct name, was the centre of village outdoor activities. Besides cricket, stoolball and the British Legion fete, the ground and pavilion were used for many other occasions including the village flower show, and the school and Cubs used it for their sports.

Like thousands of other village cricket clubs all around the country, Balcombe has been going strong ever since and Albert Constable went on to become the club's chairman.

Tasburgh Cricket Club, Norfolk, 1955. Standing left to right: E Moore (umpire), E Hardingham, R Flegg, J Reeve, F George, N Hawes. Seated left to right: B Hawes, R Moore, L Moore (scorer), H Reeve, W Moore, A Hawes, and V Barnham.

The football team

After cricket, football is undoubtedly the main team sport of villages around Great Britain. When we consider the size of some villages, it seems quite improbable that they were able to sustain a football club. Yet there were – and still are – leagues of varying sizes in every corner of the United Kingdom, embracing even tiny communities.

The main advantage that football has over most other team sports, cricket, rugby, hockey, or something else, is the fact that everyone enjoys playing it. Children and adults alike dream of scoring goals in front of an audience of adoring fans and the idea of women playing the game certainly isn't a new one either.

Like cricket clubs, many rural football clubs were also forced to disband during the war years as local men were conscripted into the armed forces to serve their country. In the late 1940s, the game saw quite a revival. At Tasburgh in Norfolk, William Moore remembers that his local team played at Rainthorpe Park, where the playing surface wasn't quite up to the same standards as Wembley or the Millenium Stadium.

'Before reaching the entrance to Rainthorpe Hall,' he notes, 'one comes to Rainthorpe Park, where Tasburgh Football Club had their pitch when the club was re-formed in the late 1940s. The pitch was very small; sloping from goal to goal with many molehills, horse dung, and rabbit holes and it was not popular with visiting teams in the Wymondham and District League. As a

youngster of about 15 I was groundsman, marking out the pitch by hand with bags of wood dust, taking my grandparent's coal shovel to dispose of the dung and molehills as best I could. Most of the players were men returning from the war including POWs. Despite this most were fairly fit. Several players came from Newton Flotman, as for many years Tasburgh could not find enough men to provide a team. I had my baptism to adult football here at the age of 15.'

Football at Tasburgh, as in most places in Britain, continued to be a great success. The team itself went from strength to strength and during the late 1940s and early 1950s, were runners up in various competitions. They also managed to recruit a good reserve team, although several players were still brought in from neighbouring villages and hamlets. In due course, the team progressed from the Wymondham and District League, to the Norwich and District League, with whom success was finally achieved in the 1956-1957 season. when they became winners.

Such was the interest in football in the village in the late 1950s, Tasburgh had enough players to

The village football team from Holbeton in Devon in 1926.

form three teams, and the number of enthusiastic supporters necessitated the hire of two coaches, in addition to the team coach, for away matches.

The Norwich and District League was first formed in 1905, and included teams from Bungay, Dereham, Diss, Fakenham, Holt, North Walsham, Swaffham and Wymondham. But with changes and the emergence of new leagues in the area, it was left with only five members, and was unable to organize a competition in the 1935-1936 season. Shortly after that the war put an end to most football in the area anyway.

The league did not reform again until the 1946-1947 season, combining with other local leagues to form a stronger and bigger group with 48 members. At its peak the Norwich and District League had over 50 member clubs and four divisions. However, as a reflection of so many other aspects of country village life, the league began to go into serious decline in the 1960s and by the 1970s it was reduced to just two divisions and less than 20 clubs. Today, the new Central and South Norfolk League, which covers a much wider geographical area, is looking healthy, with a membership of over 50 clubs again, arranged into four divisions.

Not all football was played in leagues against other villages or towns. It was sometimes a more domestic affair with local communities having their own shields, cups, and traditions. At Tasburgh, William Moore notes that local resident, Major Berny-Ficklin MC, gave a silver trophy cup to be played for annually between Upper and Lower Tasburgh. The last time this was played for was in 1970 and the result was a

The women's match during East Ilsley village sports day, 1950.

1-1 draw after extra time, with William Moore scoring for Upper Tasburgh, himself.

William Moore may have been an important goal scorer, but in the Yorkshire village of Bilton, Don Bilton found himself at the other end of the pitch. Beginning life as the goalkeeper in his school club, he would go on to greater things.

'My greatest interests in life were sporting,' says Don, 'and these pursuits were shared by my good friend Arthur Moulson. We spent as much time as we possibly could practising football and cricket. My dad had been a great sportsman in his youth and got together with some of his friends to form a football team and a cricket team. The football team was called the Bilton Tigers, and of course they played in the famous black and amber stripes of Hull City. My brother Alan became the team's dashing centre forward. As I was not old enough to play for the Tigers, I spent my time with the school team. We played against

Football fame

The village of Kintore in Aberdeenshire has a claim to great sporting fame, according to Gordon Greenlaw. 'The most famous footballer from Kintore was Andy Beattie who played for Preston North End and captained Scotland. He later went on to be the first manager appointed by Scotland, as previously the national team was run by a committee. Andy Beattie had a house built in the village for his parents and it is called Deepdale, the name of Preston North End's football ground.'

Boys v girls football match at Ash Fete, Somerset, 1951; result boys two, girls four. The girls team: back row from left: Shirley Mayled, Sheila Derrick, Gillian Dunn, Mabel Westlake. Front row from left: Marian Read, Pamela Hancock, Joy Mitchell, Jean Chedzoy.

Right: East Ilsley Football Team, winners of the Newbury and District Junior League Cup 1926-27. Back row left to right: H Mills, A Eacott, W Hibbert (captain and Rosa Hibbert's father), W Tuson, A Bartolomew, and W Turvey. Front row left to right: W Mills, H Print, F Chedzey, C Hibbert, and W Spencer.

Below: Hempnall School football team 1948-49, who were South Norfolk Schools champions. Back row left to right: W Moore, R Moore, M Warne, P Emms, J Ellis, H Smith, and E Sovereign. Front row left to right: R Youngman, W Youngman, N Day, R Warne, B Youngs, and D Etheridge.

other villages, such as Sproatley, cycling to every match.' Don Bilton goes on to describe what happened to both himself and his sporting friend Arthur Moulson. 'Arthur became a good cricketer and performed well in local teams for many years. I specialized as a goalkeeper in football, and managed to play as a professional for both Wolves and Derby County.'

In modern times, football clubs even at the highest level of the game, often find themselves in financial difficulty, so how do small village clubs continue to survive? All sports clubs need money to run efficiently. They need a ground, clubhouse, changing facilities, electricity, water, and equipment, as well as transport and all sorts of other things. But they survive, through community spirit and effort – a good example of the best qualities to found in village life.

The village sports day

It was quite common for a village to hold its own sports day, which was a bit like a school sports day, apart from the fact that adults as well as children took part. On sports day most people joined in the fun and games; mums, dads, aunts, uncles, grandparents and children all took part in conventional, and some not so conventional sports.

The event would be held on the village green, in a farmer's field, a corner of the local estate, or a recreation ground, if the village had one. As well as team sports like football, some more unusual events took place, such as a pram race, wheelbarrow race, egg and spoon race, or a three-legged race. And of course, around Britain, different areas had their own unique events.

Jack Gee, who lived in a farm near Thorney in the Isle of Ely, remembers sports day on the Fens, which seems to have been a grand occasion in the 1930s. 'Each year around the month of June, an hour a day was spent training for the local sports events, when all the lads and lassies from the Fens would enjoy competing with each other. The sports were held in a field opposite the school with all the usual tents and stalls selling food and drinks, and so on. A small funfair was held in the corner of one field well away from the roped arena, the outside of which being used for horse racing in the evening.'

Everybody was involved and the school held its own events in the afternoon when children from neighbouring schools would arrive to compete against each other. This was very much like a traditional school sports day, with various running and jumping events. However, the real fun of the games got under way later in the day.

'It was the evening events that I enjoyed the most,' recalls Jack Gee, 'when the cycle racing, horse racing, and sulky racing took place. Many of the horses taking part were hauling milk or bread vans during the day. These events were very keenly fought, and every competitor rode to win. It was quite usual to see the odd bumping and boring into the first corner. All public announcements were made by a man using a megaphone. It was a very effective piece of equipment but had one great drawback. It was so directional, making it necessary to repeat each item four or five times.'

But it was unquestionably the sulky, or chariot racing events, that were the big draw of the day. They were often dangerous and very exciting, and much money could be won or lost, as people laid bets on who would win.

Jack Gee explains that, 'a sulky was a very light, two-wheeled vehicle using cycle wheels and a pair of ash shafts. The driver sat on a seat between the wheels, resting his feet on the two pegs on the shafts. The horses used in these events were especially trained for trotting; the action was beautiful to see. Whenever the horse broke into a canter the driver corrected it, otherwise he would be disqualified. The prize was about five pounds for a first place. At that time I had never seen a five pound note and I doubt if the drivers possessed many either. Many were just paid to drive, not being the owner of the horse.'

Accidents frequently occurred when two sulky outfits became entangled with one another. 'I remember one outfit doing a complete forward somersault when the horse stumbled,' Mr Gee recalls. 'Luckily the driver was thrown clear but the horse died with a broken neck.'

These village sports continued until 1939 and as far as Jack Gee is aware, with the exception of that one horse, there were no serious accidents during that period to man or beast. The spectators were all country people from the Fens, so the death of a good horse was very depressing.

These pre-war Fenland sports days also included cycle racing which attracted younger spectators and competitors. Often the riders were semi-professional and the rivalry between them and the local farm lads ensured that the races were often highly competitive and exciting. Jack Gee recalls one occasion when this was particularly true.

'One year I remember a particular race when a young farm labourer took part using the old heavy cycle he went to work on. By the end of the second lap he was boxed-in by a bunch of riders, but holding fifth place. The spectators rose to a frenzied roar of encouragement. This was nothing compared with the applause he received as only four riders came round the final bend with our

Below: A scene from Chartham village school sports day in Kent, around 1947.

hero one length in front, and with the crowd's help he stayed ahead to the finish. The lad collapsed exhausted and the cheering crowd ran under the ropes to help him to his feet, then the policeman pushed through and escorted him to the competition tent to recover. I don't know if it was the free beer that his supporters plied him with that assisted his recovery, but he was very happy collecting his prize money.'

A local policeman often took first prize in the four hundred yards sprint and Jack Gee notes that the older boys from his school always said that he was able to do this, thanks to the training he got chasing them out of the orchards when they were scrumping apples.

At the completion of all the events, cups were presented to the winners while the brass band provided music. After that, some of the ropes would be removed and folk dancing would begin, and there would be further fun and games such as bowling for a piglet, or climbing a greasy pole. The whole occasion finally ended with a small firework display.

These village sports days were very popular all around the United Kingdom, right up until World War II, and occasionally you will still see similar things arranged today.

At Ancroft in Northumberland Mrs K Aitchison remembers the sports day arranged shortly after VE Day in 1945, with victory races keenly contested by both the children and the adults of the village. And Sheila Fullman recalls that at Bow Brickhill in Buckinghamshire, the coronation of Queen Elizabeth II was celebrated with sports, games and fancy dress. 'It was much enjoyed in spite of the rain,' she admits, proving that although times might have changed, the British weather certainly hasn't.

At Gayles, between Richmond in North Yorkshire and Barnard Castle in County Durham, Joan Foster recalls of the Queen's

Willie Graham and Tommy Waugh competing in the victory races held at the village of Ancroft in Northumberland, shortly after VE Day, in 1945.

coronation, 'There was to be a village party with sports in the afternoon and we had the day off school. Some of us got organized and practised for the sports; we rigged up a high jump, partnered off to practise the three-legged race, and the wheelbarrow race. We practised sprinting and the egg and spoon race. We were well and truly prepared.'

On Coronation Day itself it poured with rain all day, so everything was postponed until the weekend. 'Saturday following was fine and sunny,' says Joan, 'we had our party followed by the sports events. All was fine and dandy until we began to pair off with our partners for the appropriate races. We were told we weren't allowed to choose our partners and were promptly paired off with someone else. No amount of protesting brought a change of heart. The actions of those petty minded adults rankles with me to this day.'

Although team games such as cricket and football are played all around Britain, there are other sports that have a much more regional identity. Albert Constable mentioned the Balcombe stoolball club. Stoolball was an enjoyable summer game that was a cross between cricket and rounders. It was peculiar to Sussex and Kent, although it might sometimes be seen played in Hampshire and Surrey. Played traditionally on the village green, it was a game

The ladies race

Over the years many villages put on special sports days to celebrate great national events and most of the community would turn out and take part. In old photographs these events can often be identified by the lack of suitable sports wear worn by the competitors. People would turn up, often in their best clothes, and volunteer to take part in the various races dressed just as they were. This ladies race illustrates the point! It was part of the victory sports held at Ancroft in Northumberland, a short while after VE Day in 1945.

which was enjoyed by both men and women.

In Scotland there were stronger traditions of regional sport that are still upheld in the community in the form of the Highland Games, a unique variation of a village sports day. There are around 60 official Highland Games each year in Scotland, governed by The Scottish Games

Right: The egg and spoon race run by the schoolchildren of Ancroft in Northumberland, as part of the victory races held shortly after VE Day in 1945.

Below: Rosa Hibbert, on the right, and her friend Jill Taylor joined at the ankle for the three-legged race during East Ilsley sports day 1950, in Berkshire.

Association, and by far the most famous is the Braemar Gathering. The games are held between the end of the month of May and the middle of September, and some of them now attract crowds in excess of ten thousand.

Jamie Guthrie was born and brought up in the countryside, two miles from the village of New Pitsligo in Aberdeenshire, where an eventful day in the calendar was always the annual Highland Games at which many top athletes from around Scotland would come to compete.

'They were held in the pleasure park,' he says, 'always on the third Thursday of August. They were disbanded in 1935, which was a big loss to the village. On the same day, the horticultural society, held the flower show in the public hall, and the Turriff Pipe Band played on the square, and then marched up and down the streets during the afternoon and evening.'

Even though the Highland Games were discontinued in New Pitsligo, the flower show continues to this day, now held on the first Saturday in September.

The Highland Games involved much more than just tossing the caber and a tug of war, as perceived by many people in the south. There were also competitions in Highland dancing, piping, wrestling, cycling, and many light field athletics events. But perhaps the best-known events are those known as 'the heavies'. These include the hammers, throwing weights for both height and distance, tossing the caber, tossing a sheaf and the shott.

One of the longest established traditional Games, the Abernethy Highland Games, were first held at Nethy Bridge in Inverness-shire in 1880, and following a break between the two world wars, they have been held every year on the present Games field in the village since 1946. Alexander S Grant was a founder member of the revived Games and in a little book he wrote, he describes some of the atmosphere of that first occasion after the war.

'The first Games held in 1946 was a thrilling adventure. We were all enthusiastic. The Games were advertised but we had no funds, Jimmy Smith came to the rescue by guaranteeing a personal loan of £100 – quite a sum in those days when the top athletes were paid, first £4.00, second £3.00, and third £2.00.'

Everything as far as possible had been prepared and put into position the night before the Games explains Mr Grant. 'Dancing board, vaulting and high jump frames were made by the local joiners. Sand was brought in, a pit prepared for the long jump, and a good caber cut. Cosmo Stewart, who ran the pictures and was a first class electrical engineer built loud speaker

Left: A picture of the Abernethy Highland Games held at Nethy Bridge, Inverness-shire. This interesting and probably unique photograph taken in 1904, shows the Games taking place on the field that was used before World War I, it was remarkably elaborate with covered seating and more people taking part than watching by the look of things.

equipment which could be heard all over the village. The questions on everyone's lips, Will the Games be a success or failure? Will we get the crowd? Will we get the competitors?'

On the morning of the event, Mr Grant, who was the green keeper, was cutting the greens by hand, as there was no motor mower at that time. 'I can recall the sound of music wafting across the air, Jimmy Shand and his band. It made for a Highland atmosphere. I felt a thrill running through me and I am sure everyone in the village felt the same. Just then I looked up and observed the figure of a Highlander striding across Croft Croy. He was not a tall man but as he approached me I saw that he was wearing kilt and sporran with dirk at his calf, and the bonnet he was wearing was a Balmoral. After a few preliminaries he asked, "When do the Games start?" I said, "1 o'clock," but added as an afterthought, "of course the piping commences at 11 o'clock starting with the pibroch." "That," he said, "is what I have come to hear. Any fool can play a strathspey and reel but it takes a piper to play a pibroch." I did not know the man, nor have

Above right: Games officials at the Abernethy Highland Games, in 1950. Neil Sutherland, Secretary of the Games, says, 'In the centre is John M Bannerman, a Liberal politician of the day and a resident of Nethy Bridge. I think it captures quite nicely the mixture of formality with everyone dressed up, and the rather homespun quality that give the Games their charm.'

Right: A postcard showing Throwing the Hammer, one of the events at a typical Highland Games. The card was posted in 1912.

I met him since, but I gathered he came from the Badenoch area. When I eventually arrived on the field I made for the Secretary's tent. As I approached the Secretary, Cameron Craib, came rushing out shouting, "We are made, they are all here." Delighted he went on to tell me that some of the world's best pipers had arrived, also crowds of young dancers. Nor did the people of Nethy Bridge let us down. From cottage and from mansion, from hill croft and lowland farm they came. Young and old turned up. Most of the youngsters had never before seen a Highland Gathering. The older ones recalled the Games of the past when some of the finest athletes of their day competed at the Abernethy Highland Games before World War I. What a night that was, the pub did a roaring trade.'

Grasmere games

Grasmere is, of course, a beautiful village in the Lake District, famous for many different reasons, including its association with the poet William Wordsworth, and the annual ceremony of rushbearing, held at St Oswald's Church. But if you are lucky enough to be there in August, you will enjoy the thrills and spills of Grasmere Sports. This is without doubt the most important event in the village's calendar, and indeed, the most popular traditional event to be held anywhere in the Lake District. Set in the beautiful Lakeland fells, Grasmere Sports has been going strong since its inception in 1852, and pulls bigger crowds every year. The event, which is normally held on the Thursday closest to August 20th, includes local sporting traditions such as Cumberland wrestling, fell running and hound trails. This picture shows spectators with their cars at the event held in August 1919. The parking seems a little haphazard but at least the occupants can get a good view from them.

Field sports and country pursuits

Field sports basically describe the activities of hunting, shooting, and fishing, often referred to as 'blood sports' and although these were largely enjoyed by the gentry and upper middle class, they often involved many people in the village. In particular, the local meets of various fox hunts were regarded as special occasions in the calendar of the village.

Today hunting with hounds has become a very controversial issue, but in earlier decades of the 20th century the entire community would turn out to see the hunt meet in front of the pub or on the village green. Sometimes the meet would coincide with other games, community events, or special dates in the calendar such as Boxing Day. Hunting also created a certain amount of employment in villages.

Frank Hind's father was chairman of the Chipstable Hunt for many years, the village where the family farmed in West Somerset. They were true country people, and Frank's mother ran a riding school and managed a flock of breeding ewes on the hills.

'Most social life centred around the local hunt,' explains Frank, 'with dances, gymkhanas, horse trials, whist drives and the like. Chipstable lay on the boundaries of several hunts; Tiverton, Exmoor, West Somerset and Taunton Vale. It was too far to hack to meets, so in 1950 permission was given for a private pack of hounds to hunt this country and it became known as the Chipstable Hunt. My father spent the whole of his working life, apart from war service, with Westminster Bank. He was a keen horseman and was for a number of years, chairman of the Chipstable Hunt. He was also a district councillor.'

At Woodlands St Mary in Berkshire, David Andrews remembers Mr Ricketts, who lived at a large house called The Goodings, and employed a head gardener and a workforce of between 15 to 18 men. He was the master of the local hunt but hunting was just part of his varied sporting life, as there were tennis courts, a nine-hole golf course and even a swimming pool in the extensive gardens. He also had a replica – but smaller – version of the Hampton Court maze constructed in his grounds.

'For a few years Mr Ricketts was master of the Craven Hunt,' explains David Andrews. 'They had a pack of hounds, probably 20 couples. The opening meet of the season was usually held at Goodings. On one occasion Gaumont British News came to film the event, so afterwards we went to the cinema in Newbury to see ourselves on the silver screen. The film was in black and white of course, as Technicolor was yet to happen.'

Each hunt meeting was advertised in advance in the *Newbury Weekly News* giving the details for

A meet of the Chipstable Hunt at Newhouse Farm, Chipstable, on the Brendon Hills of West Somerset.

the meet on the following week, 'the venues were not at risk of hunt saboteurs in those days,' he notes. 'The hounds were kennelled at Wawcott, near to Elcot Park. Horses and hounds were walked to the arranged venue for the start. When they had finished hunting they then had to walk back home to Wawcott. It would be quite impossible to do the same thing today, with the density of traffic on the road.'

Fox hunting was just one form of hunting with hounds that took place at rural locations around the United Kingdom, not all of which involved the ultimate death of an animal. Draghunting, or hunting with bloodhounds involved a pack following a scent laid earlier in the day by a runner or horse and rider. Because the route was pre-planned it would normally include obstacles for horse and rider to jump.

An earlier chapter described the shooting parties held on country estates, where a local lord, or laird in Scotland, would invite members of the gentry to enjoy the sport of shooting game birds on his land. This was very popular all around Britain, and many of the villagers were paid to act as beaters or gun loaders. But the village folk themselves were also interested in shooting as a sport, and many farmers would use

their own land for similar events, to which other members of the community would be invited.

One estate that put on regular shooting weekends was Inholmes near Newbury in Berkshire. In October 1939, David Andrews

Hunts of the past

There was also hare hunting, with beagles or basset hounds, with the huntsmen following on foot, stag hunting, and, of course, hunting otters with otter hounds. Otters were hunted almost to the point of extinction in Britain, until in January 1978, the animal became protected in England and Wales with Scotland added at a later date. I think most people would thrill at the sight of seeing an otter in the wild today, and Mr V J Catt who lived in the village of Etchingham in East Sussex makes the point: 'I remember the lorries that came every few months, dropping horses and dogs at the Etchingham Arms. These were the otter hounds, they rode beside all the rivers looking for otters, and having killed as many as possible, the country is now spending millions of pounds trying to bring them back!'

A Buckinghamshire hunt, probably the Wadden Chase, at Oving, Buckinghamshire in 1934.

OVING. 3

remembers the weekend that he became a beater for the first time. 'On the Friday we met at Lower Poughley Farm, and covered the east end of the estate as far as Potters Corner. On the Saturday we met at Ragnalls and went over the western part of the estate. For the last drive we were taken by the estate bus to the top of Lambourn Hill, from there we walked over the fields and finished at Flint Cottages. It was all agricultural land in those days; Membury airfield

The North Staffordshire Hunt passing Charlie Harvey's butcher's shop in Barlaston during the 1920s.

hadn't been thought of then. We were paid £1 for the two days and given a bottle of beer at lunch break. With my £1 I went to a shoe shop in Newbury and bought a good pair of shoes for eight shillings and sixpence.'

There were various forms of game shooting, depending on the season. Grouse being moorland birds were mainly shot in Scotland, and the northern counties of England and continues to this day. The partridge could be targeted all over Britain, as could the pheasant. There was also duck flighting and wildfowl shooting, which took place on or off shore.

Rough and clay pigeon shooting was popular throughout the year, although in the case of rough shooting, it was often more speculative than other forms of game shooting. Clay pigeon shooting gave an opportunity to brush up your skills before the start of the other seasons.

Many of the birds that were shot during shooting parties on country estates, were reared on the land by the gamekeeper, especially for the occasion, while others were wild creatures, who inhabited the surrounding countryside. Therefore, if an estate was to be taken seriously as a venue for such events, much depended on the skill and experience of the gamekeeper, to control the wildlife, and promote the correct type of vegetation required for these animals to survive. On a typical estate during the early part of the 20th century, one could expect to 'bag' pheasant, partridge, hare, rabbit, woodcock, snipe, mallard, teal, wood pigeon, and others.

Amongst country people, fishing was always a popular pursuit and an important way of supplementing the household's diet. As a sport, there was fly-fishing for salmon or trout in rivers, as well as fishing for sea trout off shore.

Below: Shooting game was another popular field sport, with a good bag at the end of the day as this old postcard wishes.

Here's all success to your aim,
In the slaughter of this life's game
With cause to brag of the varied bag
When totalled against your name.

97

Left: Two men trout fishing in a river. The picture was taken during the war in 1944 and it is likely that they were attempting to supplement their rationed diet as well as having some sport.

Below: Ferreting was always popular in rural communities. In this picture, Mr W Hibbert, Rosa's father, who lived in East Ilsley, Berkshire, is seen with one of the animals he would take out to catch rabbits.

Rodent control

Today, modern poisons take care of rats, but Mr Lucas suggests that using such methods removes the necessity of some of the old, 'and dare one admit, enjoyable country sports. Talking of rats,' he continued, 'there was in the Highcross area of Leicester a rat pit. Women took rats along to the rat pit and sold them for training dogs as ratters. People would bet on their dogs killing the greatest number of rats. These good ladies carried the rats inside their blouses! If a rat does not feel trapped, and is kept in the dark, it will not bite. It must have been a spine-chilling sight to see their animated blouses bulging and bobbing with the movement of the rats.'

Of course, shooting and fishing were not the sole preserve of country sportsmen, they were often practised by other members of the local community as well, but in a far less gentlemanly fashion. The fact that the local big house bred its own pheasants or partridges in order to supply targets for their shooting parties, meant that there were wonderful opportunities for another local character – the poacher. All villages had them, especially those with an estate close at hand. And people poached for different reasons, some to help feed their families through difficult times, some to sell the game to butchers or private customers, and some, simply because it was inherent in their family to do so. The local poacher and the village bobby were always on the lookout for one another.

Ratting was another type of blood sport that took place in many areas. Duncan Lucas, who grew up in Wigston Magna in Leicestershire, recalls an amusing story the time when a party of men went ratting with ferrets. 'If bitten by a ferret,' he writes, 'the most immediate first aid was the crude old farm method of peeing on the wound. If a ferret got hold of anything and would not let go, you used to blow in its face and the ferret would let go. It appears a rat had bitten a young lad's ferret. On the advice of his companions he started to perform the traditional cure, but he omitted to

keep his distance. The ferret disliking what was happening, took a bite and the poor lad was in agony. The more he appealed to his colleagues to blow in the ferret's face and make it release him, the more they howled with laughter and rolled around the floor. What happened to this poor fellow's later love life I don't know, but if any of

you happen to go ferreting, please remember this lesson.'

Some country sporting pursuits existed as a direct result of the local community's interest and involvement with horses, both working and for pleasure. Gymkhanas were held all over Britain, where riders both young and old could

Above: This was the shoot that Rosa Hibbert's grandfather, Thomas Hibbert, was a member of. Thomas was known as a crack shot and is pictured fifth from left in the back row; the little dog in the front was the gun dog named Gunner.

Anxious moments on the moors, depicted in this Raphael Tuck & Sons oilette.

show off their equestrian skills. Then there were point-to-point cross-country events and, of course, many people simply enjoyed riding as a personal recreation.

Sometimes the gymkhana or point-to-point would be arranged by the local hunt. Such was the case at Woodlands St Mary in Berkshire, and David Andrews notes that one of the highlights of the year for the local children was the Craven Hunt point-to-point. But it has to be said that their interest was not solely in watching the horses compete.

'We all looked forward to this event,' he says. 'It was always held at Fishers Farm, Shefford Woodlands, where we saw more cars on that day than for the rest of the year. It was a cross-country course, and was spread over four or five fields with jumps built into the dividing hedges. It covered quite a distance. When World War II came, all those fields and many others were ploughed up and that was the end of the point-to-point at that venue.'

Margaret Kirby recalls the Kipling Cotes Derby, which was annually held on the Yorkshire Wolds near Market Weighton, and always on the third Thursday in March. She notes that this was England's oldest, longest, and most gruelling flat race at four and a half miles. Margaret, of course, lived in Burniston, but one year managed to persuade the vicar from nearby Scalby, the Reverend Tubbs, to take part. He kept a horse in a paddock at the back of the vicarage, which is now an extension to the graveyard. Margaret rode in the Kipling Cotes on several occasions, coming home first on the first occasion, second on the next, and fourth when she was pregnant.

Above: Parade of hounds (left) during a gymkhana in 1950 and a bending race (right) at the following year's event, both held at Huish Champflower in West Somerset in 1950.

Tom Wood wins the Kipling Cotes Derby on Evensong, just ahead of Mrs Bernice Holdsworth on Daniella. The race covers four and a half miles and is England's oldest, longest and most gruelling flat race. It is always held on the third Thursday in March on the Yorkshire Wolds near Market Weighton.

Above: Riding was a wartime relaxation for Phyllis Wyatt, seen in this picture wearing her Women's Land Army uniform as she exercises the local landowner's favourite hunter.

Left: Two horsemen at a point-to-point at Bratton Down on Exmoor, in the late 1950s.

Both of her daughters, Elizabeth and Susan have also ridden in the race.

Of course the description 'country pursuits' can apply to any activity that people enjoy doing in the countryside, whether they come from rural villages or towns and cities, and includes activities such as riding, rambling, cycling, hill-walking and even bird-watching. These are the ways in which rural people enjoy the peace and beauty of their surroundings.

People living in villages often have the most beautiful scenery on their doorstep as this Raphael Tuck & Sons card shows.

DARTMOOR
Tavy Cleave.

Chapter Ten
Belonging to the club

As well as the many different sports teams that existed in country villages, other clubs and organizations thrived in rural communities. Belonging to a club was another way of getting people together, helping to nurture their community spirit. Clubs for children like the Scouts and Guides instilled in young people the value of citizenship; and in later life this could be practised for the benefit of all, by being a member of the Women's Institute or the Royal British Legion. How often, today, do we hear young people in villages proclaim that they are bored because there is nothing for them to do? Well until 1960, the opposite was often the case.

Something for the children

If you want to instill a sense of community into the population of a village, the best place to start is with its children. Along with the things they learn at school, their experiences gained through the clubs they attend help to mould them as well-rounded and caring members of society.

With thousands of villages around the country it would be impossible to mention all the different organizations that existed, but children might have joined the Cubs, Scouts, Brownies or Guides; or been members of the Army Cadet Force, Air Training Corps, Sea Scouts, St John Ambulance or Junior Red Cross. All of these continue today, and many village children still belong to them, but unfortunately most will have to travel to their nearest town in order to do so. It's interesting to note that all of these clubs involve a strong ethic of discipline and respect, qualities that are all too often sadly missing in youngsters today.

Colin Russell grew up at Fradley in Staffordshire, where he went to school until reaching the age of eight, after which he attended Alrewas School, about a mile and a half away. One of the teachers, Miss Mary Ward, was also Bagheera in the Alrewas Wolf Cub pack, which

today are known as Cub Scouts. The vicar, Reverend Hugh Hodge, was the scoutmaster and also Akela in the Cub pack. At the time in question a large proportion of village men were away at war, so there were few left to run organizations for children, so the vicar doubled-up on such jobs.

'I joined the Cubs shortly after starting Alrewas School,' explains Colin Russell. 'Weekly meetings were held at the vicarage, where various activities were arranged to encourage team play and friendship. During the summer months we spent a lot of time in the fields alongside the River Trent and during the winter months games were played in one of the rooms

One of the most popular clubs for young boys in villages all around the United Kingdom, was the Boy Scouts. This photo illustrates a typical Scout den from the 1940s.

Being a member of the Boy Scouts enabled young lads to experience life away from their village, often for the first time in their lives. They went camping or took part in adventure training, such as this group from around the late 1940s.

All the clubs

The children at Merrow in Surrey took part in A Pageant of History, *in honour of the Coronation of Queen Elizabeth II, which was put on by the Sunday-school. The photograph shows some of the local clubs that took part – Cubs, Scouts and Brownies. There would appear to be other uniformed groups at the back of the photo, possibly the Air Training Corps, Sea Scouts, and Army Cadet Force.*

in the vicarage that was reserved for the Scouts and Cubs. The girls also had a room for Guide and Brownie meetings. Although I walked to school, my mother allowed me to use dad's bike to return to Alrewas for any after-school activities.'

During these Cub meetings Colin learned to do things like cleaning his shoes properly, administer basic first aid and to practise simple cooking procedures. These were all basic life-skills that helped to make children more independent. 'With food being rationed,' he goes on to point out, 'we were not allowed to cook more than the vegetables which we begged from local farmers. Roast potatoes were on the menu more often than anything else.'

From the Wolf Cub pack, it would have been normal to progress to the Boy Scouts, which in those days also had a presence in many villages. Ernest Hawkins recalls that at Barlaston, Jack Berry was the scoutmaster. In his day job, Mr

THE BOYS BRIGADE CAMP, ABOYNE, BOYS QUARTERS.

In the 1930s, Keith Watkins was a member of the Boys Brigade in the mining village of Varteg in Gwent, and he recalls going on summer camps to Usk. This old postcard shows a Boys Brigade camp at Aboyne in Aberdeenshire. It looks as though an inspection is taking place, as all of the boys are parading before their tents.

Above: Barbara Raine, Brownie Queen 1945, with the large bouquet and wearing a floral patterned dress, standing outside Wibsey Methodist church.

Right: Brownies 1940s style. June Van Dam and her sister both belonged to the Brownie pack at Hutton in Essex, a village that is 20 miles from London. June says, 'Today Hutton seems like a suburb of London. Whatever happened to this lovely village? But no amount of building can take away those happy childhood days.'

Berry was the chauffeur at Barlaston Hall and the Scout HQ was in the basement of the Hall.

'There were also Girl Guides,' he writes, 'led by Miss Joy and Miss Wedgwood, whose HQ was at Barlaston Lea, the home of the Wedgwood family. The Boy Scouts used to camp on the Downs for about a week during the summer school holidays down by Ainsworth's Farm, where the Meaford power station was later built. Our parents brought food out to us during the day for us to prepare on our open campfire. At night they joined us for a sing-song round the fire.'

Duncan Lucas, from Wigston Magna in Leicestershire, remembers how his local Scout group aided the war effort and writes, 'Sometime before the end of the war I worked as a bicycle messenger for the Home Guard. A unit was stationed at Aylestone Lane and had their barricades at the Aylestone Lane railway bridge. They slept in the old billiard hut at Uncle Les' yard. One day there were Home Guard manoeuvres and several of us Boy Scouts were

given some training with carrier pigeons by Mr Middleton on Welford Road. We were shown how to write the message and place it in a capsule which was then attached to the pigeon's leg.'

At the mining village of Varteg in Gwent, Keith Watkins was a member of the local Boys' Brigade, where the meetings were held in the Wesleyan chapel schoolroom. 'As well as our weekly meeting,' he notes, 'we attended church parades in many places; our drum and bugle band was much in demand to lead church parades and other functions. We went to Saint Paul's church in Commercial Street, Newport. After leading the parade around the streets we marched back to the church and after the service we marched to the army drill hall in Dock Street. Here we were fed by the army, with mountains of bread and butter and strawberry jam, and great slabs of cake and mugs of tea. It was great being waited on by these huge soldiers in their uniforms and hobnailed boots.'

In 1935 the Varteg Boys' Brigade helped to build a huge bonfire to commemorate the silver jubilee of King George V and Queen Mary on the mine tip above the village. It was about 20 feet high with railway sleepers built in a square all the way up and the inside filled with paper, cardboard, tree branches, and anything else that would burn.

In 1937 Keith Watkins recalls that, 'the Boys' Brigade formed a guard of honour at the old brewery in Cwmavon for the visit of Edward VIII, when he visited the valleys of Wales. In the summer we had the Boys' Brigade camps, with four large tents and all the equipment for two weeks, packed into a lorry with about 30 boys and two officers aboard. We went to Usk; it was quite a remote farm about a mile from the town centre, off the Usk to Abergavenny road. We always had a great time there, learning how to live in the open air; how to catch, clean and cook rabbits. There were hundreds of boys there, for many of whom cooking in the open was something new. We had roast rabbit, stewed rabbit, and rabbit and chips, amongst other things, including fresh trout from the stream running through the farm. We lived very well and with all the fresh air almost everything was quickly eaten.'

On the two Sundays that the Boys' Brigade was at camp, Mr Watkins recalls that church services were something special. They marched from the farm to the church in Usk town with the drums and bugles playing. 'We always attracted crowds of onlookers. After the church service we marched around the town and back to the camp, tired but well pleased with our day. We were always sad when our two weeks were over.'

If being a Wolf Cub were popular among boys, then the Brownies would appear to have been even better attended by girls. Barbara Raine was a Brownie in the village of Wibsey. Due to urban development it has now become a satellite of the city of Bradford but from its more rural past she remembers the Brownie picnic, which was always held in local woods. In particular she recalls the annual ceremony of the crowning of the Queen, especially the year when she had the honour of wearing the crown.

Audrey Purser was a Brownie in Merrow, Surrey, and remembers the group led by Miss Marjorie Elliot, where she gained lots of badges to decorate the arm of her uniform. 'Being a Brownie gave me a good start in life,' she says. 'We were told to be good to others and help our mother and father at home. We had a happy time learning new things.' Her happiest memory of the club was a trip to Chessington Zoo.

June Richards who lived at Axmouth in Devon was inspired enough to form her own pack, and explains, 'My friend Margaret Hancock was keen

June Richards' wedding at Axmouth church in Devon, on 4 April 1953. She was a founder member of the village Brownie pack that provided her with the guard of honour as she left the church.

to start up a Brownie pack. We were both Sea Rangers so we knew the whys and wherefores. It was a great time with the Brownies in Axmouth. The greatest was when I was married in Axmouth church on 4 April 1953 and all the Brownies were outside forming a guard of honour. The Sea Rangers were in Seaton and it was an easy cycle ride to attend. One memorable occasion was the All England Ranger Rally in London and we slept on the floor at Guide Headquarters in Buckingham Palace Road and then attended the

The lovely Devonshire village of Axmouth, where June Richards and her friend Margaret Hancock started up their own Brownie pack. From a postcard published by F Frith & Co Ltd.

Axmouth Village.

march past in the White City Stadium and Princess Margaret took the salute. I believe this was in 1948 or 1949.'

Just as Wolf Cubs progressed to Boy Scouts, Brownies became Girl Guides. In the late 1930s, Ruth Bennett was a Girl Guide in the village of Bucknell in Shropshire. Ruth actually lived at Stowe, which didn't have its own group, so she and her friend Roma Bodenham would cycle the four miles to the Bucknell memorial hall for meetings. 'We loved the activities,' she states, which included tracking, making campfires, taking proficiency tests, and of course the camping itself.

Camping was an opportunity for young people to experience a little more of the countryside and be more independent, and Ruth says she attended Girl Guide camps from Solva on the coast of Pembrokeshire, to Preston near Weymouth in Dorset.

Judith Nedderman, who lived in Gaydon vicarage with her parents, remembers belonging to the village Girl Guide group. One year there was a severe drought and the lawn of the vicarage had large cracks all over it. Her mother was involved with most things that were going on in the village and she had arranged a party at the vicarage for the Guides. One of the games was a treasure hunt and that particular year Judith recalls that many of the treasures were hidden inside the cracks on the lawn.

As well as these more famous clubs, what else did village children get up to? Miss Winifred Watkins from Crowthorne in Berkshire remembers a group called the King's Messengers, where children learned about an overseas mission each year and took an examination, for which they were awarded a certificate. She also recalls the Girls' Friendly Society, which was a Christian organization that taught members skills like cooking. This organization had its own holiday homes and she remembers staying at their sites in Clevedon in Somerset and Ventnor on the Isle of Wight.

Margaret Kirby from Burniston mentions the Tufty Road Safety Club for the under fives. She also recalls the village playgroup, which nine village mothers decided to start after hearing about the National Playgroup Movement in the south of England. And for those with ponies there was the Stirrup Club, which was later taken over when a branch of the Pony Club was formed.

Bruce Kean from Sandend in Banffshire notes that the Salvation Army was an attraction for many on Tuesday evenings. Their meetings were held in the school by Captain Mitchell – a brilliant storyteller who accompanied himself and could almost make the concertina sing.

From Brownie to Brown Owl

Of course for some people, joining a club as a junior is just the beginning of a life-long association, as in the case of Lynda Crotty from the village of Netley Abbey in Hampshire. Lynda says, 'at seven years old I joined the local Brownie pack. I moved to Guides at 11 years and helped as pack leader with the Brownies as part of my Queen's Guide syllabus. I moved up to Snowy, then Tawny, then Brown Owl, where I received my 30 years long service bar. When my first grandchildren were born I handed over to my daughter Beverley. The hall where the Brownies, Guides, Cubs, Scouts and Beavers are held was the old school building that Harry Crichton donated to the youth of the village.' In the picture Lynda and her sister Mo proudly show off their neat uniforms, standing each side of their brother Michael in 1959.

Most of these activities were for younger children and as teenagers they became bored with them and wanted something better suited to their age, where they weren't treated like kids. This is where the village youth club came into its own and it was normally held in the village hall.

Joan Foster, who was brought up in a village called Gayles, half way between Richmond in North Yorkshire and Barnard Castle in County Durham, remembers a group called the Sunshine

An old postcard, showing Boy Scouts giving a demonstration in hut building in a rural location.

BOY SCOUTS. HUT BUILDING.

Corner. 'When I was about 11 years old I joined the Girl Guides, as a Brownie and Guide group was newly formed in the village of Ravensworth. Another girl in our village joined the Brownies and we would walk approximately three miles there and back for the weekly meetings. Another club I remember attending was something called Sunshine Corner, it was only for a few weeks and was organized by the local Methodist Church. I think it was a travelling organization that visited villages around the area. My memory of it is very sketchy, part of the theme song was "Sunshine Corner, oh it's jolly fine, It's for children under ninety-nine." We walked to Dalton village to attend Sunshine Corner.'

Quite often these clubs only existed through the industry and efforts of one individual, who put in an enormous amount of time and energy for the benefit of local people. Pamela Gear lived in Amberley in West Sussex and remembers there being nothing for teenagers to do until a new teacher arrived at the village. He ran a youth club at nearby Houghton Bridge village hall, where she recalls playing table tennis and lawn tennis. They also put on plays, went for walks, and saw the latest films, such as *Scott of the Antarctic*.

Rosa Bowler had similar experiences when she attended the weekly youth club at her village of East Ilsley in Berkshire, where as well as table tennis and darts, many other activities were

Left: The youth club tennis team from Brent Knoll in Somerset, 1950.

enjoyed. 'Sixpenny hops were the highlight of our lives – they were fun. Music was provided by records or by someone playing a piano. We dressed up and thought we were grown up. Some of us bought make-up to put on in the cloakroom so that our mums did not see. If my father had seen me he would have told me to "Wipe that muck off your face!" We chatted amongst our friends afterwards about who we had danced with, who we liked and who had walked us home.' The village children were beginning to grow up!

Below: This adult fancy dress competition was part of the 1954 Guy Fawkes celebrations to raise money for an extension to the Young Men's Club at Stourton Caundle. Winning outfits included national costumes from Africa, Japan and Egypt and humorous pairings included a farmer with his bull, chiropodist and patient and an upside/ downside man.

Sunday-school

As well as providing for the spiritual needs of the community the church also offered certain types of recreation. There were choirs, bell-ringing groups, and even youth clubs organized by the local clergy but paramount amongst these activities would have been the Sunday-school.

Geoffrey Charge used to attend the Methodist Sunday-school at the village of Eight Ash Green in Essex. The school was held in the chapel across the road from his house, so when there was a bad snowfall he would be the only person turning up. On one occasion he recalls, 'The minister, Mr Poole, who was a plumber by trade, went through the whole hour with just me, while his wife played the organ for the hymns.' Shortly after that the Sunday-school was run by two young ladies in their twenties. They would make the children learn parts of the Bible in order to recite them out loud the following week.

'We had an evening service,' remembers Geoffrey, 'where all the parents came to see how good the children were, and what we had learned. After doing my recitation and a reading from the Bible, I decided not to go anymore as I didn't like learning verses by heart.'

At Chartridge in Buckinghamshire, Sheila Andrew was one of three sisters who played the organ at the Baptist Chapel Sunday-school, which in those days was a pedal organ. At the time of writing she was 77, still attending the chapel and still playing the organ, although now using a modern electronic keyboard. Her sisters also taught at the Sunday-school.

At Barlaston in Staffordshire, Ernest Hawkins remembers a different type of Sunday-school, a bible class which was held every Sunday afternoon at 2pm in the study at the home of Henry Johnson, one of the local gentry. It was for men only and was attended regularly by the faithful few with Mr Johnson taking the service and the occasional guest speaker. The village grocer, Mr Russell, played the organ and there was a library where the men could borrow books.

Ernest Hawkins writes, 'Henry Johnson also supplied the equipment for the bible class cricket team. The cricket ground was by the drive leading up to the Upper House and was maintained by the gardening staff. Many of us played for both the bible class team and the Barlaston village team, though there was a friendly rivalry between the two and the games were always played in good spirit. The outbreak of war in 1939 put a stop to it, as it did to so many other activities.'

As a child Ethel Fisher attended the Sunday-school anniversaries at the Rye Hill Methodist chapel in Flimby, near Maryport in Cumbria. On these occasions a temporary wooden gallery was erected either side of the pipe organ, with the girls standing on one side and boys on the other.

'It was here we stood to sing our special hymns to celebrate the Sunday-school anniversary,' she recalls, 'which was always held at Easter weekend, irrespective of the date. On Good Friday all pupils marched in procession round the village, stopping at every vantage point to sing a hymn, accompanied by a small portable organ, carried by two of the senior boys. Many of the girls carried collection tins, and we knocked at every door, collecting pennies or threepenny pieces if we were lucky, for chapel funds. After the march we all had a tea party in the Wesley Hall, before climbing on to the gallery to sing our little hearts out. The celebrations ended after the evening service on Easter Sunday, when we were each given an orange and a tiny bar of chocolate.'

Shirley Copley, as a young child, was a very active member of the Sunday-school at the village of Ash in Somerset, and later was a teacher there from the age of 12. She was also one of a gang of four who included Marian Read, John Rodford, and Gerald Bush who were always doing things to raise money for community projects. They would sell draw book tickets, hand out notices, and make collections of books, bric-a-brac and garden

The Sunday-school class at Edithmead in Somerset during the 1950s.

produce for jumble sales in aid of church and village hall funds.

Audrey Purser from Merrow in Surrey went to the Sunday-school at St John's church, and remembers Betty Randall teaching them about Jesus and drawing pictures. 'We had a stamp to stick in our books each week,' she explains. 'We always went to Little Hampton for the Sunday-school Treat. We would be picked up at the bottom of the road with our bags of sandwiches and drinks. We even had vouchers so we could go on roundabouts half price. What a great day out.' Audrey was only nine when she started Sunday-school in 1948, run by the Reverend A Ford on Sunday afternoons. Later in life the same Reverend Ford officiated at both her marriage and the baptism of one of her children.

Sheila Fullman lived in the tiny hamlet of Caldecotte, a mile from Bow Brickhill, a village which she says, 'had a real community spirit. There was a real sense of belonging.' Although there was both a church and Congregational chapel in the village, her parents were not regular churchgoers, but this didn't deter the rector from approaching her and her sister when he decided to form a Sunday-school. They both joined and went on to become Sunday-school teachers. They both also progressed to the church choir of which she recalls, 'The choir was

A Sunday-school outing to Woburn Abbey from Chartridge in Buckinghamshire, in 1956.

almost like a little club. We attended choir practice faithfully every week and we sometimes visited other churches in a kind of choir swap. The rector even took us all out for a meal one Sunday at what seemed to us then a posh hotel. Eating out in those days was only for the rich and not what little country girls did!'

At Axmouth in Devon June Richards agrees that Sunday-school treats were a joy to remember. 'We were all collected by a flat farm wagon and taken to Bindon Farm or Stedcombe Manor, where we had games and tea. Stedcombe Manor was owned by Miss Sanders Stephens of Stephen's ink fame and she had a companion, Miss Leach. The manor was enormous and still stands today. We had the run of the gardens and a field at the back for our sports and then we had our tea on the lawns – usually Devon cream teas! It was truly wonderful and although there was doom and gloom in our house and in my Gran's next door, I was too young to realize what it was all about.' It was 1939 and war had begun.

Carys Briddon, who lived at Bontgoch in Wales notes, 'There was a successful Sunday-school in the village with three teachers in charge of different classes. Every Sunday we would all take a small sum of money as savings for the annual trip in June. As in those days we didn't travel much further than Aberystwyth, which was seven miles away, everyone looked forward immensely to the trip. There was practically no one left in the village on that Saturday! I remember visiting Llandudno, Rhyl, Porthcawl, Tenby, Swansea, Caernarfon and Shrewsbury, but the day that stands out in my memory is the lovely sunny day we spent in Llandrindod in 1955 when the children had a marvellous time rowing the boats on the lake all afternoon. My grandmother was very religious, and my brother and I were not allowed to play games on Sundays.'

The Sunday-school concert

This concert was held annually in Bridge village hall, Kent, during the 1950s. 'It was a very popular concert and the whole village were anxious to buy tickets,' recalls Mrs E Ovenden. 'Proceeds would be given to St Peter's church, to help with repairs. She believes this photo was taken in 1954, and the play was called *The Bishop's Candlesticks*. All these girls attended Sunday-school and lived in the village. Performers from left to right: name unknown, Marion Setterfield, Maureen Ovenden, Barbara Hawkins, and Joan Swan.

Groups for grown-ups

As children grew into adults, it was quite common for them to maintain an interest in the clubs they had joined when young. This was probably more common with sports clubs and clubs like Brownies and Guides or Cubs and Scouts. There were, of course, other adult clubs they could join and perhaps the best known of these was the Women's Institute.

The Women's Institute contingent at the 1937 procession for the Coronation of King George VI at Stourton Caundle in Dorset. At the front are Mrs Winter, Mrs Gould, Mrs Stainer and Mrs Mullett, holding the banner.

The WI was formed in 1915, based on a concept that had begun in Canada in 1897. When originally formed in Britain it was exclusively based in rural areas and its aim was to encourage countrywomen to become involved with growing and preserving food to help the war effort. It has grown and flourished ever since to become a truly international group, whose mandate is to educate women to enable them to provide an effective presence in the community and to develop and pass on important skills.

Stanley Church, who lived at Yardley Gobion, in Northamptonshire says, 'The Women's Institute was very popular all over the country and the majority of villages had their own branch. They were very active by way of meetings in the schoolroom, approximately every month. At these meetings they would discuss such things as generally tidying up the village, arranging concerts, raffles for local organizations such as the local village band, in order to acquire instruments, uniforms, and pay for repairs.'

The first chairwoman of the national organization was Lady Denman, and it was normal for an eminent female figure in the village to be at the head of the local branch. Lynne Oakes lived in the Cheshire village of Eaton, where Mrs Antrobus, the wife of Colonel Antrobus from Eaton Hall, formed a local branch of the WI in 1954. Lynne states that there were originally more than 70 members, and although the branch still exists today, it does so with a reduced membership of 25, and although Mrs Antrobus herself has since passed away, there are still four of the original members in the group.

'Members had to go to the hall in the afternoon to light the coal fire to warm the room,' says Lynne. 'They did the washing up in the kitchen in an old tin bath until a new kitchen was added in 1970 along with two toilets and oil-fired central heating. Sheer luxury in those days.'

At New Pitsligo in a remote corner of Aberdeenshire, Jamie Guthrie remembers attending a pre-war Burns Supper put on by the women of the village. There were more than 400 people, and members and invited guests sat down to a meal of mince, tatties and haggis. 'Today there are only 37 members,' he reveals, 'they only have a Scotch night amongst themselves to celebrate Robert Burns.'

As well as the WI, there were many other organizations with rural backgrounds that flourished in country villages. Stanley Church records one of these as being the local Horticulture Society, who arranged the annual flower, and fruit and vegetable shows which were usually held in August when everything was mature. The people in the village keenly fought for prize money and a silver cup would be awarded to the person who entered the 'best exhibit in show'.

'This itself used to cause a few arguments amongst the exhibitors,' says Mr Church, 'but they had to accept the neutral judges verdict as they were mostly full-time gardeners themselves from another village.'

Then there was the Allotment Holders Association. Many villages had several fields of allotments and these were in demand because although most cottages had a decent-sized garden it was never large enough to supply all the vegetables needed to maintain the large families that were common in those days. Stanley Church says that he cannot remember himself or his parents ever buying potatoes, brassicas, onions, carrots, beetroots or parsnips.

At Cassington in Oxfordshire, Dorothy Waters says that, 'All the entertainment in the village was homespun and was always much appreciated. After the war the Women's Institute put on shows, as did the British Legion. The WI ladies also did excellent catering for functions such as weddings. There was a thriving Civil Defence Section who did haybox cookery and set up field kitchens. They were advised on what precautions to take in the event of atomic warfare, always assuming that our proximity to Harwell (headquarters of the Atomic Energy Authority) hadn't already determined our fate!'

Although the emphasis so far has been placed firmly on the Women's Institute, two other organizations are particularly worthy of special mention: the Mothers' Union and the Royal British Legion.

Mary Sumner formed the Mothers' Union in 1876, when she became a grandmother. She

The WI choir from the village of Cottingham in Leicestershire in the 1950s. Shown are the winners of the shield at the Oundle Music Festival.

established the first branch of this new organization, which believed that motherhood involved more than just providing for the physical needs of children. Her belief was that mothers should raise their children in the love of God, with their lives firmly rooted in prayer. The Mothers' Union was soon to spread, with branches being opened in villages and towns all around Britain. Today it is a Christian organization promoting the well-being of families throughout the world.

The Royal British Legion was formed in 1921 by bringing together the national organizations of ex-servicemen, which were set up as a result of World War I, in order to make the most effective use of their resources, recognizing that the public would prefer to give their allegiance to a major umbrella organization for the ex-service community.

After World War I, in particular, service in the armed forces was a common bond between most male members of the village community of a certain age group. But this service also united entire families through their grief and loss and therefore, in terms of keeping alive the memories of loved ones lost, the British Legion played a major role in even quite small settlements. Clubs were opened for recreational purposes or to help raise money for the building of memorials and other forms of remembrance. But more importantly perhaps, the Legion was there to make ex-service people and their families feel part of a larger, caring community, which united people all around the nation.

Of course during World War II, there were opportunities for villagers to take part in wartime activities. For men, the Home Guard and ARP are well recorded, but for women, perhaps the most

The Stokes sisters' stall

Around the country there were many fruit and vegetable shows arranged by the local Horticultural Society or the Allotment Holders Association where the competition was fierce. This splendid display was at the Church Fete held in 1922 in Stourton Caundle. Stanley Church from Yardley Gobion in Northamptonshire remembers, 'There was never any shortage of exhibits at the local shows, but there were very strict rules that made sure you had actually grown them. The Flower Show Committee could inspect your allotment if they or other exhibitors thought you had 'borrowed' them from a relative or friend. A competition was held every year, around July to decide which was the best allotment in the village. This really was a wonderful idea because most but not all the allotment holders used to try and win this certificate, which was signed by all the members of the parish council and carried with it six months rent for the winner.'

STOURTON CAUNDLE FETE
SEP 6ᵗʰ 1922.

important of these was in joining the local Womens' Land Army.

Phyllis Wyatt from Somerset volunteered for the Land Army early in 1941, when she was just 18 and recalls, 'Training was minimal but I did learn how to milk a cow. This left me of the opinion that to employ a land girl to do the job, was a good way for some farmers to get out of this twice daily chore. To which, I hasten to add, that this was not true of the hardworking majority. I eventually found myself on an average size farm of about one hundred acres, with a very comfortable billet in an adjoining village among people whom I already knew. There was a dairy of about 30 milking cows on the farm. The farmer, farm worker and myself milked eight or nine cows at a sitting, night and morning. We had 90 sheep which had to be regularly looked at and I was taught to recognize a ewe with foot rot or worms. I was often given the task of counting them and to report back should any require attention. I enjoyed the feeling of responsibility this entailed. Occasionally, with the help of Nip the farm dog, I would be asked to bring the whole flock back to pastures nearer the farm. This exodus of livestock invariably coincided with the 10.30am bus to town and caused a blocking of the road and at least a quarter of an hour hold up until we reached the farm a mile or so away. It was all very good natured with plenty of banter between the bus driver and myself.

Above: Members of Barlaston Mothers' Union in 1936, an organization that was formed with the belief that children should be raised in the love of God, with their lives firmly rooted in prayer.

Below: The Allandale Pipe Band leading the parade at Bonnybridge near Falkirk, at the dedication of the new colours of the Bonnybridge branch of the British Legion on Sunday 20 June 1948.

Music, drama and dance

Performing in its many different forms has always been an essential part of village culture. Music in particular can evoke regional identity and there are styles and instruments associated with each area of Britain. The more formal institution of the village band tends to make people think of northern England or the Welsh valleys, but they could be found right across the nation.

At Stourton Caundle, Frank Palmer notes that the decision to form a village band was made in 1937 for the coronation of King George VI. 'The marching rehearsals took place in Drove Road, lots of children followed us, as we marched up and down, making me feel like the Pied Piper. The band was at the head of the procession on 12 May. We started from the Jubilee Oak, paraded down through the High Street, around the Triangle, and then back to the orchard at the rear of the Hut in Drove Road, where sports and games took place. We played short selections, from a decidedly limited repertoire, during the afternoon and early evening, and the day's celebrations ended with a dance in the church hut. Our reputation must have grown, however modest our musical skills, and we were once again at the head of the procession on 11 August that same year. Members of the Slate Club had planned a revival of the annual procession that used to take place through the village on Oak Apple day, organized by members of the Friendly Society. After the procession the Reverend Fincher officiated at an open-air service in

Below: The Varteg Silver Band, who shot to fame in September 1936 when they qualified for entry into the National Band Competition held at Crystal Palace in London. Out of a total of 33 strong competitors, the Varteg Band achieved third place and brought honour to the village.

the field behind Veales Cottage, and the band provided the musical accompaniment to the hymns.'

The band would practise in the homes of its members, alternating in order that their neighbours didn't get too fed up by the noise. On one occasion as they made their way home in the early hours from a house on the outskirts of the village, having drunk a large amount of cider and feeling merry, one of the band began to play a

Above: The brass band marching up the village street of Heytesbury in Wiltshire, in this World War I postcard, is not surprisingly of military origin. The village is a few miles from the military town of Warminster on the edge of Salisbury Plain, and the soldiers appear to be Australian.

THE ANGEL INN, HEYTESBURY

colleague's trumpet, sounding like a bull elephant on the rampage. Having woken the village, one resident threatened them with his shotgun unless they 'cleared off'.

Britain as a nation boasts a proud tradition of amateur dramatic societies and in villages up and down the realm little theatrical groups have always put on wonderful shows, some better than others. Over the years these societies have entertained their rural audiences with everything from the light operas of Gilbert and Sullivan to the farces of Ray Cooney not to forget that most British of theatrical traditions – the pantomime.

From Holbeton in Devon, Jean Pearse recalls, 'We had a dramatic society and about 30 of the villagers took part. We did a pantomime each year and Mrs Collinson who lived at Flete Lodge, used to write the music and the scripts. *Cinderella* was one of the best with Iris Perring playing Cinderella and myself as Prince Charming. Albert Street and Bill Richards were the ugly sisters.'

Sheila Fullman who lived in Caldecotte in Buckinghamshire remembers appearing in two village pantomimes, *Cinderella* and *Aladdin*. Her

father also acted in both, as an ugly sister and the Grand Vizier, respectively.

Don Bilton, the goalkeeping legend from Bilton in Yorkshire recalls, 'The village hall was the home of one of the first productions I was to take part in. I had been cast as one of the principal angels in the nativity play. I was bothered by my appearance, as I was arrayed

Many villages in Scotland had their own pipe band. Shown here is the Allandale Pipe Band pictured in 1951, with the Pipe Major, John McConnachie, standing on the far left.

Carols at Christmas

The Stourton Caundle Village Band played at many village occasions. 'Our Christmas Eve date was at Haddon Lodge for carols in the courtyard,' recalls Frank Palmer. 'A servant came out with a tray of hot drinks, and we then played a few more tunes before setting off across the fields to Stalbridge Weston. A large jug full of homemade wine was given to us at our first stop. We drank the lot, which turned out to be a big mistake. We were just about to start playing outside the pub, when one young band member cried out, "I can't see...I can't see". Some of the other band members were also having great difficulty in reading the music and many a wrong note was played before the evening was out. I have never had a more enjoyable Christmas Eve, with the New Inn packed with revellers, who were far more appreciative of our efforts, than some of those we had played before on previous evenings, despite all the wrong notes.'

Eastrington Drama Group, Yorkshire, in the 1940s, which was run by Doreen Wilde's mother. Included in the cast are the local policeman, school headmaster and a school teacher – all local people. Left to right, Cecil White, Dorothy Walker, the local policeman (name unknown), Bill Bramley (school headmaster), Jean Nurse (school teacher), and Mrs Marshall: all local people.

in a short blue gauze tunic with tinsel wings. So much for my tough guy image, fostered by my role as goalkeeper of the school football team. However, Mam gave me a pep talk, stressing the importance of my part to the whole production. So encouraged, I decided to go for it. As directed, I was supposed to trip barefoot across the stage, in a fairy-like manner, and deliver my message to the shepherds in ringing angelic tones. I thought I'd done a really good job on the night. I was puzzled to see Mam in the front row of the audience, gazing at me with a horrified expression on her face, pointing at my legs. It must have been the only recorded appearance of Gabriel, wearing knee-length socks with a large hole in one and a toe peeping out. I never lived that down.'

Today local village drama groups are still widely supported by their communities, but a more traditional form of rural drama is now almost a thing of the past, though still kept alive by dedicated groups in certain areas. It was known as mumming, which in its most basic form is a very short English folk play in verse, normally performed at Christmas, Easter and some other annual festivities.

These little plays were performed in village pubs and even in the intimacy of peoples' houses. The mummers, would normally be a group of around five or six young farm lads, with blackened faces and wearing fancy dress, who would walk around the village just before Christmas knocking on doors. If you invited them in to perform their mummers' play, you experienced a five to ten minute routine. There would normally be a hero

such as St George, and in the ensuing combat he would face adversaries like Slasher or Hector. Someone would normally be killed during the play, and a comical quack doctor would bring him back to life. The whole thing rounded off with Beelzebub and Devil Doubt asking the audience for money.

There is much controversy surrounding the origins of mumming, but there were three main types of play. First there was the combat play, as already described. Then there was the recruiting sergeant's play, most popular in the East Midlands on Plough Monday – the second

A production of the pantomime *Aladdin*, staged in the village hall at Bow Brickhill in Buckinghamshire, around 1955.

Monday in January. In this play there is usually music and song, and the main story features a farm lad who falls in love with a lady. He forswears his sweetheart and joins the army, so the lady decides to marry another character in the play – the village fool.

The third main type of mummers' play was the sword dance play, found in the northeast of England, and extensively in Yorkshire. This play was a drama largely told through dance, in which the Fool is executed by putting his head through the sword lock, when the sword dancers draw their blades simultaneously. Once again a quack doctor is brought on to cure the victim, with hilarious results.

Haxby is a village some three miles north of York, and here in the 1920s, Tom Pulleyn would perform in typical mummers' plays. The following is the text of one such play, collected from Tom by his nephew Peter Walls and published in a little book called *The Return of The Blue Stots*, by Chas Marshall and Stuart

A mummers play

1st Man *In comes I who's never come afore*
With my great 'eard and my great wit
I've come tonight to please you all
Izee *In comes I Zelzebubs*
And o'er me shoulder I carry a club
In me hand a frying pan
I think myself a jolly old man
Jolly old man although I be
I've got three sons as jolly as me
If you don't believe in what I say
Step in King William and clear the way
King William *In comes King William*
King William is my name
With a sword and pistol in my hand
I'm sure to win the game
2nd Man *To win the game you are not able*
Me back's made of iron, me belly's made of steel
Me fists are made of knucklebone
And that you've got to feel
Mince Pies hot, mince pies cold
I'll knock you to the ground
Before you're ten days old
(Combat – the King is killed)
2nd Man *Where's the little doctor?*
Doctor *I'm the little doctor*
2nd Man *How came you to be the doctor?*
Doctor *By my travels*
2nd Man *Where have you travelled?*
Doctor *Hittle-te Pittle-te France and Spain*
Round to me mother's back door again
2nd Man *What did you see there?*
Doctor *Little pigs running with straws in their duffs*
Shouting 'Anybody wants pork today?'
2nd Man *Can you cure this man?*
Doctor *Yes, shove a little jiff jiff up his little sniff sniff*
Rise up Jack and beg.
(Prods the King up his backside with a bottle – the King is resurrected)
All sing *I am an old Roger with me rags and me tags*
For the sake of the money I wear these old rags
Me hat it's an old 'un and me boots are all worn
Me breeches are wroven me stockings are torn
All say *Patronise the Plough Boys please!*
(A collection is taken)

Rankin, and is reproduced with their permission.

All around the country different areas also have their own styles of country dancing, from traditional Highland dancing to clog dancing. Both children and adults alike became members of dance groups and would flock to attend any new dance classes being put on in the village or church hall.

The best-known form of rural dancing is Morris Dancing, yet it's surprising to discover that during the period covered in this book there was very little indigenous Morris Dancing in country villages. Although it was an ancient craft, in most places it had died out by the beginning of World War I. Its current revival really began in the 1960s. So it's rare to encounter someone who belonged to a Morris Dancing group before 1959.

Alford Morris from Lincolnshire provides the following explanation as to what Morris Dancing consists of. 'This is a hotly debated question to which we don't offer a pat answer, though we favour the idea that it began naturally as a set of pre-Christian dance rituals intended to encourage the sunrise, crop success, victory in battle, fertility and so on; surviving and altering until the present day. We feel that the men and women of a particular village passed down the style of dance from one generation to the next,

Above: A scene from a Haxby mummers play, from the 1920s. The village of Haxby is some three miles north of York, and the play was performed by village lads on Plough Monday, which was the second Monday in January.

Below: A performance by The West Somerset Morris Men at Halsway Manor in Somerset, on 22 May 1968.

rather than formally teaching it, and this is borne out by the fact that there are distinct village traditions in places such as Brackley, Field Town, Bledington and Lichfield, with distinctive figures and steps.'

Although there was little Morris Dancing in villages from the 1920s to the 1950s, country dancing in schools at least kept an element of this tradition alive and fresh. With integral characters such as the Squire, Bagman, and Foreman, it has become Britain's most instantly recognizable form of rural dance.

Whether joined as a child or as an adult, all of these clubs and organizations once again gave people an opportunity to meet, helped to bind the village community together, to give it an identity and contributed to the preservation of its local traditions and history.

Left: Kirkby Malzeard Longsword Team from North Yorkshire, pictured at Grantley Hall in 1932.

Left: Twenty years later the women's longsword team took part in the Kirkby Malzeard centenary celebrations on 21 June, 1952. The sword dancers display the type of sword lock used in a mummers play to execute The Fool. Left to right, Lena Clarkson, Margaret Kitching, Joan Dent, Marion Metcalfe, Winnie Thirkill & Elizabeth Drewer.

Above: The West Somerset Morris Men, holding a Boar's Head ceremony in the 1960s. This ceremony may date from the 16th century.

Chapter Eleven

High days and holidays

Every year villages up and down the country held fetes, fairs, carnivals, and other similar events. These annual festivals provided an opportunity for the people in the village to reinstate their commitment to each other. Fairs on the other hand, often brought outside colour into the life of the village, although they were largely descended from ancient markets, where farmers brought their stock into the village to sell. Taking a fleeting glance at many of the traditions that flowered throughout the rural calendar it is apparent that they were vitally important to village life, keeping alive community spirit, and in a sense are a link to the present and future.

Village fetes and shows

Most people in the village got involved in the annual fete, either making things to sell or taking part in the activities such as fancy dress, tombola, tug-of-war – many of which were traditonal throughout the country. In this way community spirit was kept alive and fund raising for a village project was combined with fun for all.

The village fete was traditionally a community activity where people helped to raise money for community projects. It was normally a smallish affair held in the village hall or on the village green. Sometimes the local gentry would hold a fete in their garden in a marquee, or if there was a vicarage in the village it might be held there. Local people would often make things to sell, such as cakes, biscuits, or jam, and the money they raised would be contributed to a project like repairing the village hall, building a bus shelter, or re-hanging the church bells.

Margaret Wilce recalls that in her village of Walford in Herefordshire, the church fete was once the high point of the summer. Her mother and two friends always manned the ice cream and lemonade stall, and were kept very busy if the weather was hot and dry. Another lady made hundreds of pounds of jam, which was always a great attraction. Sadly, Walford's annual fete, like so many others, has been discontinued.

In East Ilsley in Berkshire, Rosa Bowler fondly

Above: The ladies of Caldecotte in Buckinghamshire attend the village fete dressed in summer frocks and hats. Sheila Fullman's mother is examining something on the stall.

Left: A fete was held annually in the grounds of Sway Place, a large house opposite the church and school in the village of Sway in Hampshire. Each year the school provided a display of country dancing and PE, shown here. This photo was taken in either 1956 or 1957.

remembers the annual fete that was held on the rectory lawn. A brass band played and there was either country dancing or dancing round the maypole. Stalls included coconut shies, darts, shooting, bowling for a pig, and there were, of course, teas and homemade cakes. 'My uncle won a pig at a local fete one year,' she says, 'and had to bring it home in his bread van.' She remembers the hilarious journey home with the pig, and a van full of people, although she wonders about the hygiene regarding the bread delivery round the next day!

Not all fetes were annual events. Others were periodically arranged in support of an urgent village project. William Moore who grew up in Tasburgh in Norfolk, notes that when the village badly needed a new bus shelter, a special fete was arranged. It raised two hundred pounds and this money was put in the village hall fund, awaiting other funds to be raised to complete the amount needed. Meanwhile the village hall committee, the majority of which were church members, 'decided to borrow the money lodged for the bus shelter to buy and have erected fine-mesh wire netting around the churchyard, to stop rabbits desecrating the graveyard.'

As well as fetes, many villages also had flower shows. In East Ilsley, Rosa Bowler mentions that each year, 'there was fierce competition in all classes from the villagers. My father was the treasurer. He would fill up the little brown envelopes with the prize money, which he kept in a little cash box. I was allowed to help sometimes. One pound for the first prize, ten shillings for the second, five shillings for the third and two shillings for the fourth. A cup was awarded each

Decorated bicycles on display at Swinefleet Gala, East Yorkshire, in 1930. The Gala was held each year in July or August. There would be a parade around the village led by the Swinefleet Brass Band, and various classes of fancy dress, including these cycles.

The baby show at the church fete at Stourton Caundle in Dorset, held on 6 September, 1922.

Below: The Silverdale village carnival queen, Doreen Berry, and her retinue outside Bethel chapel in Silverdale, North Staffordshire, at the start of the village's annual carnival procession in August 1957.

year to the person who had won most points overall, and this would be inscribed later with their name.' The winner was allowed to keep this cup for a year, until the next show, when the competitors fought to win it away from them.

Judith Nedderman lived in the vicarage at Gaydon in Warwickshire, where her father was the rector. Her mother was heavily involved with all village activities, as she explains, 'The village fete was always a great occasion and held on the vicarage lawn, with someone special coming to open it. My mother had working parties with

many of the village ladies coming along each week to sew clothes of all descriptions. A cake competition was usually held with recipes given out and followed through to the finished product. These were then judged by a "professional" from Stratford or Leamington.'

There was also a fancy dress parade for all ages, a common feature of fetes and galas, which would be judged by the principal guest. Then there were numerous stalls and sideshows, many of the latter being built by the vicar himself, in the style of similar ones he had seen elsewhere.

Above: Fancy dress parade held during a fete at Oving recreation ground, in Buckinghamshire, in the early 1920s.

A fancy dress group at the Swinefleet Gala, East Yorkshire, around 1933.

Fancy dress parade

Another annual event at Burniston was the fancy dress and sports day. 'One year,' Margaret Kirby says, 'the fancy dress competitors would parade through the village from our garage and the next from the Three Jolly Sailors pub. Always following the magical notes of bagpipes. There were a variety of classes for different age groups of children, and a best decorated hat for adults. This was judged in front of the Burniston Dairy bungalow (a replacement for the farm-house that was badly damaged by a bomb in the war). Then everyone would file through the farmyard into a long field at the back, for an afternoon of traditional sports. The afternoon concluded with tea served in one of the barns, especially cleaned out and decorated for the day. Tea was on trestles and seating was on the prickly bales of straw.'

Fancy dress line-up at the Swinefleet Gala. Mr L A Reed who supplied the picture ran a haulage business in the village, which he started in 1936 with one Bedford lorry, transporting mainly farm produce. The business is still going strong today run by his son and has 18 heavy goods vehicles and 54 trailers. He married a local girl, Edna, who is on the left of the picture.

The fete observed a strict etiquette, and nothing was allowed to start, or be sold, before the official opening. Teas were served under the trees, an area well mown and cleared by the rector and a band of willing helpers.

'Many people came from the surrounding villages to our fetes,' Judith claims, 'and grandmother always came with many people from the Clifford Chambers and Stratford areas, to swell the crowds. I don't remember there ever being a wet day, so we were very lucky!'

Over the years some village shows have become celebrated even outside their immediate vicinity. Such is true of the Burniston Agricultural and Horticultural Show in Yorkshire, which has existed annually for well over a hundred years. The show also includes classes for horses, ponies, cattle, sheep, and show jumping.

Margaret Kirby says, 'I remember taking part in a pony and cart driving competition using a borrowed donkey-cart and a borrowed pony. I came fourth and still have the RSPCA medal.'

'Ye Olde Village Wedding', a decorated float at the Swinefleet Gala in Yorkshire, approximately 1922.

Fairs and funfairs

The travelling fairground was a feature of the summer months in many country villages. They may seem tame compared with today's thrilling rides in theme parks but they brought an excitement and glamour to many rural lives and were often combined with the selling of sheep or horses.

Village fairs differed around Britain and were held for many different reasons. More often than not, in their original form they were based on agriculture. There were sheep fairs, cattle fairs, horse fairs, and fairs to celebrate the harvest. There was even a Strawberry Fayre in the village of Draycott in Somerset. Sometimes the funfair would roll into the village with huge steam traction engines pulling the rides. The rides would be set up, and the following morning the engines trundled off to the next village.

Rosa Bowler explains that a unique early feature of East Ilsley was its sheep fair. It was a trading centre that began in the 13th century. The fairs were held in the village between April and October, with the sheep kept in pens in the streets. The last of these was held in 1934. Such fairs were also the reason why many small villages had several public houses. Sid Green, who lived in Donnington in Lincolnshire, recalls similarly that fair days were held in May and October, when herds of horses were driven in to the high street for sale. He also recalls that, 'The fair often led to fights.'

Barbara Raine remembers that the most

exciting day of the year in Wibsey was 5 October, which was the annual fair day. On that day the school closed at lunchtime (for safety reasons they said). This meant that Barbara and her friends could go along and watch the horses showing their paces along Folly Hall Road. 'That was a mixture of thrill and fright,' she admits.

Stoneleigh is a small village in Warwickshire, where each year at nearby Stoneleigh Park, The Royal Show is staged, one of the biggest national annual celebrations of all that is best about the British countryside. This old postcard showing the stock lines, dates from the early 1960s.

The Burniston Show in North Yorkshire, taken just before World War II. The photograph shows the Heavy Horse Class parading at Townend Field.

Thorney's annual funfair, in the Isle of Ely, was held on the village green beside the Abbey remembers Jack Gee. 'The fair would arrive just before midday with gaily-painted steam traction engines pulling one or more trailers behind them. These contained the carousels or the next big attraction known as the Cakewalk.'

Motor lorries brought the darts and other stalls, and by the time the villagers had finished their dinner, the fair would be in full swing, with music blasting out of fair organs attracting men, women and children to attend.

Bruce Kean notes that at Sandend in Banffshire in the late 1940s, 'One of the really big events was the arrival of Willie Biddal and his Swing Boats and Side Shows. We bairns could see the old Foden lorry and caravan passing the school window prior to turning into the Haughies and our excitement knew no bounds. Willie was always guaranteed a good audience as he spat on his hands before wielding the big hammer with which he drove in the steel pegs that held the whole contraption together. Once he got the barrel organ going with "Skinny Malinky Langlegs Umbrella Feet", we were almost bursting with joy, and even that pleasure was surpassed when we were allowed to spend our first threepenny bit on the swing boats. Willie's shouts of "hold tight" as he gamely lifted the plank which ground the swing boat to a halt, was a particularly unique feature of the fair.'

Happy days indeed were to be had at the fair and as children Bruce Kean and his friends thought they would never end. 'But not even Willie could go on forever,' he states. 'I had a fascinating conversation with his nephew (also a showman) many years later who related, "my uncle Billy gave up his travels when he arrived at the Keith Show to find that his traditional stand had been given to another showman." In later life Willie lost both his legs to gangrene but was of cheerful disposition till his death.'

Apparently Willie Biddal finished up in Coventry assisting a family member in the rag trade, and his beautiful barrel organ was sold for a pittance. As the 20th century rolled on, the nature of funfairs changed in order to appeal and to entertain a modern audience, with new and ever more exciting rides, and traditional showmen like Willie Biddal slipped quietly into the annals of history. Sometimes we can hear their barrel organs, renovated by enthusiasts and put on display at country shows, helping to give us a feel for what it must have been like at one of these wonderful occasions, not so long ago.

All the fun of the fair

'We children had to walk around the whole fair and calculate our cash flow with great care,' notes Jack Gee. This was to make sure, of course, that they could afford to go on the best rides. If they couldn't, they needed to waylay an aunt, uncle, brother or sister for any petty cash they could spare. On the Sunday morning, a service was held on the village green with all the villagers and stallholders taking part. By the following morning the fair had packed up and was gone, and all that remained to be done, was to write the inevitable school essay entitled, 'What I did at the fair'.

Dates in the rural calendar

Of annual rural events perhaps Harvest Festival was the most important, when people brought their produce to church as a thank you to God for blessing another harvest. Up until 1960 when there were many more productive farms and the majority of village houses had cultivated gardens, Harvest Festival meant much more than it does today.

Stephen English, who has lived in the village of Adderbury in Oxfordshire for some 50 years, has seen many changes in the way the festival is celebrated. Today, the gifts that people present before the altar can happily sit on a single table, but 'a look back across the years,' he says, 'paints quite a different picture of a harvest celebration.' The chapel resembled a market garden, or a smallholding, and with all the produce on display it was a wonderful sight to behold.

He recalls sheaves of wheat and barley still tightly bound, brought straight from the fields and lashed to the pulpit rails. Whole sacks of potatoes leant heavily on the pew ends, and there were overflowing baskets of apples, pears, and plums. All types of freshly produced vegetables added to this wondrous display; cabbages, onions, carrots, and parsnips, to name a few.

'From the domestic source' continues Stephen, 'came the jams, preserves, Victoria sponges, pickled onions, milk, eggs, and tomatoes. From the hedgerows came the blackberries, wild strawberries, and mushrooms. Flowers by the bunch! Masses of chrysanthemums, dahlias and daisies filled every available space left grudgingly by the fruit and veg. The fragrance of the flowers mingled with the rich smell of the produce lingers in the nostrils after all these years. It was a Garden of Eden in the village of Adderbury.'

Following the Sunday service, all the items on display were moved from the church to the schoolroom, which must have been some considerable undertaking. This was to make ready for the auction of all the goods on the Monday evening.

The auction itself was quite a village event, where everybody entered into the spirit of the occasion, by bidding for the items with offers that were well above their value. Great fun was had by all and the proceeds of the sale went to the Methodist Famine Relief Fund. Today, of course, the few token gifts presented at Harvest Festival are hurried away to a local nursing home for the benefit of the residents, and the community has lost another chance of celebrating together and enjoying an evening of fun and competition which helped to bind them together.

Celebrated in the West Country, Harvest Home

was another annual celebration. Joan Nipper from Rooksbridge in Somerset remembers it being the highlight of her village's year, and it was always held on the last Thursday in August. There would be a church service, which was later followed by a luncheon held in a massive marquee, with speeches given first by the local MP and then the farmers.

'But what a lunch!' she recalls. 'There was beef and home-cooked ham, plus salads and crusty bread and butter. A six-foot loaf was carried shoulder-high by four strong young men, then an equally large-size locally made Cheddar cheese (not six-foot long of course, but round). The best

An illustration from a magazine published in about 1918 showing a parish church beautifully decorated for a Harvest Festival service.

Dancing round the maypole

Children dressed in their best show off their dancing skills at Barlaston Hall in Staffordshire in June 1912. This traditional dance was enacted throughout the country. 'May Day was the best day of the year at Yardley Gobion in Northamptonshire,' remembers Stanley Church. 'This was usually arranged for the first or second Saturday in May. It was a day when all age groups throughout the village would take part. The schoolteachers would organize a maypole dance display by the students several times during the day, and between these professional displays, would encourage the onlookers to have a go. The result would be quite a laugh as they tried to disentangle themselves.'

the band in the same marquee. All the ladies wore long evening dresses, doing the waltz, the foxtrot, and so on, none of this rock and roll, twist, or head banging stuff.'

She also recalls that after the dancing, usually around midnight, all the neighbours would walk home together. She attended her first Harvest Home at Rooksbridge in 1925, when she was five years old. 'The last Harvest Home was held in 1939,' she remembers, 'when war was imminent. They were cancelled then, and started again many years later. I went with my daughter just two years ago. The luncheon was just as good as all those years ago but the difference is in the cost – in the 1920s the lunch was 7/6d old money, but now it's £12.50.'

'One more thing' she concludes. 'This is the village where, 'tis said, they put the pigs on the wall to watch the band go by.'

Yardley Gobion May Day involved stalls of various types, where people could display and sell things like homemade jam, wine, lacework, or even bread and cakes that had been made at home on the old kitchen range. Local artists might also exhibit their work. Stanley Church described some of the games and competitions that were available. There would be the old

part of the lunch was the parade to it, through the village, of the Christmas Puddings, held shoulder-high by local ladies in their very pretty dresses. What a feast, with cream or custard, loads of beer or soft drinks brought around by the jug filler. There was a fancy dress parade for local schoolchildren and a sports event, also for local children. Three years running I won the egg and spoon race. Then from 8pm there was dancing to

skittle table from one of the pubs, and at a penny for three goes you had a chance to win £1. For the highest score with three balls, the prize was a cheese. A ten-pin bowling alley was also in big demand, but the piece of grass used for this would become very rough as the day wore on, and if you left it a bit late before you had a go, you'd be lucky to hit any of the skittles at all.

Other competitions included slinging the wellie, which involved throwing an old wellington boot as far as you could from a marker rope. Women and children were given a few yards advantage on their throw, and everybody had great fun.

'Another good laugh,' recalls Mr Church, 'was the old village chimney sweep, still with his sooty clothes on and his face black with soot. He would walk up and down behind two solid garden fence panels, measuring six feet by six feet, with a very tall top hat on, and the idea was for the public to try and knock the hat off his head with a tennis ball. You could only see about half his hat and he could walk as fast or slow as he pleased, so it really was good fun for anyone young or old. There was no prize involved, of course, but the charge of one penny for three balls went to central May Day funds.'

Then there was the Hobby Horse, when a man would put on a specially made outfit, the top half of which looked like a horse, made from wood

and leather. It was held up by two straps, and gave the impression that the man was actually riding the old Hobby Horse. It had reins, girth and saddle and looked like the real thing to the small children. However, if you were an adult and you got too close, he would snatch the horse's head up and at the same time hit you on the head with three pigs' bladders that he had attached to a six-foot pole. His actual job on the day, was to

Below: May Queen procession from a village near Sheffield in the 1950s. The traditonal farm cart is pulled by a colourfully decorated Shire horse.

lead the village band through the streets, but every now and then he would allow the band to pass by, and then give the bass drum a whack or two with his bladders.

Bonfire night, held on 5 November, was another big event in the rural calendar. At Merrow in Surrey, Audrey Purser recalls collecting for the village bonfire in October. To do this they borrowed a handcart from the local builder and decorator and gathered garden and other rubbish from all the village houses. Having built their large bonfire, they would then collect for the Guy in order to buy fireworks. 'One of our parents would light the bonfire at 6pm,' she notes. 'We ate crisps and drank lemonade bought at the off-licence, which has since been returned to an ordinary house.'

At Sandend in Banffshire, Bruce Kean notes that the weeks running up to Bonfire night, 'were an exciting time, and the whole of the tattie holidays was devoted to finding and storing items for the bonfire.' This was only interrupted by Halloween, when the children visited every house in the village, hoping to get a penny from the occupant, usually with success.

'It wasn't safe to build the bonfire at "the heich craig", the traditional site, until the final couple of days,' he points out, 'as it would invariably be prematurely set alight by the big loons. Instead, whins would be cut down and stacked in the gunhouse, and old tyres would be located and booked at Andy Thomson's and the Broom for later collection, then all hands would roll them with a stick from source to bonfire on a dry

weekend near the event. Rolling a tractor tyre from Glassaugh garage to the muckle house needed a fair degree of skill, as the tyre, much bigger and heavier than the driver, could very easily career out of control and end up where it wasn't supposed to be.'

For children though, whether in village or town, Christmas was the high point of the year. 'I always asked for a *Nipper Annual*,' states Margaret Wilce. The Nippers were cartoon characters of two little brothers, published by the *Daily Mail*. 'I always got it,' she continues, 'even through the war years. I also had nuts and an apple. We had a walnut tree and apples in the orchard, but of course Father Christmas didn't know this! We always walked to my paternal grandparents in the morning, after the animals had been let out and fed. Here a game bird or possibly poultry would be turning on a spit in

The carnival queen and her retinue seated on the rear of a coal lorry outside Bethel chapel, at the start of the village's annual carnival procession.

East Ilsley's 1953 May Queen and her attendants are taken on a tour of the village on a trailer pulled by a tractor, following her coronation.

Children hanging their stockings above the fireplace on Christmas Eve, in the hope that Father Christmas will fill them with presents overnight.

and spent most of the rest of the day either celebrating or commiserating with his friends in the pub. Her mother on the other hand hated Boxing Day, as she had all the animals to feed. Margaret says that in those days, 'neither nice ladies or children went into a pub.'

At Imber on Salisbury Plain, Doreen Charles remembers how Christmas was celebrated before the MOD took over the village and evicted all its inhabitants in 1943. 'What wonderful Christmasses we had; not a lot of presents, just one small one and not much in your stocking, perhaps an apple, an orange, a few nuts, a sugar mouse, and chocolate money, but we had lots of fun. We had Christmas dinner at home, which included Christmas pudding made by Grandma. I used to help her make them (well I gave them a stir). They were really lovely and she always put a silver threepenny piece in each one: I don't know why. We had to be very careful and make sure we didn't swallow it. No fear of that, because my two brothers and I were always on the look-out for it.'

Joan Foster from Gayles notes an entry in one of her father's diaries for Christmas, which reads, 'going to whist drive, first prize a goose.' The next entry on Christmas Day itself reads, 'had pork for dinner.' So he obviously didn't win.

At Sandend in Banffshire, Bruce Kean explains that presents weren't unwrapped until New Year's Day, when people went out visiting each other and doors were open throughout the village. 'A much more pleasant side to Hogmanay,' he notes, 'was hanging up your granda's seaboot stocking from the mantelpiece. An added bonus for my sister and I was a handful of change in the foot of each stocking beside the apple and orange. Radiograms were making an appearance in the village, and ours would be on full blast, an open invitation to first footers who would get a dram, (only a thimbleful in those days), and spend a happy hour or so listening to Jimmy Shand or singing along with Guy Mitchell, Bing Crosby and the other recording stars of the day. Before leaving us at No 8, the visitor invariably dropped a coin or two in each stocking, then the whole company moved to the next stop at No 5, and then on to the next place. Our dad didn't get to bed at all that night, going straight from the party to his milk round, once he had seen us open the presents at 5am. Mam would then spend most of the morning preparing the one special meal of the year. Like most families we had our chicken on 1 January rather than Christmas Day.'

In Cornwall, Martin Skin says that their New Year's custom was to place a sixpence on the windowsill, then leave the front door open to let the old year out, and the new year in.

front of the fire. We had lunch with them then walked back home.'

Margaret also remembers that sometimes other members of the family would be there. There was always a Christmas tree, and in those days it had real candles on it, so they had to watch carefully to make sure they didn't burn too low and set the tree on fire. One of her uncles could play the banjo and her aunt the piano, so they all sang carols and the popular songs of the time. They also played party games, and had cold meat sandwiches before starting the long climb back up the hill. Her father always said that Boxing Day was his day. He went to a football match, usually to see one of the village teams,

Singing for pennies

At Bontgoch in Ceredigion, Carys Briddon notes that all the children would get up early on New Year's Day to go round the village to sing for Calennig, which was an old Welsh custom. This involved visiting each house to wish everyone a 'Happy New Year', and in return hopefully be given some money. 'The girls and boys would go their separate ways on this day,' she explains, 'and we used to race each other to be first to reach the farms – the first ones to sing at certain farms would have more money than the others. Some people would give us a penny, others threepence, and if we were very lucky, sixpence. As there were so many farms in the district, it was quite a challenge to reach them all before midday. We always aimed to reach Werndeg last, as we knew that Mrs Jones would give us something to eat, and by that time we were really hungry! After all the walking and running we had done during the morning, it was a treat to go to the shop in the afternoon to buy sweets with some of the money we had collected.'

Local customs

All around the United Kingdom, villages often celebrate with their own unique customs, and although it would be impossible to briefly describe all of these, a few are chosen to give a flavour of the many traditions prevalent in different areas. Some, like Arbor Day in Aston on Clun date back hundreds of years.

In ancient times, a tree, well placed at the head of several valleys was decorated for the fertility rites practised by the pastoral shepherds living in the hills of the Clun Forest. In its modern form the festival began after the restoration of the English crown in the 1660s, when King Charles II declared a national holiday on 29 May, his birthday. All around the British Isles this festival became known as Oak Apple Day. Trees were dressed in flags and there was dancing, eating and drinking. However, in Aston on Clun, they adapted the date to coincide with their more ancient tradition, and Oak Apple Day there became known as Arbor Day.

On Arbor Day in 1786, a local squire, John Marston, arrived back at Aston following his wedding. He was so taken with the joyful celebration taking place in the village, that he set up a trust to pay for the care of the tree and the flags, which lasted until the mid 1950s, when Hopesay Parish Council took up the task.

In 1859, the tree-dressing holiday was abolished, and all around the country the tradition slowly died out but in Aston on Clun, Arbor Day continued. Since then, the Arbor Day festival has seen many ups and downs in its fortunes, and although the original tree, which was over 300 years old, was blown down in a storm in 1995 and was replaced by a 20 year old sapling, Aston on Clun is the only known village in Britain where the tree-dressing custom still survives annually. In the 1950s, it evolved into an annual wedding pageant when children dressed up in the clothes worn in the days of Squire Marston. There was a colourful procession, containing a bride, groom, vicar and villagers. But it was not until the Queen's Silver Jubilee year of 1977, that the wedding pageant was truly revitalized, and ever since then this ancient festival has thrived.

In many places during the period covered by this book, the original Oak Apple Day was still much in evidence. For instance, on 29 May each year at the Dorset village of Stourton Caundle,

A policeman stands before the ancient tree at Aston on Clun in South Shropshire in 1900. Aston is the only remaining village to celebrate the annual event of Arbor Day, when a tree was decorated by local pastoral shepherds to aid fertility. This over 300-year-old tree fell down in 1995, and was replaced by a 20-year-old sapling.

Left: The Arbor Tree at Aston on Clun in South Shropshire pictured in 1911. The tree is shown decorated with flags and buntings.

Below: The 1922 Oak Apple Day procession at Stourton Caundle in Dorset. Oak Apple Day was celebrated on 29 May each year with a procession through the village to commemorate the restoration of the monarchy in 1660.

the occasion was celebated by a procession through the village to commemorate the restoration of the monarchy in 1660. The day's celebrations were organized by the Friendly Society, which was founded in 1836, with the members contributing to provide some money in the event of a member's sickness, unemployment, or other misfortune. Any surplus funds were paid out to members after the procession, which in turn was followed by a fete, tea and dancing in the tithe barn at Court Barton. The society's emblem was mounted on a banner carried at the

head of the procession, and it bore the inscription 'May we all strive together like bees of a hive and never sting each other.' The entire village turned out for this procession, marching behind the village band.

Another hugely popular event takes place on Cooper's Hill near Brockworth in the county of Gloucestershire. The annual Cheese Rolling and Wake has been taking place on this site, quite possibly in use since the time of the Ancient Britons. There is certainly evidence of a Celtic hill fort, which stood at the top of the hill, later inhabited by the Romans. By the early 1800s it was already recorded as an ancient festival.

The event takes place at midday on Spring Bank Holiday Monday. There are four downhill races, when a 7-8lb Double Gloucester cheese is released down the hill, after a count of three by the Master of Ceremonies. During the war, and up until the end of rationing in 1954, a wooden substitute was used. On the count of 'and four to be off!' the competitors hurl themselves down the precipitous slope. The first person to arrive at the foot of the hill wins the cheese. The slope has a gradient in places of 1-in-2, and it is almost impossible to remain upright on foot during the descent. Each year there are many minor injuries to the competitors.

The cheese rolling itself is only part of the Wake, which in the past has also included dancing for ribbons; grinning through a horse's collar for a cake; dipping in a tub of water for oranges and apples; bobbing for penny loaves smeared with treacle; and shin-kicking – ouch! In later years there was also a flower show, climbing the maypole and a tug-of-war. Cheese Rolling on

Above: A village child demands a toll from a bridal party after a wedding in 1938. Tying the church gates was the local custom at Henbury Church near Bristol, and it is also to be found at other Somerset churches.

Ancient beliefs

This postcard published by F Frith & Co Ltd, shows the famous village green at Manaton in Devon. At one time, there was a fine granite cross in the village, and the local custom when somebody died, was to carry the corpse the way of the sun three times round the cross, before lowering it into the grave. As this was a remnant of local pagan beliefs, and unable to stop the practice with his sermons, the rector at the time went out in the night and smashed the cross.

A view of the annual ceremony of 'Clipping Sunday' performed in Painswick, Gloucestershire in 1934. The local children march through the avenue of yew trees and form a large circle by holding hands around the church. The custom is said to date from pagan times.

Cooper's Hill has taken place every year, at least since the early 1800s. Twice in recent years, the public event has been cancelled over safety concerns, but on both occasions a small ceremony took place with a single cheese being rolled, to maintain the tradition.

Gertie May recalls that in Clovelly in Devon, on Shrove Tuesday, the young children would drag tins down the street in the evening to drive away the Devil before Lent. And Ethel Fisher from Flimby in Cumbria, says that, 'Pasch-eggs were a Cumbrian delicacy, made by wrapping hens eggs in newspaper previously lined with either gorse flowers or onion skins. These were

The Parade of the Flitch, (a side of pork salted or cured), at Ilford, a custom originating in Saxon times. It takes place every year to find the happiest married couple. Shown here in 1926 are Mr and Mrs Wood and six of their ten children taking part in the parade.

boiled for an hour then unwrapped to reveal beautifully patterned eggs, which were then rubbed with butter, producing a glaze. Pasch-egg competitions were usually held on Easter Monday. This entailed all available children standing on top of a hill, then rolling their individual eggs down the grassy slope. First egg to reach the bottom was the winner. All the winners from each group raced their eggs in the final, amid loud cheers and much laughter. The eventual winner would probably receive a penny. Afterwards we ate our eggs with relish, despite them being battered, cracked and grass-stained. Food poisoning? We'd never heard of it!'

Local characters would also feature in customs, such as Molly Grimes in Glentham, Lincolnshire, remembered by Mary Cooper. 'The church had a stone figure inside of a lady called Molly Grimes and when we were at school we played a game of sticking a pin in the church door and running round the outside of the church seven times and Molly was supposed to appear. To this day one tradition is still observed and that is also to do with Molly Grimes – every Good Friday seven spinsters had to fetch water from Newell's Well and wash the statue. Now it's part of our summer fete, as cross-country runners fetch water from the well in balloons.'

Funerary customs

Alfriston is a charming village in Sussex, steeped in ancient folklore and rural customs, one of which was to lay a white wreath called the Virgin Garland on the coffins of unmarried women during the funeral service. Afterwards they would be displayed in the church, sometimes with a white glove or a piece of paper in the shape of a glove. Another funerary custom practised until the 1930s, was to bury a shepherd holding a small piece of fleece in his hand, so that when he got to heaven, St. Peter would see he was a shepherd and would forgive his lack of attendance at church because of the demands of his job. From a postcard dating from the 1960s.

Traditional celebrations

These are just a few of the wonderful traditions that existed all around Britain, and many still do. For those with appetites wetted, who wish to discover more, the following list represents a few further examples, although they are not necessarily associated with villages, as some are rural town celebrations. These are merely a few, picked at random.

Bedfordshire – Orange Rolling and Wilkes Walk
Berkshire – Hock Tide Ceremony
Buckinghamshire – Swan Upping and Weighing the Mayor
Cambridgeshire – Dicing for Bibles, John Clare Day Cushion Ceremony and Straw Bear
Cheshire – Bawming the Thorn, Jack in the Green, High Spen Rapper Sword Dance and Souling Play
Cornwall – Hurling the Silver Ball, Mazey Day, Furry Dance, Gorsedd Kerno, St Pirian's Day and Starry Gazie Pie
Cumbria – Egremont Crab Fair, Rushbearing and Gurning
Derbyshire – Maiden's Garland, Plague Service and Well Dressing
Devon – Barrel Rolling, Turning the Devil's Stone and Pretty Maid
Dorset – Ale Tasting, the Sherborne Dole and the Marblers and Stonecutters Annual Meeting
Dumfries & Galloway – Common Riding
Durham – Shrovetide Football
Dyfed – Coracle Racing
Essex –Dunmow Flitch Trial and Old Man of Braughing
Glamorgan – Mari Lwyd
Gloucestershire – Church Clipping, Scuttlebrooke Wake and Torchlight Procession
Grampian – Burning the Clavie and Swinging the Fire Balls
Hampshire – Knighthood of the Old Green, Bellringers' Feast, Wayfarer's Dole and Maiden's Garland
Hereford and Worcester – Boy Bishop, Fownhope Walk and Pax Cakes
Hertfordshire – Bakers & Sweeps Football
Highlands – St Mary's Clootie Well
Humberside – Hood Game and Sword Dancing
Kent – The Bartlemas Bun and Chulkhurst Charity
Lancashire – Britannia Coconut Dancers and Egg Rolling
Leicestershire – Bottle Kicking and the Hare Pie Scramble
Lincolnshire – Good Friday Bridge Sermon
Lothian – Beltane Festival, Burry Man and Fisherman's Walk
Norfolk – Blessing the Plough
Northamptonshire – Corby Pole Fair and Tin Can Band
Northumberland – Blessing the Salmon Nets
Nottinghamshire – Cradle Rocking
Orkney Islands – Boy Ploughmen
Oxfordshire – Bounds Beating and Yarnton Meadow Mowing Rights
Shetland – Up-Helly-Aa
Skye – Dunvegan Day
Somerset – Burning the Ashen Faggot, Punky Night and Wassailing
Staffordshire – Horn Dance and Sheriff's Ride
Strathclyde – Orange Parade and Sma' Shot Day
Surrey – Dicing for the Maid's Money
The Borders – Blanket Preaching
Wiltshire – Duck Feast and Grovely Day
Yorkshire – Horn Blower and Shrovetide Skipping

Celebrating national events

Not only were village events celebrated in a local capacity, but there were also occasions when they were made to feel part of a much wider national community. These were the times when the whole of Britain celebrated together: coronations, jubilees, royal weddings, VE and VJ Days, and more recently the new Millenium.

At Edithmead in Somerset, Phyllis Wyatt recalls the Silver Jubilee of King George V and Queen Mary in 1935. Edithmead was a small community and she recalls these celebrations as being the last big event to be held in the village. Edithmead was later ripped apart by the building of the M5 motorway. There was a large wooden building in the village called The Rabbitry, which was cleaned of its accumulation of rubbish, and with the help of a large tarpaulin sheet to block off the adjacent cow stalls, it was made into a temporary village hall. 'Everyone rallied around with tables and chairs and the ladies cooked and baked for days. Flags, bunting and banners transformed the look of the whole village and sports were held,' notes Phyllis.

On Jubilee Day 1935 at Church Knowle in Dorset, Fred Simpson recalls that there was a tea party in the school, where all the children were

A fancy dress competition as part of the celebrations at Dulcote in Somerset in 1935, to mark the Silver Jubilee of King George V and Queen Mary.

The whole village pictured outside the marquee to celebrate the Silver Jubilee of King George V and Queen Mary at Dulcote in Somerset.

Inside the decorated marquee for the celebrations at Dulcote in Somerset in 1935, to mark the Silver Jubilee of King George V and Queen Mary.

given a mug with King George V engraved on it. 'I don't know if it coincided with May Day,' he contemplates, 'but I do remember there were sports and dancing round the maypole, when the villagers attended at the school.'

One of the most important and widely celebrated occasions of the entire 20th century was VE Day, 8th May 1945, a day which was celebrated from Trafalgar Square in London, to the tiniest hamlet of the realm. Marie Litchfield

who lived in Ashcott, in Somerset, has vivid recollections of this long-awaited event, when six years of war in Europe finally came to an end. It was a day for which she and her family had prayed and hoped, and worked towards.

'In the end,' she writes, 'it really happened. The taut band of tension snapped, and everyone was free at last. A mighty surge of relief, untranslatable into words and impossible to describe to anyone who has never experienced it,

Carnival float depicting the village King and Queen; part of the 1935 Silver Jubilee celebrations at Bridge in Kent. Mr Hogben played the King, but the name of the Queen (another man) is unknown. The float was driven by Ernest Ovenden, standing by the float in a suit and flat hat.

swept through the land. Exteriorly, nothing had changed, apart from the fact that the air raid sirens were heard no more, and the blackout was ended. Rationing went on for almost as long again as it had already lasted. Everything was in as short supply as before. But oh, the lads came home demobbed, and the girls from the ATS and other services. Ashcott was complete again and everyone could celebrate. Families put out flags and bunting and 'Welcome Home' signs outside their houses when they knew their dear ones would return. During the First World War the village had suffered heavy casualties. Unless my memory serves me false, I don't think we lost any of our men in this one. Some had been taken prisoner, and took longer to get back, but I think they all eventually came home.'

Marie goes on to explain that there were parties, street by street, and lots of events. 'Not this time,' she points out, 'to get money from people in order to make more weapons, but simply for joy. Everything was free, those who had any cash handing out prizes to the children when they won races, those who hadn't helping to collect tables together or lending cups, or at least a hand. There was relief and great happiness on every face. I know that for those elsewhere, who had lost one or more members of their families – and there were so very, very many – there must have been an even greater sense of loss as they witnessed the home-comings and reunions. That pain was all around us, and even those who were most energetic in the celebrations were aware of this other side – the price that had been paid.'

Marie was nearly 16 when VE Day brought peace in Europe, and not long after her birthday the war against the Japanese also came to an end. VJ Day, 15th August 1945 was hardly even noted in many places, let alone celebrated, but it meant that World War II was finally over.

However, even though hostilities had come to an end, people throughout rural Britain continued to feel their effects for some time. This was another way in which remote villages were able to share experiences with the rest of the country.

'Life was still just as curtailed by shortage of goods and of money as it had been,' Marie expands, 'but by now we were getting quite clever at managing. Everybody still had to be. It was common practice to take an old, worn-out jumper or cardigan carefully to pieces, unpick the parts that were still good, wash the wool, and then knit it up into another garment. Fathers' worn trousers were cut down to make smaller ones for their sons; ladies' dresses made children's skirts or frocks; and even furnishing materials like cretonne and butter-muslin, which were not on

coupons, were used to make clothing. In our house, if we needed something that cost money, we knew we would have to use our ingenuity to create it ourselves – or go without. But it took a lot to beat us! Making things out of next to nothing was a challenge and usually fun. We made rugs out of snipped-up rags – not elegant but long-lasting and serviceable. Nothing at all was wasted. Once in a while a rag-and-bone man still came round, as of yore. He paid a few pence for a bundle of rags, but we never had any bones for him. What few well-stewed bones we had finished with were eagerly snapped up by our dog, or someone else's.'

Newspapers were never thrown away continues Marie, 'They had several uses before being either composted or used as firelighters. A folded paper was always used as a chopping-board for vegetables; another as a stand for hot saucepans, and others for putting on the floor to soak up spilt washing water. They were used under mats and carpets to help keep the cold of the stone floors a little further from our feet; and of course they were always used as toilet paper. Toilet rolls were rarely seen – in fact, it would have been considered unpatriotic to use them. Even public conveniences only offered newspaper, cut ready into squares. Shops, too, were always glad of any spare papers to use as wrapping paper for their

Children help to put up bunting and flags for the VE Day celebrations 8th May 1945.

wares. When I see all the paper that is wasted today, and hear the few voices raised to try to tell people to save it, I remember those days. We knew well enough how to save and use every scrap of paper then. It is a skill that needs to be re-learnt – possibly not quite to the same extent, but at least in moderation.'

In spite of all this making and mending and all the work that had to be done, with no labour-saving devices whatsoever, not even an electric iron or kettle, Marie admits that life was not pressurised in Ashcott, or at any rate not in her family home. 'Looking back,' she concludes, 'I see how almost all the teaching our parents gave us was by example rather than in words. It stood us in good stead in later years.'

But there is no doubt that the final great event that took place during the period covered in this book, and still remembered by many people, was the Coronation of Queen Elizabeth II, on 2 June, 1953. At Holbeton in Devon, Jean Pearse remembers lovely celebrations where everybody decorated their houses. The village also had a fancy dress parade. 'Mary Potter,' she recalls, 'dressed up as Edmund Hillary who had just conquered Mount Everest. I was dressed up as a coronation flower girl. I was dressed in red, white and blue. Mary had first prize and I had third prize. We also had a huge bonfire in the hut field near Machinery Farm, the biggest bonfire the village had ever seen.'

At the village of Merrow in Surrey, the church Sunday-school put on *A Pageant of History* to celebrate the Queen's coronation, which was written by Mr J Gould, an old Merrow man. Audrey Purser, who was 14 at the time played the part of Queen Elizabeth I. Auditions were held in the church room, and Audrey was chosen to play Elizabeth as they said she was the one who looked most like her. The pageant itself was held at an old house in Merrow called The Cedars, but she also recalls that the rest of the houses were decked with bunting and flags as they paraded through the village.

At some places the activities in celebration of the coronation didn't go quite to plan. At New Pitsligo in Aberdeenshire, Jamie Guthrie remembers it being a terrible day, with the wind howling and the rain pouring down. Everything that had been arranged to take place in the open had to be cancelled, and the village had to suffice with activities inside the village hall.

Another common occurrence at the time of the Queen's Coronation was that many people purchased their first television, which must have made them feel even more a part of what was going on around Britain. At Auchengray in Lanarkshire Jim Dunlop notes that 1953 was the

year that the village was finally linked to the national grid, with electricity being supplied to all homes. 'My parents in the week before the coronation,' he recalls, 'purchased a 12-inch TV console. The cabinet of which was three times larger than the screen. This was the only set in the village, which had 18 houses, and consequently the whole village converged on the house to witness this marvel which produced an extremely grainy black and white picture.'

At Skirling village in the Scottish Borders, Elizabeth Stodart's father was on the Coronation Celebration Committee. Peebleshire County

Children enjoying a street party at Netley Abbey, Hampshire, to celebrate the coronation of Queen Elizabeth II in 1953.

Pamela Gear and her brother pictured during celebrations in the village of Amberley, West Sussex. She doesn't remember the occasion, but as she was born in November 1934, it could be a coronation or jubilee – but which?

Council provided commemorative items to be distributed – mugs for the children and tins containing tea for the elderly. Other celebrations were organized and paid for at village level. Raffles and other fund-raising enabled the hire of a TV for the schoolchildren to see the Coronation.

'I went with my family to an aunt and uncle in the village who owned a TV,' notes Elizabeth, 'it was one of only a few in the place. There was a fancy dress competition for the children followed by a picnic in the garden of the Big House. This was owned by the Carmichael family – at one time owners of most of the area around Skirling but by 1953 their land holdings were mostly sold off and they were by no means so "grand". I was dressed as a nurse in the fancy dress competition with a large white handkerchief folded in a triangle for a headdress. During the picnic one of the smaller schoolchildren fell against the corner of a form on which we had sat, bled profusely from a head wound and my head-dress was pressed into service to stem the flow!'

At Skirling the day was rounded off with a bonfire on the highest ground in the village, which was the traditional way of marking such events. Elizabeth Stodart admits to being too young to attend the 1953 bonfire, but she did attend the one on the same spot in June 2002 to celebrate the Golden Jubilee.

There was also a bonfire at Forgandenny in Perthshire, but it was only part of the village's celebrations, some aspects of which are best not remembered. Joan Blue says, 'A coronation tree was planted by Lady Anne Hutchinson, assisted by one of the village children.' That was the good bit, as she goes on to explain, 'The bonfire, which had been built over the previous weeks, was lit by local youths on the night before coronation day. The band that was engaged to play at a dance in the village hall on coronation night did not turn up and were eventually found, drunk, in a pub in

The children of Bramdean in Hampshire wearing fancy dress to celebrate the coronation in 1953.

Close up of the doorway of a cottage in the village of Oving in Buckinghamshire, decorated for the coronation of King George VI in 1937.

the next village. Not a very auspicious Coronation Day in Forgandenny!'

And finally, at the other end of the country at Piddletrenthide in Dorset, Janet Burt was only five and a half on Coronation Day, but says, 'I do remember watching it on our new television together with various friends and neighbours. The sun came out in the afternoon and the whole village was invited to the Manor House grounds for a giant picnic. Everyone took along some food, which was pooled and enjoyed by all. There were fun and games organized for all ages, including a fancy dress for the children. I was dressed in my old bridesmaid dress with Commonwealth flags pinned all over the bodice. Every time I moved the pins stuck into my chest; it was most uncomfortable!'

The Coronation of Queen Elizabeth II in 1953

was perhaps the last great event to be celebrated around the country in villages that had remained unchanged for years and whose inhabitants were descended from those who had lived there for centuries. Since then, other national events have been celebrated in similar ways, but with decreasing enthusiasm. At the village where I live in Somerset for instance, we celebrated the Queen's Golden Jubilee in 2002 with a half-hearted street party, only arranged at the very last minute the day before. But other than my own family, and our nearest neighbours, no one else in the street even originates from Somerset. In a sense, this situation on my very own doorstep, sums up the theme of this book, but also sadly underlines the fact that we can never return again to the world described by so many of the contributors to this book.

Coronation celebrations

Many people, who were children at the time, still have the commemorative mugs they were presented at school, but on the day itself at Bow Brickhill in Buckinghamshire, Sheila Fullman was more interested in the bar of Dairy Milk chocolate that came with it. She also remembers it raining, but not enough to prevent the sports, games and fancy dress taking place. Although she went to school in Bow Brickhill, she actually lived in the nearby hamlet of Caldecotte, where few outsiders ventured, but that didn't subdue their national pride. 'At home,' she says, 'my sister who was then 13, and I, who was 11, insisted on decorating the outside of our house. We used red, white and blue ribbons and crepe paper, which rapidly disintegrated in the inclement weather at that time. What we seemed to fail to recognize was the fact that living in a small hamlet of only eight houses, it would only be the few delivery men who ventured down our lane that would be likely to see our handiwork!'

REFLECTING ON CHANGE

In all aspects of life, it's inevitable that things change, sometimes for the good, and sometimes for the bad. Many of the changes that have occurred in traditional village life in the past 40 years, are certainly regrettable, but perhaps the improvements to the way in which we live can at least help to compensate for this. In this final section, one or two of the people who have told us about their villages between 1900 and 1960, reflect on some of those changes. But ultimately, for those who can remember what it was like in those bygone days, you will have to draw your own conclusion, as to whether life was better then – or now!

Ernest Hawkins grew up in the village of Barlaston in Staffordshire, which similar to many other rural villages, has seen nearby towns getting ever closer as they grow in size.

'It was inevitable that the urban sprawl would eventually reach Barlaston due to its proximity to Stoke on Trent; the old village would no longer be tranquil, so we all had to learn to live with it, as other villagers throughout the country have done. I don't think any of us thought it would be as extensive as it has been. Before the war, except for the Old Road, Meaford Road, and properties alongside the canal, Barlaston was the village at the top of the hill and confined to little more than a square mile, with amenities that were sufficient for the needs of almost everyone who lived there.'

Chipstable in West Somerset, where Frank Hind grew up, can still boast to having a rural location, but apart from that almost everything else has changed.

'Everybody knew and greeted everyone else; there was a real sense of community; most locals spoke Exmoor dialect or were bi-lingual in the Queen's English, and most were engaged in agriculture or related enterprises. On the day I was de-mobbed from National Service, a beautiful May day in 1957, I caught the train from Taunton and had a real song in my heart as we came along the valley between Milverton and Wiveliscombe. I was returning to my beloved Brendon Hills, after 19 months in Berlin, to the sound of a mewing buzzard soaring on a thermal, and the baa-ing of sheep. I still drive over the moor to Chipstable to visit my parents' grave, but sad to relate the village has changed beyond recognition. Not at first glance but insofar as the life has gone out of it. There is no village school; no parson; no squire; no shops; no Post Office; no builder; no policeman and no taxi service. You would be lucky to hear any dialect and most people commute to Taunton or other towns – I don't know a soul there now.'

The increase in the volume and type of traffic at Snitterfield in Warwickshire prompts Valerie Marlow to suggest:

'I am sure most people here would agree that the worst aspect of change for us, as for other roads in Snitterfield, has been the increase in traffic over these last few years. Dangerous speeds, often more like 60 than 30, with heavy lorries, transporters and the like, all making it difficult for walkers to safely use the pavements – especially for the young mothers with prams and toddlers. This is a far cry from 200 years ago when, according to our much-respected local historian, the late John Shelby, Smiths Lane was known as Farrs Lane, and there would only have been horses and carts rumbling along on it.'

Phyllis Wyatt from Edithmead in Somerset, a village decimated by the construction of a motorway, remembers so many wonderful aspects of life in the 1920s and 1930s.

'It has become very clear to me that the best times of all were the 1920s and 1930s. Born in 1922 I can still vividly recall the feel and flavour of that era. Wartime songs from a war to end all wars; wounded Tommies in hospital blue; the Charleston, Black Bottom, cloche hats and poverty; Empire Day at school; singing patriotic songs and saluting the Union flag; proud of being part of an empire on which the sun never sets. Old-fashioned values prevailed and were adhered to. Times were hard, but life had a certain indefinable quality about it, which sadly is no longer with us.'

Many parts of Britain have strong regional identities, which quite rightly nurture a sense of local patriotism. In England, this is probably most true of Cornwall, but no matter where we live, the overwhelming changes to village life, are a unifying factor we can all identify with and appreciate. Martin Skin lived at the hamlet of Doddycross near Menheniot in Cornwall and his conclusion in a way, is representative of many regions of Britain, where the local people have moved away to be replaced by foreign invaders from other parts.

'People never locked their doors or windows and nothing was ever stolen. On reflection, I was fortunate enough to have grown up in an area where people still cared about each other, where a way of life was as it should be, working with nature and working with each other. The people around me, such as hamlet and village dwellers, farmers, weekly visiting tradespeople and suppliers, and travelling Romanies, were my teachers and protectors, their workshops, sitting rooms, caravans, gardens and surrounding land were my classroom. I learnt new and important skills from each type of person, for which I am truly grateful. I look back with many happy memories. I miss those smiling faces and kind words and I feel great sadness for the younger generations that will never know the true meaning of a true country way of life.

'Community spirit consists of experiencing love for what is around you; love made up of deriving and giving highly positive feelings and emotions through touch, feeling, caring, congruence, with ones-self and outside of ones-self, sight, hearing, smelling and respecting, combined with a very large position of understanding the ergonomics, culture and ways of life which surround a person growing up in that environment. Because the true Cornish people, their blood line, culture and way of life has been so greatly diluted by people moving into the area, the true community spirit has been seriously damaged and often totally destroyed. Sadly many people who have moved to Cornwall for a better way of life have played a major role in destroying the very way of life that they have moved to Cornwall to enjoy.'

Jim Dunlop, who hailed from the hamlet of Auchengray, Lanarkshire in Scotland, feels that the dilution of community spirit is one of the gravest losses from traditional village life.

'I suspect that in today's society the little hamlet of Auchengray would be seen as the backwoods, but surprisingly it is growing in population and a number of new houses have been built over the past ten years. This is the main result of land being cheap in relative terms. However, many of the new inhabitants use it solely as a commuter base to Edinburgh and Glasgow. In the 1940s and 1950s, residents appeared to be, and were content, and there was a strong community spirit. There was no vandalism, and crime was limited to an occasional bit of poaching. My mother continued to live there for ten years after being widowed and I can honestly say that in her final years when she was virtually housebound, never a day passed without some member of the village calling to see if she required any assistance. I suggest that few places in Britain today could make such a boast.'

Mr Charles, who has told us much about life in his corner of southwest Wales, through living between the two Pembrokeshire villages of Porthgain and Llanrhian, has also observed many changes.

'In the 1970s, a transition took place at an ever-increasing rate. Gone are the old characters, the smallholders and the fishermen. The harbour at Porthgain is full of boats for pleasure and trips, with maybe one or two fishing boats.

There has been a change of ownership at the pub and it has been developed out of all recognition, catering for maybe 500 to 600 people per day. There is ample parking space for up to 100 cars. This together with the harbour is a great attraction for visitors. In fact the village is now a holiday resort. The coastal footpath rises up from either side of the harbour. The National Park Authority does not allow any development, so any properties for sale fetch a very high price. Some villagers have sold up and moved and by now about one third of the 27 houses are either holiday homes or occupied by incomers.

'In Llanrhian the transition has been slower and less dramatic; besides the school and church there are only seven houses. But gone is the school, which has become a church hall (the church owned it anyway). The schoolhouse is owned by someone from abroad who visits it about four times a year. The shop and Post Office have long since closed and are occupied by incomers, who arrived there about 20 years ago. The mill, as well as the mill outbuildings, is being rented to summer visitors. Another house is similarly rented so there is only one old resident in the village today. Ten council houses have been built adjacent to the village and these are occupied by locals.'

From the start of the book, we explained about the lack of amenities to ordinary houses. There was no water, for instance, and no gas or electricity. Nobody can deny that life improved for everyone as these things were brought into peoples' homes. But perhaps, in a subtle way, it was these particular advances that were the catalyst for some of the most profound changes in the way in which we lived our lives. Carys Briddon, who lived in the little village of Bontgoch in Ceredigion, makes the final analysis:

'The way of life in rural areas was definitely changed with the coming of electricity; for the better, because it eased some of the workload of the housewife who was lucky enough to be able to buy all the latest equipment, but also for worse, because it killed off many of the social gatherings in the community with the coming of television to the home. I suppose that by now most of us who experienced life before the coming of electricity wouldn't want to return to that old way of life. Nowadays people seem to be rushing around with no time on their hands, and mothers don't stay at home to bring up their children any more. Therefore, there's a lot to be said for the old days and the old ways, with regard to village life.'

Acknowledgments

I would like to thank the following people, who have provided their memories for this book: Margaret Wilce, David Andrews, Mr E Fairweather, Diana Phillips, Ken Rennison, Rosa Bowler, Frank Hind, Richard Shimmin, Martin Skin, Geoffrey Charge, Mrs J Peacock, Mrs M Williams, Peter Waite, Phyllis Wyatt, Stanley Church, Christine Harber, Jessie Lockhart, Ruth Bennett, Jean Pearse, Bill Wilson, Ewen Gillies, Joanne Cousins, Mr G Thacker, Elizabeth Crowe, Audrey Blake, Dot Hunt, Lynne Oakes, Molly Kinghorn, The Lord Digby, Charles Littlefair, Donald Patience, Wilfred Login, James Jamieson, Arthur William Henry Charles, Ken Carruthers, Keith Watkins, Mr O F Evans, Glyn Dumphy, Christine Arnold, Doreen Charles, Frank Stanford, Iris Sanders, Margaret Kirby, Marion Cooke, Gordon Greenlaw, Irene Foster, Fred Gallacher, Peggy Shepherd, Pamela Gear, Janet Burt, Mr VJ Catt, Gertie May, Ethel Fisher, Audrey Purser, Janet Beer, Dorothy Waters, Carys Briddon, Ken Sleight, Maurice Hoile, Ted Tudor, Lynda Crotty, Doreen Wilde, Jim Dunlop, Allan George, Hilary Price, Shirley Payne, Sheila Andrew, Elizabeth Stodart, Mr L A Reed, Kathleen White, Valerie Blackburn, Judith Nedderman, Denys Damen, Don Bilton, John Wood, Audrey Battersby, Sid Green, Fred Simpson, Albert Constable, Mrs K Aitchison, Sheila Fullman, Jamie Guthrie, Barbara Raine, June Richards, Winifred Watkins, Bruce Kean, Joan Foster, Shirley Copley, Stephen English, Joan Nipper, Mary Cooper, and Joan Blue.

I would also like to thank Harry Marlow for sending the thoughts of his wife Valerie, which were first published in *The Snipe Newsletter*, the village magazine of Snitterfield. Thanks also to Ginny Crow the editor for her permission. Thanks to John Stanley Woodcock, for supplying his own memories, and those of Fred Shore. Thanks to Colin Russell for his own memories and those of John Radford Cartwright. Thanks to Helen Rendall, for writing up the memories of her husband Charlie Rendall. Thanks to Lyn Gower for sending me the memories of her mother Beryl Haywood. Thanks to Phil Knott, for the memories of Ken Knott and Frank Palmer. And thanks to Heather Cave, for the memories of Mary Cave.

Thanks to Ernest Hawkins for letting me use quotes from his booklets, *Memories of my life 1920–1946*, and *More Memories of Barlaston*: copyright Ernest Hawkins. Thanks to Marie Langford, for her booklet *Cattistock – A Dorset Village*: copyright Marie Langford. Thanks to William Moore, for his booklet *Hard Times and Humour*: copyright William Moore. Thanks to Marie Litchfield, for allowing me to quote from her book *Countryside & Cloister*, published by Family Publications: copyright Family Publications. Thanks also to Family Publications, 6a King Street, Oxford, OX2 6DF, for their permission. Thanks to Duncan Lucas, for his book *One Man's Wigston*, published by Sutton Publishing: copyright O D Lucas. Thanks to Jack Gee, for his book *Memories of a Fenman*, from which all of his extracts are taken: copyright Jack Gee. Thanks to Bill McKay, for his book *Migvie*, published by Dilstreetee Books: copyright Bill McKay. Thanks to Chas Marshall for his book *Return of the Blue Stots* by Chas Marshall and Stuart Ranking. Thanks to Alford Morris for their booklet, *25 Years of Alford Morris*. Thanks to Rosie Evans, Secretary to the Aston on Clun Arbor Tree Festival Committee, and Neil Sutherland, Secretary of the Abernethy Highland Games Association. Thanks also to James A Grant, for permission to quote from his late father's book *NethyBridge – The Games & Its Characters*: copyright A S Grant.

Thanks also to the following people who have aided my research by providing photographs, information, or by helping in some other way: June Mill, Ian Parris, John Allen, Lorna Delanoy, Bryan Avery, Jo Moran, Rose Docherty, G Barley, Mrs E Ovenden, Ted Dodsworth, Myrtle Hind, Nick Fletcher, Mrs F Francis, Reginald Enticknap, Graham Bebbington, Bernard Foster, June Van Dam, Mrs D Lunn, Audrey Battersby, Peter Walls, Raymond Hunt, John Hoggard, Linda Walsh, Mr S Baker, Bill Johnson, and Mr C Licquorish. Thanks also to Lance Jordan Photography of Glastonbury, Somerset, for copying lots of old photographs for me.

Picture credits

The author and publishers would like to thank the following people for the use of their photographs in this book:

Mrs K Aitchison: 49 (bottom), 194, 195 (top); John Allen: 192–3; Sheila Andrew: 215 (top); Brian Avery: 24 (bottom); G Barley: 229 (top), 230 (bottom); Audrey Blake: 248 (top); Rosa Bowler: 17 (top right), 104 (bottom), 106 (bottom), 151 (bottom), 156 (top), 177 (bottom), 182 (top), 190 (top), 191 (top), 195 (bottom), 202 (right), 203 (top), 233 (top), 236 (top), 237 (bottom); Carys Briddon: 18 (bottom), 117 (bottom); Ken Carruthers: 84, 85 (bottom), 86, 89 (top right); Heather Cave: 50 (top); Doreen Charles: 98, 99; Albert Constable: 186; Marion Cooke: 149 (top), 166 (bottom); Shirley Copley: 160 (bottom); Lynda Crotty: 31 (bottom), 212 (top), 247 (top); Rose Docherty: 244, 245 (top); Ted Dodsworth: 225 (top and bottom left); Glyn Dumphy: 93; O F Evans: 91 (top); Rosie Evans/Arbor Tree Festival Committee: 239, 240 (top); Bernard Foster: 14 (top), 15 (top), 16 (middle), 17 (top left), 23 (top), 27, 40 (top), 48 (top), 113 (top), 114 (top), 161 (top), 172 (bottom), 174 (centre), 199, 230 (top right), 248 (bottom); Mrs F Francis: 213 (top); Fred Gallacher: 107 (bottom), 109 (bottom); Pamela Gear: 174 (top), 247 (bottom); Allan George: 142 (bottom), 143; Gordon Greenlaw: 108 (top right and left), 109 (top right and left); Ernest Hawkins: 63 (bottom), 106 (top), 110 (top), 150 (bottom), 152 (top), 153 (top), 171 (bottom), 201 (top), 219 (top), 235; Frank Hind: 40 (bottom), 46 (top), 49 (top), 111, 163 (bottom right), 198, 204 (top left and right), 205 (top left); John Hoggard: 17 (bottom), 32–3, 44; Maurice Hoile: 128 (top left and right); Raymond Hunt: 224 (bottom), 225 (bottom right); James Jamieson: 83, 219 (bottom), 221 (top); Dr F H Jardine/Hallaton Museum/Duncan Lucas: 12; Bill Johnson: 73 (bottom), 107 (top), 145 (top), 188 (top); Margaret Kirby: 133 (bottom), 200 (bottom), 204 (bottom), 232 (bottom); Molly Kinghorn: 15 (bottom left), 47 (top), 49 (centre), 67 (bottom), 68 (top left and bottom), 69; Phil Knott: 16 (bottom), 25 (top), 30, 35 (top), 36, 48 (bottom), 108 (bottom), 119, 136 (bottom), 139 (top), 157, 159, 178 (bottom), 179 (bottom), 181, 213 (bottom), 216, 218, 221 (bottom), 229 (bottom), 240 (bottom); Marie Langford: 175; Mr C Licquorish: 149 (bottom), 174 (bottom), 217; Charles Littlefair: 76 (bottom); Jessie Lockhart: 29 (bottom); Wilfred Login: 79, 80 (top), 81 (top); Duncan Lucas: 39 (top), 113 (bottom), 154 (top), 180; Mrs D Lunn: 92 (top), 94 (bottom), 95 (top); Gertie May: 112, 114 (bottom), 137 (centre left); William Moore: 118 (top), 121, 188 (bottom), 191 (bottom); Jo Moran: 25 (bottom left); Judith Nedderman: 163 (top), 171 (top right and left); Lynne Oakes: 62, 104 (top); Mrs E Ovenden: 215 (bottom), 245 (bottom); Ian Parris: 46 (bottom), 103 (top); Donald Patience: 78, 160 (bottom); Shirley Payne: 228 (bottom); Mrs J Peacock: 9 (bottom), 35 (bottom), 37 (top left and right), 38, 40 (centre), 43 (bottom), 127 (bottom), 141, 150 (top), 177 (top), 236 (bottom); Jean Pearse: 133 (top), 189; Audrey Purser: 105 (top), 209 (top); Barbara Raine: 210 (top); L A Reed: 123 (bottom), 162 (bottom), 176 (top), 231; Helen Rendall: 60 (top), 67 (top), 68 (top right); Ken Rennison: 122 (top right); June Richards: 211 (top); Colin Russell: 126 (left), 127 (top), 128 (bottom), 131 (top); Fred Simpson: 138, 139 (bottom); Frank Stanford: 102; Neil Sutherland: 196 (top and centre); G Thacker: 37 (bottom), 51 (top), 60 (bottom), 65 (top); Ted Tudor: 129 (bottom), 130 (bottom left); Peter Waite: 24 (top), 118 (bottom); June Van Dam: 210 (bottom); Peter J Walls: 224 (top); Lynda Walsh: 148, 233 (bottom); Keith Watkins: 87, 88 (top), 89 (bottom), 154 (bottom), 166 (top), 220 (bottom); Kathleen White: 167; Margaret Wilce: 18 (top), 21 (top), 26, 28, 64, 77 (top), 155 (bottom), 158 (bottom), 163 (bottom left); Doreen Wilde: 82, 222 (top); John Stanley Woodcock: 56, 57, 58, 59 (top), 61 (top); Phyllis Wyatt: 15 (bottom right), 19 (top), 21 (bottom), 205 (top right), 214.

The Bebbington Collection: 91 (bottom), 230 (top right), 237 (top)

The Citizen: 241 (top)

Hulton-Deutsch Collection/Corbis: cover (backround – Widecombe-in-the-Moor), 6

Getty Images/Hulton Archive: cover (girl on swing), frontispiece, 7, 8, 9 (top), 10, 11, 20 (bottom), 23 (bottom), 53 (top), 70, 71, 72 (bottom), 95 (bottom), 96, 97 (top), 115 (top), 116, 120, 134, 135 (top), 140 (top), 142 (top left), 153 (bottom), 187 (bottom), 197, 202 (left), 238, 241 (centre), 242, 246.

Kent Messenger Group: 129 (top)

Lorna Delanoy/The Farmland Museum: 22 (top)

Mary Evans Picture Library: 29 (top), 31 (top), 51 (bottom), 52, 169 (bottom), 179 (top), 183 (top)

North Bucks Times/Bletchley District Gazette: 169 (top), 222 (bottom), 223, 228 (top), 249

Scarborough Evening News: 103 (bottom), 173 (bottom)

The Scout Association/Basil Green 208 (top), R B Herbert 208 (bottom)

Times & Citizen, Bedford: 168

The author and publisher have endeavoured to contact all contributors of pictures for permission to reproduce.

Index